Ethical Dilemmas in Management

This exciting new text engages with the issue of ethical dilemmas encountered in different organizations. Rather than exploring the definition of ethical conduct, this book focuses on the way in which the process of organization produces dilemmas of ethical behaviour. Using illustrative accounts from corporate settings as a basis, the book explores the conditions that lead to ethical dilemmas and the strategies organizations adopt to deal with these dilemmas or steer away from them. The book suggests that ethical dilemmas are often dealt with by directing attention away from the core problem, rather than engaging with and solving them.

This is a fascinating text, which raises important questions and provides a deeper understanding of the dynamics of ethical processes. A company's ethical behaviour is a major criterion by which the company, its products and services are judged and is therefore crucial to sound management in today's organizations. *Ethical Dilemmas in Management* is essential reading for all students of business and management and ethics.

Christina Garsten is Professor and Chair of the Department of Social Anthropology at Stockholm University, Sweden.

Tor Hernes is Professor in the Department of Organization at Copenhagen Business School, Denmark.

Ethical Dilemmas in Management

Edited by
Christina Garsten and
Tor Hernes

LONDON AND NEW YORK

First published 2009
by Routledge
2 Park Square, Milton Park, Abingdon, Oxon OX14 4RN

Simultaneously published in the USA and Canada
by Routledge
270 Madison Ave, New York, NY 10016

Routledge is an imprint of the Taylor & Francis Group, an informa business

© 2009 Editorial matter and selection, Christina Garsten and
Tor Hernes; individual chapters, the contributors

Typeset in Times New Roman by
Bookcraft Ltd, Stroud, Gloucestershire
Printed and bound in Great Britain by
TJ International, Padstow, Cornwall

British Library Cataloguing in Publication Data
A catalogue record for this book is available from the British Library

Library of Congress Cataloging in Publication Data
Ethical dilemmas in management / edited by Christina Garsten and Tor Hernes.
    p. cm.
    Includes bibliographical references and index.
    1. Management—Moral and ethical aspects.
    2. Business ethics. I. Garsten, Christina. II. Hernes, Tor.
HF5387.E776 2008
174'.4—dc22   2008016078

ISBN10: 0-415-43759-8 (hbk)
ISBN10: 0-415-43760-1 (pbk)
ISBN10: 0-203-89156-2 (ebk)

ISBN13: 978-0-415-43759-2 (hbk)
ISBN13: 978-0-415-43760-8 (pbk)
ISBN13: 978-0-203-89156-8 (ebk)

Contents

Illustrations

Figures

Tables

Contributors

Tore Bakken is Professor of Sociology in the Department of Innovation and Economic Organization at the Norwegian School of Management, Oslo, Norway. He has published books and articles within the field of modern systems theory. His current empirical work includes a study of risk communication in food production, and an examination of the notions of mind and social reality in John Searle's philosophy of language and Niklas Luhmann's sociology of communication.

Todd Bridgman is Senior Lecturer in Organizational Behaviour at the Victoria Management School, Victoria University of Wellington, New Zealand. He completed his PhD at the University of Cambridge and held research fellowships at Judge Business School and Wolfson College, University of Cambridge. His PhD examined the changing relationships between business school faculty and non-academic organizations, and developed Laclau and Mouffe's discourse theory as a framework for organizational analysis. The PhD was judged best doctoral dissertation in 2005 by the critical management studies interest group at the Academy of Management and it also won the 2006 Emerald/EFMD outstanding doctoral research award in the category of organizational change and development.

Johannes Brinkmann is Professor of Business Ethics in the Department of Strategy and Logistics at the Norwegian School of Management in Oslo, Norway. During the last ten years, he has published articles in the *Journal of Business Ethics* and other business ethics journals, most recently related to the insurance industry and ethics.

Christina Garsten is Professor and Chair of the Department of Social Anthropology, and Research Director at Stockholm Centre for Organizational Research (Score), Stockholm University. Her research interests lie in the anthropology of organizations and markets, with a current focus on new forms of regulation and accountability in the labour market and in transnational trade. Her particular research concentrations are the varieties of cultural articulation at the interface of market and community: organization and sociality. She has published in the areas of organizational culture, flexibilization of employment, and corporate social responsibility. Among her most recent books are *Workplace Vagabonds*: *Career and Community in Changing Worlds of Work* (Palgrave Macmillan, 2008) and *Organizing Transnational Accountability* (co-edited with Magnus Boström, Edward Elgar Publishing, 2008).

Steven Grover is Professor at the Department of Management and Deputy Dean of the School of Business, University of Otago, New Zealand. He has studied honesty and dishonesty in organizations for over 15 years. His current research programme examines the effect of honest and dishonest leader behaviour on followers. This programme examines multiple issues in leader honesty, including how to measure it, how value congruence influences perceptions of honesty, and how different motives for dishonest behaviour influence followers.

Tor Hernes is Professor of Organization Studies at the Copenhagen Business School, Denmark. He previously worked at the Department of Innovation and Economic Organization at the Norwegian School of Management, Oslo. His research aims to apply various forms of process perspectives to the study of organizations. He has published the following books: *Understanding Organization as Process: Theory for a Tangled World*; *The Spatial Construction of Organization: Autopoietic Organization Theory* (edited with Tore Bakken), *Actor-network Theory and Organizing* (edited with Barbara Czarniawska) and *Managing Boundaries in Organizations* (edited with Neil Paulsen). Current works relate to the application of phenomenological perspectives to organizational processes.

Lane La Mure holds a PhD in Government from Harvard University and an MBA from the Harvard Business School. He works in the investment management industry and lives in New York City.

Hervé Laroche, PhD, is Professor in the Department of Strategy, Organizational Behaviour and Human Resources of ESCP–EAP European School of Management, France. He was Associate Dean for Research (1994–1998) and is currently Editor in Chief of the *European Management Journal*. From first studying strategic decision processes and cognitive processes in organizations, with particular attention to the structuring of strategic issues and the strategic agenda, he then became interested in issues of organizational reliability, trying to account for accidents and failures. He also investigated the contribution of middle managers to the conduct of action in organizations. On these topics he developed teachings and published or co-published articles in various journals (*Organization Science*, *MIT Sloan Management Review*, *Journal of Risk Research*, etc.) as well as books (*Moi manager*, *Repenser la stratégie*) and chapters in edited books. He was a president of the AIMS (Association Internationale de Management Stratégique – the French-speaking academic society in the field of strategic management) from 2003 to 2006.

Monica Lindh de Montoya is Associate Professor in Social Anthropology at Stockholm University, Sweden. Her interests include markets, entrepreneurship, and microfinance. She has carried out fieldwork in Sweden, Venezuela and in Bosnia-Herzegovina, contributed chapters to a number of books, and has also worked as a consultant in the field of international development for USAID, CGAP and Sida. Recent publications include *Market Matters: Exploring Cultural Processes in the Global Marketplace* (co-edited with Christina Garsten, Palgrave Macmillan, 2004).

Steve McKenna is Associate Professor of Human Resource Management at York University, Toronto, Canada. His research interests include the analysis of managerial narratives; the role of conscience in ethical workplace behaviour and ethical dimensions of international human resource management. He has worked as a senior manager in multinational corporations and small and medium-sized businesses in North America, Europe and Asia. He is currently working on a funded project investigating the 'HRM textbook as fact or fiction'.

Robert H. Moorman is the Robert Daugherty Chair in Management and Associate Dean for Graduate Business Programs at Creighton University. He is also the founding director of the Anna Tyler Waite Center for Leadership. Professor Moorman's research interests include the study of leader integrity, organizational justice, and organizational citizenship behaviours. He has also taught undergraduate, graduate, and professional classes on leadership, organizational behaviour, human resource management and entrepreneurship.

Gerhard Emil Schjelderup is Lecturer in the Department of Innovation and Economic Organization and a PhD Fellow at the Norwegian School of Management, Oslo. His primary research interest lies in the area of communication, organization studies and sociology. Previous publications include: *Forbrukersosiologi, Makt, Tegn, og Mening i Forbrukersamfunnet* (2007), Gerhard Emil Schjelderup and Morten William Knudsen (eds), Oslo: Cappelen.

Ronald R. Sims is the Floyd Dewey Gottwald Senior Professor in the Mason School of Business at the College of William and Mary, Virginia, USA, where he teaches leadership and change management, business ethics, human resource management and organizational behaviour. He received his PhD in organizational behaviour from Case Western Reserve University. His research focuses on a variety of topics to include leadership and change management, HRM, business ethics, employee training, and management and leadership development (i.e. Human Resource Development), learning styles, and experiential learning. Dr Sims is the author or co-author of twenty-eight books and more than eighty articles that have appeared in a wide variety of scholarly and practitioner journals.

Debora Spar is the President of Barnard College. Prior to that, she was the Spangler Family Professor at Harvard Business School where her research focused on the political economy of international business. She is the author of numerous books and articles including, most recently, *The Baby Business: How Money,*

Science, and Politics Drive the Commerce of Conception (Harvard Business School Press, 2006) and *Ruling the Waves: Cycles of Discovery, Chaos, and Wealth from the Compass to the Internet.*

Anne Live Vaagaasar is an Associate Professor at the Department of Leadership and Organizational Management at the Norwegian School of Management, Oslo, Norway. She teaches and does research in the area of project management and project organization.

Foreword

This book has been on a long journey, starting with the initial idea of writing a book on 'organizational conscience', which was the theme of a track at the European Group for Organization Studies conference in Ljubljana in July 2004. At that conference track, several people took part, who provided major stimulation to thinking about conscience, morality and ethics in the context of organization. Without those enlightening discussions this book would not have seen the light of day. Since 2004 the focus of the book has changed somewhat, becoming more explicitly focused on ethical dilemmas inherent in organization and management. We have benefited from advice from Routledge editors in sharpening the focus of the book, especially Francesca Heslop. We are also grateful to Ola Håkansson and Tor Paulson, who were important discussion partners in the early stages of the book.

Christina Garsten and Tor Hernes

1 Introduction

Dilemmas of ethical organizing

Christina Garsten and Tor Hernes

From (ir)responsibility to accountability

Years ago, big businesses would be content simply to earn money and capture large market shares. In fact, the hypothesis advanced by the famous sociologist Max Weber in his classic *The Protestant Ethic and the Spirit of Capitalism*, first published in 1904–1905, was that the rise of Western capitalism was based on the idea that earning more money was legitimately seen as an end in itself. In other words, there were no moral or ethical considerations that were placed above that of earning money. Thus, until quite recently, it has seldom been asked if the operations of large companies or public institutions were harmful in any way or if they served dubious political agendas. Being big, powerful and appealing to the consumers seemed an end in itself, and company strategies could be formed with the exclusive aim to be more effective, which is why slogans such as 'What is good for General Motors is good for America, and vice versa' was seen as a legitimate slogan in the 1950s.[1] The 1970s witnessed a rising concern with civil rights, a growing focus on the environment and an increasing awareness of human rights and equality. The 1970s is perhaps the decade when questions began to be raised about the role of big business in politics. The International Telephone and Telegraph Corporation (ITT), under Harold Geneen, came under sharp criticism when it was allegedly involved in the military coup and overthrow of the democratically elected Chilean president Salvador Allende in 1972. Geneen, famous for his ruthless management style, fell into disrepute perhaps from sticking to his dictum: *The only unforgivable sin in business is to run out of cash.* In other spheres of society people began to ask if there were not other sins of which businesses might be guilty. The US was no exception. In Europe in the 1970s, for example, banks came under attack for their investments and operations linked to the apartheid regime in South Africa.

A decade later, the responsibility of big business in preserving the environment became a reality, with the Bhopal disaster in India in 1984. Thousands of local inhabitants were killed or mutilated when methyl isocyanate gas leaked out from the Union Carbide plant. With falling profits, the safety measures at the plant had become increasingly lax. The Bhopal disaster served to raise the issue of the *accountability* of corporate actors in society, and not just their responsibility.

Responsibility in the Bhopal case became subject to court rulings. However, legal sanctions could not be enforced, due to failures of the international legal regime to handle issues of accountability in a globalized business corporation such as Union Carbide. The invoking of court jurisdiction was, nevertheless, highly significant, because with accountability comes *legal responsibility*. Legal responsibility means that a company's practices, and by association its image, may be deemed harmful to the environment or society through a court ruling.

Court rulings about misconduct are potentially more harmful to a company's image than any other event, and have decisive negative effects on the company's economic viability. It is not surprising, therefore, that companies have, during the last decade, increasingly imposed standards of conduct upon themselves by introducing in-house Corporate Social Responsibility (CSR) systems. The costs of not appearing to be a responsible company are just too big in a mediacized, brand-conscious society. It is possible to see a self-reinforcing loop of factors at work here. A heightened awareness in society in the 1970s made it easier for the judicial system to consider legal sanctions against corporate misconduct. The power of legal actions opened up the perception of a need to respond to pressures for accountability among companies, and sometimes also for a feeling of wanting to be accountable. This need to be accountable to society at large has in turn stimulated people inside and outside corporations to search for ways of being socially responsible.

Such developments do not belong to the corporate world alone. Parallel developments have taken place in public institutions, forcing them to become more accountable to their constituents. Accountability applies to politicians, private organizations and public agencies, such as schools and universities, as much as it applies to corporations. It is all part of the trend which is referred to as 'the audit society' (Power 1997). An audit society implies a growth of new administrative-style control systems that play an important public role. As part of this development, organizational performance becomes increasingly formalized and auditable. Today, a huge variety of experiments and research are undertaken with the aim of making companies auditable and thereby accountable to the wider public. The extent to which they produce accountability is, however, open to question.

Some deeper questions

Organizations are powerful actors. To a large extent, transnational corporations, states, international organizations and non-governmental organizations fashion and control the everyday contexts in which we lead our lives. Spar and La Mure (in this book), for example, point out how the agendas of large corporations may influence the policies set by nation states in different parts of the world. Many organizations, though not all, also have missions and rules intended to reduce risks of wrongdoing. However, organizations are not only 'do-gooders', but also make decisions and choices that could have harmful effects. Why do some organizations act in ways that harm people in their neighbourhood, their employees or their competitors? Why do organizations sometimes choose not to act responsibly?

How is it that people in organizations can become greedy automatons when placed in powerful positions? Perhaps it is not in the nature of organizational leaders to be able to choose 'right' from 'wrong'.

Part of the answer to these questions may be found in social transformations at large. In his work on postmodernity and morality, sociologist Zygmunt Bauman (1995) sketches a world of individuals afloat in society. They have lost their bearings and are no longer investing in other individuals, only in themselves. In Bauman's view, when the organization of society moves from community logics to market logics, there is a loss of morality and an irretrievable loss of conscience. He also speaks of how formal organizations may simply 'suspend' moral responsibility, pretending it is not an issue. In this way, they do what the church did with certain issues in the Middle Ages, declaring them not related to faith, so they could be declared neither sinful nor virtuous (Bauman 1989). The question, however, is whether companies can declare that they go about their business, i.e. earning money, leaving others to decide what is right or wrong.

Although Bauman is critical of the moral standards achieved by modern organizations, he also talks with some optimism about our age as 'the age of morality'. As organizational boundaries and areas of societal and individual responsibility are being redrawn, when the risks of society take on global proportions and force people to deal with them in new ways, then critical reflection and social responsibility will increase, with chances of moral togetherness, according to Bauman. Conscience will again be reconstructed because people recognize the social, i.e. the interpersonal, as being the very core of our lives. In other words, here lies a challenge to modern business because they are populated by people who care and know that there are other values than bottom line results.

Businesses committing themselves to ethical rules of conduct may be a reality today, but it is not entirely new. Some early founders were more than just corporate owners; they took paternal interest in the welfare of their workers and their families. Although this was the exception rather than the rule, in many societies they were a substitute for a non-existent public welfare system. Another measure of achieving some degree of ethics in business was the formation of various types of cooperative movements in the second half of the nineteenth century. Cooperatives were formed by consumers, farmers, fishermen, workers, etc. to provide some protection from exploitation by industrialists, traders and finance institutions.

Thus the role of corporations in society is a question of long standing, and one that has become ever more pertinent today, with increasing globalization and emerging governance gaps in the system of international jurisdiction. Large corporations, for example, may avoid thorny ethical issues by moving their activities to less visible corners of the world, or they may simply outsource activities to companies that are less concerned with ethical standards. This raises poignant questions such as 'How do corporate actors respond to pressures of responsibility and accountability?'; 'What practices and procedures are initiated to negotiate accountability and corporate business priorities?'; and 'What dilemmas emerge and how are these dealt with?' These questions deserve critical attention from managers, researchers and students alike. This book does not provide definitive answers, but offers an initial basis for reflection and questioning.

Faith in formal standards and structure

In the last few decades, one trend has become increasingly dominant in social life, notably what is called the institutionalization of standards (Brunsson and Jacobsson 2000). Standards seem to guide the lives of individuals as well as the lives of companies to an ever greater extent. Standards developed by governments and the EU as well as agencies such as the ILO, WTO, etc., serve to protect rights, to facilitate coordination and to assure fair play among market actors. Standards exist in different forms. As such, standards can be voluntary in nature and may complement systems of binding rules when these rules are not sufficient. Standards for ethical conduct and social responsibility of corporations belong to this category. Over time, standards may become compulsory. Standards on emissions and pollution, for example, are set through international agreements and subsequently through national legislation, which means that they then become compulsory rules. Some standards are produced by national or international organizations, such as the International Organization for Standardization (ISO), and are then offered to, or imposed on, other organizations to follow. They are what we would call *exogenous* standards; they are imposed by external bodies such as regulatory agencies. *Endogenous* standards are standards developed in-house by companies that choose to apply them to their own operations. They are self-imposed for a variety of reasons.

One important reason is to promote the image of the company to the public and their customers. In an increasingly globalized marketplace it has been recognized that large corporate actors as well as governments may evade national and regional regulations. At the same time, large brand-based actors, such as Nike, H&M, IKEA and others depend on being perceived by the public as ethically responsible in order to prosper in their respective markets. Hence a number of organizations have enrolled in the Corporate Social Responsibility (CSR) movement, which has created large opportunities for consultants as well as research agendas for academics and teaching curricula in business schools. CSR has been hailed as a major means by which corporate actors develop their internal capacity for auditing their impact on targeted areas (environment, labour relations, human rights). Until the Enron/Andersen scandal erupted, it was thought that there was a correlation between a corporation's commitment to CSR and its 'real' commitment to being ethically responsible.

CSR standards (and other standards) are essentially based on the idea that problems are avoided by imposing rules. An important trend in past years has been to leave it to standards to ensure ethical conduct. Standards may be an effective means of ensuring some degree of ethical conduct, but although enforcement through standards may improve the overall level of ethical conduct, they similarly may allow for more perverse breaches of ethical conduct to emerge. Standards are double-edged swords. One edge is *explicit*. It sets the minimum lower limits for conduct. Not falling below this level basically means that the company is 'OK' and it will normally keep it out of trouble. An advantage of the explicit minimum standard is that people inside the company as well as people from outside are able to assess its performance. It means that the very existence of the standard helps create *awareness* of the importance of ethical conduct. The other edge of the sword, however, is more problematic. This is about the *implicit* effects of standards of conduct. It basically implies that as long as the company apparently performs well enough, and attention is focused on those operations where it does well enough, other operations may be performed that are ethically irresponsible. This is not just because actors in the company wilfully perform deceptive operations. It may just be that because organizational operations are very complex, it is difficult to know what is really ethically defensible.

However, let us deal with intentional misconduct first. In the pre-Enron scandal era, for example, CSR was seen by many writers and practitioners as a way to infuse corporations and public organizations with a sense of ethics. Paradoxically (or maybe not so paradoxical after all), Enron scored very high CSR indicators and was seen as an example worth following in terms of exercising their social responsibility. We know the story. The consequences were disastrous for thousands of employees and small investors. Authorities, institutions and individuals were tricked into believing the good intentions of Enron. What was at play behind the sincere facade was a remarkable deftness with which select individuals could lure huge numbers of people around the world. Their CSR was bogus. However, we could also turn the phrase around and say that CSR *allowed* their practices to be bogus. The example suggests how CSR standards, along with many other standards, may sometimes serve as smokescreens. Enron stuck to the explicit standards which they could – and would – measure. As smokescreens, such standards may deflect attention from practices that are condemnable; but as smokescreens they serve a different function, which is to make people believe that the company operates in an ethically responsible manner (or at least more or less so). However, what is at stake is not so much Enron. It is how they could trick the world with the help of CSR technologies when CSR is intended to prevent exactly this. We would argue that it is the conceptualization of CSR that is problematic, more precisely the foundations from which CSR is developed.

We are not arguing that CSR (or other rule-based approaches) is a mistake. What we are arguing is that CSR has its limits, and it is at its limits that the consequences of mischief are potentially most disastrous. The Enron story shows us that with some deftness and ingenuity, corporations may actually use instruments such as CSR *in order to* circumvent the responsibilities that CSR is meant to instil. Part of the explanation lies in the functionalist logic of CSR, which demands that corporations put into place a certain number of functions to ensure that codes of ethics are followed. One example is 'environmental accounting' which demands that the corporation monitors its effects on the natural environment. Such measures have their obvious strengths. It is not easy for management to ignore data that are produced through institutionalized structures instigated by themselves. There are, in fact, many arguments why such structures are a good idea. They do not just perform regulatory functions internally, but are also educational in the sense that they serve to sensitize organizational members to issues of global concern.

On the whole, corporations and public agencies have a long history of applying a good dose of 'discretion' when it comes to their functions. It might be useful to employ the metaphor of CSR functions as 'corporate lightning rods'. Lightning rods serve to deflect the lightning from the main building. For example, a strategy that is becoming increasingly common in the globalized economy is to outsource activities that could prove to be harmful to the image of the corporation. Outsourcing, or decoupling effectively moves the responsibility for questionable practices to another corporate actor and hence outside the reach of the corporation's own monitoring responsibility. A common practice is to move production to companies operating in countries where public disapproval does not engender sanctions. Thus, as long as CSR remains functional in nature, it may be subject to manipulation in the sense that organizational actors may follow rules, but still perform what, under closer scrutiny, would appear as ethically questionable. We will return to the 'lightning rod' chapter in our concluding chapter.

The power of dilemmas

So far, we have assumed that misconduct is a result of wilful actions, and that CSR or other types of corporate rules sometimes cannot prevent it. However, invoking rules may sometimes make it worse, because the invoking of rules may activate standards as smokescreens behind which some companies hide operations that might be condemnable. Beyond standards, beyond the mere application of CSR, emerge the complexities of doing right or wrong. The fact is that companies operate in a world of multiple standards of what is right and wrong, and when different, sometimes mutually contradictory standards manifest themselves, behaving ethically soon becomes a dilemma.

Protecting the environment and society through reduction of emissions is a laudable goal. The same goes for ensuring a secure and healthy work environment, and staying loyal to the local community as well as to the workforce. For each one of these issues, deciding what is good or bad may not necessarily be overly problematic. However, organizations have to deal with these issues and many more, and have to reach a compromise between many factors, where what is good for one may be bad for the other. For example, it may be environmentally more ethical to move production to a place with access to cleaner energy, but that might also necessitate laying off the workforce, causing harm to staff and their families. Another example is that agricultural products may be imported from developing countries in order to facilitate their access to foreign exchange. On the other hand, importing produce entails transport over long distances, with increased pollution of the atmosphere, which in turn harms the agricultural production and consequently the livestock of developing countries, which the measure of importation was supposed to help in the first place. Hence, in many different ways, companies are forever facing the challenge of actually distinguishing right from wrong where there are no readily discernible answers.

We believe that, rather than suggesting definite answers or rules of thumb about what is and what is not responsible corporate conduct, an alternative is to study examples in different organizations and management settings. Thus the aim of this book is to explore the ethical issues that confront organizational actors and how the actors deal with them, while, at the same time, trying to understand how ethical dilemmas come about. We explore how actions and structures of organizations may emerge, cause dilemmas and find solutions – or, how they may be 'organized away' through formal organizational functions and technologies of responsibility. We aim principally to identify dilemmas and paradoxes and ponder some implications that these may have for organizational management. Thus, rather than provide guidelines of solutions, we provide questions to ponder. The rationale for being open and reflective rather than prescriptive lies in our belief that questions of ethics in organizations are best pursued though reflexivity. Organizations may well have developed structures and functions to take care of CSR questions, but beyond the sphere of influence of such structures and functions, questions of importance can only be handled adequately through enhanced reflexivity.

The basic assumption behind this book is that organizing processes inevitably involve balancing the different implications and scenarios resulting from the effects of decisions. It involves sorting out ambiguities and reducing complexity. However, in this very process, management runs into dilemmas of ethical decision making where the prescribed rules and procedures risk not simplifying the task, but actually exacerbating the dilemmas. These are the very dilemmas to which we wish to draw attention.

The basic premise of the book is that *any* action of organizing creates ethical dilemmas. The reason for this is that organizations have a tangled reality (Hernes 2007). By 'tangled' we mean that processes and intentions that may be intended not to interfere with each other, inevitably do so. For example, the intention to use ecologically sound technologies may interfere with budgets and costs, which may cause lay-offs of personnel. What is then ethical – to use less ecologically sound technologies, or to lay off personnel? Evidently, there is no ready-made answer to such a question. Faced with such a dilemma, a decision has to be made for better or for worse; not to make a decision is not an option.

Decisions are distinguished from one another based on the premises from which they are made. One premise is that of rules, and most decisions made in organizations are based on rules. In the case of ethical considerations, rules may be invoked on the ethical principles by which the company is run. One example is not to engage in any form of bribery under any circumstances. With this type of decision premise, the dilemma of making a decision is effectively avoided; the decision makers make use of standard rules to navigate and impose those rules on a relevant situation.

Another main type of premise on which decisions are based is to consider the context that lies behind the decision and explore what led to the dilemma. In this, rules are not useful and standard answers are not sought. The premise is not external to the dilemma, such as rules. Instead, the premise lies in the context in which the dilemma is understood, as well as some causes that actors believe lead to it.

The word 'dilemma' may seem a negative term, something to be avoided by managers. Dilemmas, however, are not so much to be seen as 'necessary evils' of organization, but rather as natural consequences of organization, as challenges that foster organizational survival and change. We could even say that dilemmas are prerequisites for organizing. A dilemma forces organizational actors to rethink the basis of how they organize and the effects of organizing in that specific way. Dilemmas, therefore, may trigger reflection and learning, and once decisions are made between alternatives, they provide a foundation for explaining future actions and decisions. Organizational actors may choose to avoid dilemmas, a point made by James March (1988). March suggests that decision makers frequently ignore problems; they simply pretend that the problems are not there and one way to do so is by invoking rules. Applying standard rules may allow them to dispense with the problem, at least in the short term. However, it does not follow that by invoking rules, the problem goes away. On the contrary, sometimes it is necessary to explore and investigate the conditions in which the problem or dilemma arose rather than rely on rules. This is particularly true for ethical dilemmas, which may be particularly harmful to the organization if not dealt with carefully.

Several types of dilemmas and how they are engendered are presented in this book. The chapter by Bakken sets the stage by discussing the broader perspective of ethics and organization. Bakken explores the philosophical foundations of thinking in terms of ethics in our post-industrial society, notably by relating ethical considerations to the question of risk. Modern organizations live in a situation where decision making may be seen through the lens of risk-taking. Any decision related to ethical considerations is a risk that organizations take, and creates a dilemma that cannot be settled by following rules, but requires that the social *context* be brought into the analysis. Bakken effectively suggests that the only way to resolve ethical issues in a complex, fast-changing world is by trying to understand the context in which they arise.

The remaining chapters are based on examples from various types of organizational settings. Hernes, Schjelderup and Vaagaasar consider the aspect of history in their study of a dairy corporation, illustrating how features of a corporation which, at some point in time, were considered non-problematic in relation to ethical considerations, may become a dilemma at a later stage in the life of the corporation. In this case, the corporation evolved from being primarily directed at solving the logistical problems of producing and transporting milk, to becoming an important actor in society having to resolve ethical concerns about health, the environment and their primary business.

Quite a different type of dilemma is presented by McKenna, who takes a look at behaviour at the level of individuals in an IT corporation. Rather than consider history, as do Hernes, Schjelderup and Vaagaasar, McKenna enters the realm of actual behaviour, using one person's narrative to examine how a story of personal harassment unfolded in a small unit. McKenna's study enables us to ask pertinent questions about the effectiveness of behavioural rules that are widespread in modern corporations.

Grover and Moorman explore the role of individual leaders and how their integrity influences the ethical positioning of the organization as a whole. The dilemma in question is the transfer of ethical standards among individual leaders and the organization – a question that is central to any theory or practice related to organizational development.

Garsten and Lindh de Montoya explore the effects of organizational ideology in engendering ethical dilemmas. In this case, they discuss the notion of transparency, which is not just a question of organizational ideology, but, as they say, a significant feature of our modern, post-industrial society. Transparency is no doubt a virtue, but pursuing virtue in itself may create conditions in which dilemmas are produced.

Spar and La Mure take the analysis to a different level, looking at how corporations respond to ethical pressures created by non-governmental organizations (NGOs). Their chapter illustrates how dilemmas may be resolved differently by organizational actors, by explaining what accounts for the variation in how firms respond to activist pressure. Why do some firms take extremely proactive measures, engaging activist groups and anticipating their protests, while others stand defiant? Why do some firms capitulate to NGO demands while others refuse? In their analysis, Spar and La Mure explore the different ways in which firms respond to activism.

Brinkmann and Sims discuss the well-known debacle of the Enron Corporation, and follow the effects of corporate culture in their analysis. They demonstrate how Enron, although pursuing a rule-based logic of behaviour, was able to maintain a culture of misconduct. Through a systematic analysis of the organizational culture, the chapter highlights how the company's culture resulted in a series of ethical missteps by staff, which eventually led to the fall of the corporation and its auditing firm, Arthur Andersen.

Bridgman discusses ethical dilemmas emerging in an increasingly professionalized and commodified university. The chapter describes how an educational institution that actually engages in defending the integrity of knowledge and ethical behaviour is entangled with demands from constituents obliging it to make sacrifices in the quest for income. He explores the reasons behind this development as well as how business schools position themselves with regard to this conflict.

Laroche discusses ethical behaviour through the lenses of management and work practice. He argues that moral consciousness may be lacking, not because of intrinsic or learned indifference, but mostly because of difficulties in developing and sustaining the context of managerial work. The chapter works from the idea that ethical dilemmas are engendered by the tendency of corporations to practise 'overmanagement'. This is seen as a pattern of self-reinforcing management practices that give rise to opportunistic behaviour, resulting in a lack of learning in the organization.

Together the chapters illustrate how ethical dilemmas form an important part of the backdrop of organizational life. They imply that ethical dilemmas are not to be easily eliminated, but constitute challenges for organizations that actually give them an opportunity for endurance and renewal. Thus, to understand better the dilemmas faced by organizational leaders, we invite the reader to explore the particular characteristics of organization that create ethical dilemmas, and courses of action taken by organizational actors to deal with them. We propose that ethical dilemmas are not unique or rare, but intrinsic to organizing processes and, hence, part of the challenges that management have to address. The proliferation of rules, standards, policies, and the like, intended to simplify organizing and decision making, may sometimes lead to new dilemmas and challenges. Similarly, enhanced globalization and relativization of rules and norms contribute to the presence of ethical dilemmas for managers. In the concluding chapter, we return to the issues raised in the introduction to provide a broader scenario of implications for organization and management, building on the discussions put forth in the contributing chapters.

Notes

1 Pronounced in front of the US Senate in 1955 by General Motors' CEO, Charlie Wilson. It should be noted, however, that businesses were not entirely independent of public opinion. Herbert Simon remarked in 1947 that 'an increasing number of private businesses are becoming "affected with public interest"' (Simon, 1947). Moreover, President Dwight D. Eisenhower warned in his 'leaving office' speech in 1961 that the US had to be careful of the growing power of the relationship between the military and the industrial complex.

References

Bauman, Z. (1989) *Modernity and the Holocaust,* Cambridge: Polity.
—— (1995) *Life in Fragments*, Oxford: Blackwell.
Brunsson, N. and Jacobsson, B. (2000) *A World of Standards*, Oxford: Oxford University Press.
Hernes, T. (2007) *Understanding Organization as Process: Theory for a Tangled World*, London: Routledge.
March, J. G. (1988) *Decisions and Organizations*, Oxford: Blackwell.
Power, M. (1997) *The Audit Society: Rituals of Verification*, Oxford: Oxford University Press.
Simon, H. (1947) *Administrative Behavior*, New York: The Macmillan Company.
Wikipedia, ITT and Harold Geneen. Available online at http://en.wikipedia.org/wiki/Harold_Geneen (accessed February 15 2007).

2 Risk, responsibility and conscience

How does one communicate about morality in the risk society?

Tore Bakken

Introduction

This chapter critically engages with problems of consequentialist ethics in modern risk society. The main question which will be discussed is 'How can we act responsibly as decision makers in a society that is increasingly unpredictable and unknown to us?' It is well known that moral philosophers have long insisted that they can solve this problem by finding valid arguments for what is good and evil and on this basis formulate rules for responsible action. The aim of this chapter is to give an argumentation for the inadequacy of the moral philosophers' standpoint. Instead we should reflect upon the conditions themselves that declare an action to be moral. But this requires that the social context for morality and ethics be brought into analysis. Rather than giving principles for right and wrong behaviour, we should reflect upon how we communicate morality in risk society. This point of departure leads us into an investigation of the sociology of morality.

We are witness in the modern risk society to a tension between two opposing trends. While on the one hand we have become more skilful at 'gestalting' our life relationships by making them safer and more predictable, at the same time we register that these relationships are becoming progressively more complex, a development that is making it increasingly difficult to control society and its social systems. Max Weber (1904/1991) has described the first trend, and shown how science, technology, law and organization have contributed to an advancing rationalization of our lives. As a result of our ability to see *causal* relationships between social phenomena, we are now better able to predict specific events and their consequences. This knowledge-and-control optimism is well illustrated in Frank Knight's classic study *Risk, Uncertainty and Profit* from 1921, where our ability to calculate risk and master uncertainty is discussed as a distinctive feature of modernity. Consequences that earlier affected the individual are now treated as 'risks' and understood as *calculable risk*; the calculus of risks can be applied to almost everything – from the risks of nuclear power to the risks of smoking. It is in this sense, Ulrich Beck (1995) says, that the calculus of risks exemplifies a kind of morality without morality, the 'mathematical morality' of the technological age. It permits a type of technological moralization which no longer directly employs moral and ethical imperatives; for instance, mortality rates, under certain conditions of air pollution, replace Kant's 'Categorical Imperative'.

Complementary, and often opposed, to this development optimism we can identify the second trend. The complexity of social processes has distorted their predictability to such an extent that we can no longer rely on causal explanations of risk. This is a central theme in Charles Perrow's celebrated study from 1984, *Normal Accidents: Living with High-risk Technologies*. When investigating commissions assess the causes of an accident, the normal practice is to show how damages can be traced back causally to specific decisions and persons. However, according to Perrow, few technical risk-bearing systems are themselves *linear* systems; that is to say, systems where one can operate with indubitable calculations of if-then consequences. Instead of predictability we need to get used to the notion of unexpected effects, and this applies not only to the technological and industrial world, but also to the social and political world. There are good reasons for believing that decision makers behave in completely different ways from those presupposed by the models of rational risk calculation. The magnitude of a risk depends not merely upon the probability that a specific event will occur combined with the extent of the possible damages, but upon the *extent of the possible consequences of the event itself.* And the possible consequences of a decision can be extended ad infinitum. Moreover, with this increased complexity and unpredictability comes the awareness that it is society itself – through its actions, decisions and omissions – that must be assigned blame for the fact that damages occur. Our descriptions of society are themselves a part of that society. This will be a central argument in the following discussion. The challenge lies at the social level. It is the modern society itself that produces the damages that society in turn must address, and society can only learn to comprehend this fact as future risk is immanent in present action.

The question is: How can we act responsibly (as decision makers) in a world that is fundamentally unknown to us? Moral philosophers have long insisted that they can solve the problem by finding valid arguments for what is good and evil and on that basis formulate rules for responsible action. I will argue, however, that rather than looking for valid arguments for good and evil we should instead reflect upon the conditions themselves that declare an action to be moral. This requires that the social *context* for morality and ethics be brought into the analysis. We must be able to assume that the moral code of a society reflects the social structures of that society. We might follow moral principles in good conscience, but we cannot exempt ourselves from the negative consequences of our decisions in today's risk society. In what follows, two central concepts in particular – responsibility and conscience – will be examined in the light of such a social context.

Morality and responsibility

'Business ethics' is an attempt to examine the concept of responsibility within a socio-economic context. It represents the most widely expressed form for social ethics today (rights and duties that members of a society have, not towards themselves, but in relation to social norms, institutions and social systems) with a practical aim that targets the question of *responsibility*. It constitutes the combination of ethical principles for a good life with the economic imperatives of efficiency, utility maximization and value appreciation. Just as the growing number of ecological problems speaks of the increasing danger to the environment, so too on a growing scale are critical voices being raised for a fairer and more collectively responsible economic relationship that will ensure a sustainable future. It is not only individuals who are being urged to review their profit maximization schemes within a context of social practice, companies are now also expected to show responsibility towards employees, customers and competitors by protecting them from possible adverse effects of a company's business activities. In best Kantian terms: one should act such that the economic action corresponds to the economy's two-fold task; namely, to ensure an effective provision of goods while contributing to an improved self-realization and humane practice (Koslowski 1984: 304). If we follow Kant (1785/1964), it is not sufficient only to do the right things – an action has moral value *only* if it is done from *duty*, that is to say, from the need to do the right things because they are good in themselves. Duty is to act with due respect for the moral law. Responsibility presupposes here a duty of faultless action with respect to prescribed norms. A clear demand for sanction is thus implied against those who do not follow duty; and that which binds norm and sanction is responsibility.

When compared to 'business ethics', 'corporate social responsibility' plays down, to some degree, the duty aspect of our actions while retaining the importance of the responsibility aspect. The demand for sanctions is relaxed. Instead, it is argued that business corporations are social institutions and that owners therefore have a responsibility to their 'stakeholders'. Conditions for large international companies in today's global economy are constantly improving; it is well known that companies extract huge profits from the economy while the public poverty increases. As the public sector declines, demands are made upon private companies to provide financial assistance in areas previously covered by the public sector. This takes place in the form of sponsoring of sport, culture, scientific research and so on.

In many ways it is difficult to find fault with the motives of 'business ethics' and 'corporate social responsibility'. Of course one might point out that by weakening the public sector these movements increase the power of the private sector, but I will not take up this argument in the present discussion. What is more interesting for our purpose is to take a closer look at the kinds of sanctions one has at one's disposal when ethical demands are laid down as the basis for action. What 'regulatory authority' has morality in the modern risk society? To answer this question we will need to examine more closely what it is to communicate morally. There are essentially three dimensions that stand out.

1   The first dimension is bound up with the fact that moral communication is based upon *censure*.[1] Morality – understood as a form of communication within a social context – communicates the opposition between esteem and contempt. Esteem should be understood here not as a personal trait but rather

as a quality conferred upon one or that one confers upon others. It wins and loses, increases and decreases in social systems. From the legal world the concept of responsibility is familiar to us as the basis for deciding what consequences a norm violation will have for those violating the norm. When it comes to morality, however, the sanctions never go further than censure. One can rebuke a company for not acting morally, but one cannot oblige a company to act morally through morality. Only laws are legally binding for *all parties*. Morality and ethics will always have the sense of being a personal matter. Of course, there abound those moralists who would make their moral programmes into more than just a personal matter. They are prominent whenever legislation is passed on issues that have moral overtones: abortion, gene manipulation, euthanasia, the environment, etc. But such campaigns can never be more than an attempt by an ethical programme to provide grounds for legislation. The law can only exist in relation to the enforcement power of the state. The demand for a legal virtue is therefore difficult to implement in a modern society. So this is where one stands with censure as a means of sanction: censure of business leaders who say that they have a responsibility primarily towards owners and employees, but not towards the environment and society. Morality censures others for their indifference while it craves the opposite for itself: devotion, sympathy, or, to quote Sartre, 'identification with the Other'. Censure can be painful, especially for those directly affected by it, for instance in the form of a tarnished reputation. However, it has no legally binding effect.

2   The second dimension of moral communication is that it generates *conflict*. It is characterized not only by integration but also by conflict creation. It would seem safe to say that the nature of morality is to seek peace and harmony. In terms of society, however, this is by no means the case, either historically or empirically. It is not unusual for morality to champion a cause against an enemy, to reinforce 'in-group'/'out-group' differences and dissent to other points of view. Morality excludes. It may be true that one can no longer exclude others from the modern society, but one can still exclude them from a community of kindred thinkers. Morality can thus compensate for the impossibility of absolute exclusion by providing a milder form of censure. And it is precisely the impossibility of excluding a person from society (for example by killing the person) that induces morality to act all the more intensely and emotionally. When one cannot exclude absolutely, one can judge and evaluate. And this leads quickly to contention and conflict. Instead of excluding by purging or killing, one can do something else; for example, one can devalue others' communication. This is a part of morality's conflict-creation function.

3   The third dimension is morality's *paradoxical* character. I am referring here not so much to the kinds of paradoxes exhibited in the Enron scandal, where ethical rules were clearly in place but not observed by the company when it came to the crunch. My objective is more to point out the significance of, and to reflect upon, the distinctions we are operating. What happens if we reflect

upon the distinction between good and evil? The first thing that strikes us is that the distinction operates with a presupposition of exclusion of contraries: only good actions are worthy of being associated with a humane society. Bad actions are regarded as isolated incidents, so that 'good' represents both the positive side of the distinction *and the distinction as such*. This constitutes a notion of unity within a contrary. The Norwegian labour relations scholar Philip Herbst (1976) has shown in his study of 'Manichean logic' how the proposition 'deliver us from evil' creates a monolithic structure that compels the separation of good from evil in an absolute sense. Paradoxically enough, however, the result can be the exact opposite of the intention; namely, that instead of promoting the good we end up with a totalitarian regime. Totalitarian logic, which sets out to establish absolute certainty over what is good and what is evil, as a result of its own premises will fail to establish that certainty.

My point is that we cannot a priori take for granted that morality inheres within certain contexts or that it is always fitting. I say that morality is decidedly not fitting when it is converted into a lucrative investment to increase the profits of a company or when it in itself essentially degenerates into an independent profit source. 'Business ethics' becomes a means of amassing profits by selling symbols and values attached to products and services for which we, as consumers, create the demand. I am not suggesting that we abdicate our responsibility for the consequences of our actions, be they linked to persons or to companies; the perpetrator of the crime will naturally be held responsible for his or her crime. Indeed, such self-evident truths are difficult to disagree with. The risk society's problem, however, consists in the fact that a demand for responsibility is made for damages that have not occurred, or that we fear may occur. The challenge lies in explaining how risk and morality can be linked. This increases the complexity of the task, for not only do we need to examine the morality of risk, but also the risk of morality.

First, let us look more closely at some suggested solutions to the problem posed by responsibility in the risk society. I will outline two solutions, the first from philosopher Hans Jonas based on the morality of risk, and the second from sociologist Niklas Luhmann based on the risk of morality. The two different approaches to morality and ethics in risk society form the basis of the following discussion. On the one hand, Hans Jonas's approach which presents a new way of thinking about morality and ethics which is meant to be more adequate to problems concerning introduction of new technology in modern societies; and on the other hand Niklas Luhmann's more sceptical contribution which emphasizes the risk by using moralistic communication in a complex society.

The morality of risk

The book by German philosopher Hans Jonas *The Imperative of Responsibility* (1979) is an interesting attempt to combine consequentialist ethics with the question of risk as it pertains to the introduction of new technology. The idea is to develop a code of ethics that justifies humanity's obligations to its environment *objectively*, and that humanity, by observing this code, will save itself from environmental disaster. After all, we do not know the effects gene manipulation will have on food products over the long term, when it comes, for example, to altering both animals and humans. The 'new' in modern technology is its cumulative nature, which creates 'unprecedented situations' and abolishes earlier essential conditions. Herein lies a critique of ethical utilitarianism, which, according to Jonas, regards nature as a laboratory that one can manipulate. In this way ethical utilitarianism becomes 'an accessory' to, for example, the gene manipulation of food. The injunction to 'respect nature' thus becomes more valid than ever. However, this creates a problem of knowledge. We would prefer our knowledge to be equal to the *causal* dimensions of our actions. Causes and effects should be known (or at least known to the extent of Knight's risk-conception), but this, Jonas claims, becomes a problem in the age of technology. The gulf between our powers of prediction and our power to act creates a new ethical problem that classical anthropocentric ethics can no longer solve.

In this respect one can say that Jonas's ethics of responsibility is also an ethics of the future. It functions as a kind of 'lobby' for the non-existent, for the unborn, for that which *may* occur in the future (for example, as a result of gene manipulation). Instead of utilitarian thinking, nature's 'moral infallibility' must be defended. It means encapsulating in an ethical reflection the conditions for life and future life, a standpoint very close to Habermas (2001) in his contribution to the ethical debate on gene technology. Habermas's premise is that the power that alters organisms is different from the power that intervenes into dead or passive matter. The knowledge that one's genotype is programmed will restrict a person's ability to exercise his or her autonomy. The person becomes alien-determined from the outset; the relationship between person (life) and parent (life determiner) changes radically from what we are accustomed to and this creates a new power relationship, namely the power of existing persons over those yet to be, the latter having no power to influence existing choices. The relationship between these two parties – programmers and programmed (the clone) – is asymmetrical with no prospect of reciprocity.

What makes Jonas's solution especially interesting, however, is his proposal for the means of ensuring nature's 'moral infallibility'. Ethics based on 'moral contracts' must be more than simply a demonstration of a virtuous disposition or good intentions. It must possess a *regulating* power. It must have an ontological basis and this basis must extend to the metaphysical; it must explain how the instinctive imperative to ensure humanity's existence for the future is valid. This demands a break with all forms of value-subjectivism. Instead, humanity's new duties must be anchored in being; that is to say, in the doctrine of being and becoming, and in the idea that humanity is part of this process. Jonas attempts to establish a *binding code of behaviour*, but without anchoring the code in the categories of either the divine or of religion. This entails coming up with an 'imaginary casuistry', which, unlike the normal casuistry within law and morality, does not seek to test already known principles but rather to identify the yet to be known (for example, what we do not yet know about gene manipulation). There emerges thus the possibility of ethics still to come. Those who fear the future must also have a sense of the potential dangers that the future holds in store. In this way Jonas's ethics of responsibility leads directly into the discourse of risk. He proposes a mode of thought based on the 'heuristic of fear', for precisely in that fear is the *no* revealed to non-being (for example, gene-manipulated food) as a primary *duty* – not unlike Thomas Aquinas, where fear corresponds to prudence, hence as an opposite to lust's desire and debauchery's delights. For Jonas, then, it is a question of an ethics of duty that applies to the life possibilities of future generations. And the point of the 'heuristic of fear' is to render the menace of the future *determinable*. For fear is determinable; if we are afraid of something there is something specific we can point to. In this way Jonas provides us with an important contribution to the morality of risk.

The risk of morality

Jonas's argument for the role of fear in establishing a regulatory ethics can be challenged. Clearly if something can be rendered determinable then many of the problems besetting the risk society in regard to the future consequences of present decisions can be resolved. The question is, however, whether we possess the means to bridge the gap between the consequences of actions and our powers of the imagination as Jonas describes them. Luhmann's approach to this problem in his book *Paradigm Lost* (1990) is interesting because, in virtual opposition to the concept of fear, he argues for the concept of *angst*. He focuses not upon the morality of risk but upon the risk of morality. Unlike fear, angst is indeterminable; it can be neither justified nor specified. Luhmann thus asserts that to regard hypothetical threats that await us in the future as fear is problematical. The dangers of the future (for example, gene-manipulated food products) should be more correctly characterized as angst, precisely because of their indeterminacy and contingency (different-possible). If we go along with Jonas, living an angst-free life becomes a possibility, providing that we adhere to a determined norm. According to Luhmann, however, this would be difficult in today's society, for there no longer exists a superordinate norm for the way we should conduct our lives. For angst cannot be monitored or regulated, nor can it be scientifically refuted. Luhmann writes that 'angst (anxiety) resists any kind of critique of pure reason. It is the modern apriorism – not empirical but transcendental' (1986/1989), and adds that '(It) seems to have a great political and moral future' (p. 128). If Jonas's fear is determinable, one cannot say the same for angst. 'Angst reveals the nothingness', says Heidegger (1927/1962), meaning that in a state of angst the world around us is totally irrelevant. For that which threatens is *nowhere*; it is at one and the same time near and nowhere. For when angst relaxes its grip, 'it was really nothing at all'. What angst agonizes over is the very fact of being in the world. 'Humanity is angst', says Sartre in *Existentialism and Humanism* (1973), and by this he means that people who become involved in human relationships cannot escape the feeling of deep and utter *responsibility*. This is how angst leads humanity to self-knowledge, for everyone feels angst for the decisions that he or she takes. Anyone who has held an executive position knows the angst produced by having to choose one course of action from a range of possible alternatives. It is an angst that springs from being responsible for other people. The aspect of the free (the contingent) in our existence, the feeling that things might have been done differently, produces angst. However, angst applies not only to decision makers, it applies also to those affected by the decisions; that is to say, to the victims of the decisions. We can say with Richard Sennett (1998), that in today's 'New Economy' the old fears of dependency and loss of self-realization in the business world have given way to the angst of becoming redundant, of being made useless.

Angst-based communication thus tears down Jonas's vision to render the dangers of the future determinable. For such communication is difficult to monitor, not least for its selectivity in its choice of topics. What is more, it focuses on making things worse, not better – without one being able to say that this is irrational. And finally, those who have angst are home and dry morally speaking, especially if they feel angst for others. Against this, theoretical analyses, plausible explanations of causality, and probability calculations often have very little to offer. Angst can achieve an irresistible self-confidence, a phenomenon perhaps best expressed in the workings of the mass media.

Mass media have a special preference for moral judgements, where violations of the norm are accorded particular attention (Luhmann 1986/1989). This is especially evident when politicians or prominent business figures are accused of financial improprieties, or when sporting stars are caught taking performance-enhancing drugs, etc. Such violations, moreover, are usually portrayed as scandal; for one censures and condemns the offenders morally. This happens because the media want to assign responsibility for specific events and actions. And as a method for their reality portrayals so-called 'scripts' are often used. Such scripts simplify and reduce complexity; they have their own special technique of cutting back to familiar images, and in this way they help to produce a stereotyping of events. One creates 'scripts' for 'causal attribution', either in the form of 'question and answer' or 'cause and effect'; for example, government subsidies reduce unemployment; scuttling the Brent Spar oil platform will pollute the environment; people who eat BSE-contaminated meat can contract the brain disease CJD. One is alarmed by the fact that nothing is being done, a powerlessness that soon gives way to an appeal to do something. Something has to be done about the environment, about food contamination, about unemployment, about the war, etc. And *who* is responsible for this parlous state of affairs? The mass media's use of 'scripts' oversimplifies to the extreme the complex interdependencies of reality: it is the unemployment statistics, for example, that are examined, not the question of employment and job creation as in Keynes's day. With environmental pollution, it is the sinning polluters who must be caught; nature's self-polluting and self-cleansing cycles are kept out of the picture, for example, when it comes to natural radiation, etc. The fact that 'scripts' present an oversimplified version of a complex set of circumstances produces both a playing down and an overdramatizing of political decision-making problems. They play down the issue by finding simple solutions and they overdramatize by communicating morally. Blame must be assigned and scapegoats must be identified. In such cases moral communication can be lethal.

Conscience and responsibility

In the foregoing discussion I have attempted to identify some of the problems associated with moral communication. In the risk society, despite our having accommodated ourselves to a set of specific moral principles, there is no escaping the fact that our moral apparatus is no longer adjusted to the way the modern society functions. For while on the one hand moral principles are independent of time and events fixed in the past, decisions are acutely time-dependent and adapted expressly for the future. A constant tension is thus created between morality and decision making, a fact not difficult to verify, be it in the business world, politics or science. The consequences of the risk society's decisions seem to escape our human powers of perception completely. More risks accumulate at the centre, which for an entire lifetime will remain unseen and incomprehensible to those exposed to them, only to become known finally to succeeding generations. The moralizing of the mass media over who has the final responsibility becomes slightly comical in such a context. For the problem lies at another level, where, to paraphrase Ulrich Beck (1986), one has sinners without sins, criminals without crimes, offenders without offences; or where, as Bauman (1993) says, the final responsibility has become *fluid*.

Responsibility has no natural anchorage. We must be prepared to acknowledge that responsibility rests with the *role*, and not with the *person* playing that role. Our own era is characterized as a time of *deep moral ambiguity* despite the attempts of moral philosophers to diminish pluralism and to reject moral pluralism. Bauman's description recalls Robert Musil's critique of nineteenth-century Europe, where Musil (1980) says:

> Who can be interested any longer in the age-old idle talk about good and evil when it has been established that good and evil are not 'constants' at all, but 'functional values', so that the goodness of works depends on the historical circumstances, and the goodness of human beings on the psycho-technical skill with which their qualities are exploited? (vol. 1, p. 37)

The German philosopher Odo Marquard (1981/1989) calls this a 'departure from principles':

> We cannot spend our lives waiting for principled permission finally to begin living, because our death comes more quickly than the principles do – which is why we are forced to bid them farewell. This is why the finite human creature – with a provisional ethics for the long being, which is to say, in any case, until its death – must live without principled justification (so that conscience is always more solitary than a universal thing, and maturity is

above all the capacity for solitariness). This finite being must be contingent, and base its life on contingencies. (p. 16)

We find a common thread running through Bauman, Musil and Marquard, namely, that even if with good conscience we might follow moral principles, we have no guarantee that we will avoid damaging consequences.

The problem in truth lies in acknowledging the complexities within the things we take for granted rather than coming up with our easy tailor-made solutions. I am therefore in favour of more scepticism, not as a counter position to optimism, but rather as a strategy for identifying the contingent in every situation. A sceptic is decidedly not a person who does not know anything or who wishes not to know anything – for example, about the future. The sceptic is a person who does not know something on principle. However, the question that then poses itself is that if we do not wish to know something on principle, then where should we turn when so-called ethical dilemmas arise? The most obvious answer is that we should listen to our conscience. But what is conscience? How does it work and what problems are associated with it?

The conscience of the individual

Conscience stands as a last line of defence for our moral justifications. When we justify our actions through conscience, no arbitrary answers are admissible. For the burden of proof rests with that which pleads conscience as a justification for its action. For example, I refuse to do military service because taking the lives of other people – even in war – runs contrary to my conscience.

Conscience is clearly articulated in Thomas Aquinas's moral philosophy, and has subsequently been integrated into the tenets of the Catholic Church. Through conscience the individual is alone with God, and the voice of God is one of the premises for humanity's actions. The individual is thus freed from the demands of external social groups and institutions. In the controversy over birth control in the Catholic Church (the use of condoms when one's partner is HIV positive, etc.), many bishops went against Pope Paul VI, arguing that the voice of their conscience is a higher authority than the prescriptions of the Catholic Church. For what they were listening to was the voice of God and the voice of God is above even the Catholic Church. For when the voice of God speaks to us there is no reciprocity. In morality there is no room for reciprocity, and in this respect the relationship is fundamentally *asymmetrical*.

It is in contrast to this asymmetrical view of morality, one can say, that Heidegger's concept of *being-with* (Mitsein) (1927/1962) is revolutionary, for from the outset it carries an assumption of *symmetry*. 'The world of Dasein is a *with-world*. Being-in is *being-with* others' (p. 118). This kind of *being-with* others is much more fundamental than what is usually meant by 'intersubjectivity' or 'mutual knowledge'. I am with the other so that we – the other and I – are there *together*. This is non-substantial ethics for which Heidegger has been sharply criticized by moralists and which can be derived from interdependency without content – interdependency *before* morality. This interdependency has its foundation in *being-with*. As Xenophon writes in his introduction to a new period in the life of Socrates: 'Also upon these matters will I recount what I know in concert with him'; that is to say, with-knowledge or together-knowledge, which in Latin corresponds to *con-scienta* which forms the basis for the English word. It is a case of pure intellectual knowledge that one shares with others, such that the word is ethically neutral and in moral terms it is impossible to separate neutrality from indifference. Conscience becomes therefore a fundamental concept that can be conceived neither in psychological terms (Freud) nor in theological terms (the voice of God). The interesting thing about conscience, however, is not so much that it speaks to us, but that humanity wants to hear what it has to say. Conscience is to choose oneself 'in resolve'; that is to say, to choose responsibility. Conscience calls to people when they ignore the summons to take charge of their own lives and to live with *resolve*; but this voice is devoid of content, an emptiness that Kierkegaard experiences as 'unrest'. For Heidegger, however, such unrest does not demand that one should do one thing or neglect the other. Indeed, unrest speaks through its own silence. However, there is never any doubt over what it will say; it will call humanity back to its true responsibility. The voice of conscience is therefore not *ignored*, for humanity flees from the voice's call into an unreal existence. Duplicity thus emerges: there is nothing external to me that speaks to me but my own *being* (Dasein); but at the same time there is something that I cannot grasp – the voice comes at once from and to me. The tone of voice is often importunate and censorious, not so strange considering it springs from the 'unearthly' and the *angst* of existence, which again stems from humanity's attempt to flee from itself. In order to speak, paradoxically, conscience must remain silent; that is to say, to convey *non*-meaning. Only in this way can nothingness be revealed from an existence that finds meaning in necessity and external circumstances. Conscience cannot therefore be the voice of God or the 'public conscience'. Hence, according to Heidegger, the everyday experience that the voice of conscience comes after the event (as a judgement over an action) is wrong. The real obligation lies long before a concrete action. Heidegger rejects the medieval assumption that conscience can be a guide for our actions: that it can tell us something about the good that we should follow and that it can provide a list of safe calculable alternatives that stand ready at our disposal. Conscience cannot provide prognosis or counsel, but only urge us to live responsibly in resolve. There is no freedom that can be liberally bestowed upon humanity. Humanity must find its own freedom through 'resolve'.

This is not unlike the situation in Mark Twain's *The Adventures of Huckleberry Finn* (1967) when Huck takes the journey down the river with his friend Jim, the slave. The closer they get to the place where Jim can be legally released from his slave status, the more intensely Huck feels guilt for helping Jim. There is something from outside that calls to Huck – and that something is conscience. Huck feels guilty for an action that later everyone will agree was the right thing to do. However, Huck is merely a young boy whose conscience reflects the principles he has uncritically acquired from a society based on slave ownership. Unable to think through on his own what is right and wrong, Huck finally decides to ignore his conscience. He follows his instincts for what is right there and then, and runs away with his friend the slave. What we learn from this example is not that we should ignore our conscience but rather that its voice should be examined critically. The voice of conscience is like a warning; one should stop to consider the justness of one's actions, but one can never justify one's actions by merely following one's conscience.

Sartre's (1973) dialectic between *plea* and *help* – understood as an alternative to prayer and the ethical claim – might also bring us closer to an understanding of what it means to live responsibly in resolve. Responsibility is present, says Sartre, in whatever state one places oneself and this creates an angst-charged situation. However, to carry out a single action with moral relevance demands choice. Sartre illustrates the point with the following scene from the streets of Paris. A man runs to catch a bus that has begun to move off. Another man stands on the platform of the moving bus. The man running stretches out a pleading hand to be helped up onto the platform, while the man on the platform reaches out to help him up. Hence, one person helps the other even though they are perfect strangers and are most likely not travelling to the same destination. They both acknowledge the immediate goal of the other and therefore every person's right to live his or her life as a free individual. The help is a gift, but the one who pleads for help also gives something. He gives his confidence by entrusting his freedom to another person without ceasing to be himself. Both perceive riches in the freedom of the other. Neither attempts to make the other into an object of control. Morality must therefore manifest itself politically as a struggle to overcome every inequality in living conditions and to help establish a humane world where any plea from any person is always possible.

The strength of Heidegger and Sartre's existential ethics of responsibility is that they both come down to the level of immediate life. However, this is also a limitation. Ethics which relate only to the immediate meeting between people say little of how we live our lives removed in time and space. This is a question that cannot be escaped from in a technical age where we can injure or help one another, even if the one in need may be far away or even yet to be born. What happens when we move from an individual basis for conscience to a social level?

The conscience of society

One approach to the study of these kinds of problems is Emile Durkheim's (1958) claim that the subject of morality must be of a supra-individual character. The moral goals are thus those *with a society* as their subject. To act morally is to act with an eye towards the common good. This is so because society is not of the same order as individuals. Hence, when conscience speaks to us it is society that speaks to us from within; or in Heidegger's terms, it is the 'public' voice to which we listen.

This collective mentality is challenged by the two American researchers into organization, Goodpaster and Matthews (1982), who raise the question: 'Can corporations have a conscience?' Their basic premise is that corporations should not be less responsible than individuals and that therefore an analogy between individuals and corporations should be valid. 'If we analyse the concept of moral responsibility as it applies to persons, we find that projecting it to corporations as agents in society is possible' (p. 148). While it may be argued that corporations are not the same as individuals, corporations are still 'made up of persons' (p. 149). Plato's method is thus invoked: justice as a moral standard for 'community' is used as a model for justice for the individual (p. 150). The fact that corporations are 'artificial legal constructions' makes little difference, for 'goals, economic values, strategies, and other such personal attributes are often usefully projected to the corporate level by managers and researchers. Why should we not project the functions of the conscience in the same way?' (p. 153).

It is perhaps not so surprising that American writers focus so strongly upon the aspect of the individual in organizations. In contrast, an approach that takes into account the tradition from Durkheim, which focuses upon the tension itself between the individual and society, can be found in the literary texts of Robert Musil (1957/1980). In *The Man Without Qualities*, the businessman Arnheim says to the protagonist Ulrich (the man without qualities):

> Wherever there are two such forces, on the one side the person who really wields the power, on the other the board of governors, what automatically appears is the phenomenon that every possible means of profit-making is exploited, whether it be moral and pleasant to contemplate or no. When I say 'automatically', I mean it literally, for this phenomenon is to a high degree independent of the personal element. The person who really wields the power does not directly take a hand in the carrying out of his directions, and the individual members of the management are covered by the fact that they act not on personal grounds but as functionaries. This relationship is one you find on all sides nowadays, and not by any means exclusively in the financial sphere. You can be sure that our friend Tuzzi would give the signal for war with the clearest conscience in the world, even if, as a man, he may be incapable of shooting an old dog. And thousands of people will send your protégé Moosbrugger to his death because none of them but three need to do it with their own hands! This system of 'indirectness', developed to the point of virtuosity, is what nowadays guarantees each individual, and society as a whole, the possession of a clear conscience ... I should almost go so far as to say that what is manifested here, in the form of social division of labour, is nothing but the dualism in man's conscience between the end that is approved and the means that are tolerated – it is the same thing, even if in a form that is grand and dangerous. (vol. 2, pp. 420–421)

Musil continues:

> Ulrich had shrugged his shoulders in answer to Arnheim's question whether he found all this abominable. The split in the moral consciousness, of which Arnheim spoke, this most frightful of the phenomena in modern life, was

something that had always existed, but it had acquired its appallingly clear conscience only in recent times, as a consequence of the universal division of labour, and in this form it also had something of the magnificent inevitability of the latter. It went against the grain with Ulrich to indulge in indignation about this. On the contrary, and as though in defiance, he had the comical and pleasant sensation that one can get from tearing along at sixty miles an hour, leaving a dust-bespattered moralist standing by the wayside, cursing. (ibid. p. 421).

The division of labour understood as social differentiation – as it is so aptly described in Durkheim's texts – acquires thus in Musil a direct relevance for how we should understand the social character of conscience in modern societies.

Luhmann (1965) also provides a clearer picture of the kinds of social mechanisms which come into effect when conscience is protected by law, and thus might be seen as following up the arguments of both Durkheim and Musil. From an historical perspective one might say that since the nineteenth century conscience has become interiorized, while law has become exteriorized. Luhmann's premise is that a differentiation has taken place within law, science and ethics. The reasoning is that all functional systems such as law, the economy, politics, science and so on, have detached themselves from morality, that the systems are drained of moral content. They are amoral. In this way conscience is made highly personal, and it constrains only personally. One expects no inter-subjective truth from it. As a result of differentiation, in legal questions we can no longer base ourselves upon scientific truths, and in questions of scientific truth we can no longer base ourselves upon conscience, and vice versa. The manner of argumentation in the one area must be sealed off from the manner of argumentation in the other area. At the same time, however, the personality needs protection from the pressure of the outside world, and in this way conscience constitutes a control mechanism that can secure the single individual identity; that is to say, the possibility for the individual to represent himself or herself within a society.

One can thus say that in the modern society the general control of the personality is left to conscience. With conscience humanity now has in its possession the possibility of re-examining its actions against agreed norms. Moreover, this is how one's personal identity can be made into a basis for *reflection*. One can say that conscience places the confidence of its own integrity at risk. It makes things uncertain. Through conscience one can make oneself intolerable, for one can question one's own identity, which can take one to the brink of death: for in conscience one 'resolves upon one's own identity' (Heidegger). In the final analysis, the possibility of choosing one's own death radically renders humanity independent of the world around it, and renders it therefore also free. Humanity is thus made responsible for its actions. In the presence of conscience there are no excuses.

What we have described above is the conventional understanding of conscience; that is to say, the right to act in accordance with one's own conscience. If we go a step further and inquire into the latent functions of the institutionalization of the freedom of conscience, then the relationship between freedom and conscience automatically becomes an issue; but then we come to considerations that pull in the opposite direction, which brings us to the point that Luhmann makes: the freedom of conscience shall save society from too much conscience.

Hence, there emerges a tension between presiding over oneself according to the dictates of conscience and presiding over conscience within a social context (social systems). Conscience is limited in two ways: firstly by the consequences of one's actions and secondly by the conditions or the possibilities for making use of conscience. Therefore, in a social context, studying how conscience *cannot* control our actions is just as important as studying how it can control them. For example, the person who, due to the dictates of conscience, will not kill others in war will be an unreliable comrade, for the conflict of conscience could harm a role-context. Further, one is bound by one's family. One who is loved by others feels this as a constraint in other role-contexts, for example in government–political life or other contexts (in the business world), where one is unable to decide according to one's conscience out of consideration for one's family. This is especially evident in totalitarian states where one neglects to act according to one's conscience on the grounds that it might adversely affect not only oneself but also one's family and friends. In constitutional democracies too, one cannot simply turn the dictates of one's conscience upon the state without exposing one's family to harmful repercussions, which could eventually lead to financial ruin. Every professional role has, as Musil describes above, a clear obligation to conform. One is free, one can say and believe what one likes, one can practice 'exit' or 'voice', as Hirschman (1970) says – but not with impunity. One cannot withdraw from the field while at the same time retaining one's gains.

In this sense then, with Bauman, Musil and Luhmann, we can conclude that in a differentiated society one must, in various ways, be cautious about orientating oneself too rigidly according to one's conscience. Society – as institutional context – helps in evading the incalculable freedom of choice that conscience offers. Society immunizes against too much conscience. For example, a vendor does not need to feel pangs of conscience because a potential buyer cannot afford his merchandise. This is one of the reasons why so few young people claim conscience as grounds for exemption from military service. The point is that the social systems we operate in cannot impose themselves upon the personality function of conscience, but they can be immunized against it. For conscience will not only make itself known, it will also be responsible and it is the social structures that discipline conscience, that demand that it behave responsibly.

From the above reasoning then, we can conclude that in a social context conscience is an inner voice that humanity should heed, but at the same time not heed, a contradiction which naturally leads to uncertainties and controversies of great practical significance. In this sense, perhaps it is better to say that conscience is not a 'voice', but a *function*.

Conclusion

So what are we left then with? Should all forms of moral communication in the risk society be rejected? The answer is that it is more a case of playing down the importance of our need for principles of moral communication and for the allocation of responsibility, needs that derive more from self-justification than from actual circumstances, and instead look towards the contingent aspects of our existence where the challenge is to handle greater complexity more competently. We need to reduce the influence of Kant's 'categorical imperative' while taking up again the work of Hegel, which consists in reflecting on morality and how it communicates in society. There are too many people with pretensions to moral responsibility; they have all the right answers without having asked the questions. One question we must ask is the following: Are we applying moral communication intelligently? In this way we might follow Foucault's (1988) instructions when he says that he considers himself a moralist to the extent that he believes that one of life's tasks is never to accept anything as final, as something that shall not be tampered with, as an open-and-shut case, as unshakeable. There is a fundamental shortcoming in the traditional ethics of responsibility, and this shortcoming is one of self-application, or perhaps we might say, of the prohibition against 'self-exemption'. To defeat this shortcoming we need ethics which can make us more sensitive to how we communicate morality, rather than giving principles for right and wrong behaviour.

Notes

1 The word 'censure' is not to be confounded with 'censorship'. 'Censure' refers to *expression* of disapproval or condemnation, whereas censorship refers to the act whereby an authority suppresses something that has been – or is in the process of being – expressed.

References

Bauman, Z. (1993) *Postmodern Ethics*, Oxford: Blackwell.

Beck, U. (1986/1992) *Risk Society: towards a new modernity*, London: Sage.

—— (1995) *Ecological Enlightenment. Essays on the politics of the risk society*, Humanity Books: New York.

Donaldson, T. (1982) *Corporations and Morality*, London: Prentice-Hall.

Durkheim, E. (1958) *Professional Ethics and Civic Morals*, Glencoe, IL: Free Press.

Foucault, M. (1998) 'Power, moral values and the intellectual', *History of the Present*, 4, Spring: 1.

French, P. (1979) 'The corporation as a moral person', *American Philosophical Quarterly*, July: 207.

Goodpaster, K. E. and Matthews, J. B., Jr. (1982) 'Can a corporation have a conscience?', *Harvard Business Review*, 60: 132.

Habermas, J. (2003) *The Future of Human Nature*, Cambridge: Polity Press.

Hegel, G. W. F. (1832/1971) *Phänomenologie des Geistes*, Frankfurt am Main: Suhrkamp.

Hirschman, A. O. (1970) *Exit, Voice and Loyalty*, Cambridge: Harvard University Press.

Heidegger, M. (1927/1962) *Being and Time*, New York: Harper and Row.

Herbst, P. (1976) *Alternatives to Hierarchies*, Leiden: Martinus Nijhoff.

Jonas, H. (1979/1984) *The Imperative of Responsibility*, Chicago: The University of Chicago Press.

—— (1985) *Technik, Medizin und Ethik. Zur Praxis des Prinzips Verantwortung*, Frankfurt am Main: Insel Verlag.

Kant, I. (1964) *Fundamental Principles of the Metaphysics of Morals*, New York: Harper and Row.

Knight, F. H. (1921/1971) *Risk, Uncertainty and Profit*, Chicago: The University of Chicago Press.

Koslowski, P. (1984) *Ethik des Kapitalismus*, Tübingen: Mohr Siebeck.

Ladd, J. (1970) 'Morality and the ideal of rationality in formal organizations', *The Monist*, 54(4): 499.

Langston, D. C. (2001) *Conscience and Other Virtues: from Bonaventure to MacIntyre*, University Park, PA: The Pennsylvania State University Press.

Luhmann, N. (1965) 'Die Gewissensfreiheit und das Gewissen', *Archiv des öffentlichen Rechts*, 90(3) Tübingen: J.C.B. Mohr, pp. 257–287.

—— (1986/1989) *Ecological Communication*, Cambridge: Polity Press.

—— (1990) *Paradigm lost: Über die ethische Reflexion der Moral*, Frankfurt am Main: Suhrkamp.

—— (1993) *Risk: a sociological theory*, Berlin: Walter de Gruyter.

—— (2000) *The Reality of the Mass Media*, Stanford: Stanford University Press.

Luhmann, N. and Pfürtner, S. H. (1978) *Theorietechnik und Moral*, Frankfurt am Main: Suhrkamp.

Marquard, O. (1981/1989) *Farewell to Matters of Principle*, Oxford University Press: Oxford.

Musil, R. (1957/1980) *The Man without Qualities*, New York: Putnam.

Perrow, C. (1984) *Normal Accidents: living with high-risk technologies*, New York: Basic Books.

Sartre, J. P. (1973) *Existentialism and Humanism*, London: Eyre Methuen.

Sennett, R. (1998) *The Corrosion of Character: the personal consequences of work in the new capitalism*, New York: W. W. Norton.

Twain, M. (1967) *Adventures of Huckleberry Finn*, New York: Bobbs-Merrill.

Weber, M. (1904/1991) *The Protestant Ethic and the Spirit of Capitalism*, London: Harper Collins.

3 White as snow or milk?

Strategies for handling ethical dilemmas in a dairy corporation

Tor Hernes, Gerhard E. Schjelderup and Anne Live Vaagaasar

Managers have to incorporate an increasing number of stakeholders' concerns in their decision-making processes. Stakeholders, such as mass media, public authorities, business partners, customers, activist groups, shareholders and employees create demands that pose increasingly complex challenges to managers. Today, managers face challenges related to factors such as business ethics, environmental issues and staff welfare among many others. Faced with a multiplicity of demands, managers employ various strategies. We refer to these strategies as 'discursive' strategies in the sense that they consist of actions intended to communicate intentions about actions to stakeholder groups. We identify essentially five types of strategies: diversification, countering, repackaging, decoupling and cover-up. Each one of these is a distinct strategy type serving to deal with ethical dilemmas in management. We illustrate the types of strategies with observations of the evolution of a large dairy corporation.

Companies and presentation

Corporate actors can be seen as performing for two primary reasons. One reason is simply to get things done. Companies are formed in order to get things done more efficiently than if individuals were to go about the task without being organized. Organizing humans is as old as human history. A very early example of large scale human organization was the building of the first cities, more precisely the cities of the Maya in Peru. Building a city required that actions were coordinated among many people so that buildings, roads and public places could be created in a reasonably orderly fashion. It required that clergy, army, artisans, commercial establishments and family dwellings were positioned in relation to each other so that the city could fulfil the purposes of a city, such as to promote commerce, ensure production of goods and ensure protection against enemies. If we take the leap to today's modern corporation, organization is still about getting things done in an efficient manner, such as delivering goods and services on schedule, adhering to plans and budgets, motivating staff and making the most of available technologies. Annual reports usually contain numerous graphs and figures that represent the performance of the company.

Efficiency is, however, not the only aim of organizing. Organized actions also *convey* another message to actors who are concerned with what is being done. When the Mayas built cities, the very act of building cities *conveyed* not only that organized housing was being provided, but also that something safe and functional was being made for the inhabitants. The fact that building activities were coordinated expressed the message that the developing city would respond to the concerns of those who were to inhabit it. Not only was the efficiency of building the city important, but the very value of the city in itself. To switch back to the modern corporation again, when something is produced on time and according to specifications, this very fact communicates that those behind the production are able to produce on time and according to specifications. Moreover, it expresses that those who did it then can do it again. In other words, getting it right was not an accident, but was the result of how the resources were organized, hence communicating a certain level of reliability. Moving from individual companies to the market, the very value of the stocks of a company is based on what the company conveys to the stock market as assets and performance that are relevant.

Hence every action, in addition to being an action in itself, conveys a message to other actors, whether explicitly intended or not. We would argue, in fact, that in today's consumer-oriented society, it is often more important what actions actually convey than what they 'are'. When a company, for example, launches a new product to a segment of the consumer market, it is important that this activity conveys the message that the product is made by the company especially to meet the specific needs of a particular consumer segment.

What is it that companies convey? Conveying is more than presenting the company in terms of words and images, such as through its catalogue of products and/or services. Conveying is *representing* the company in such a way that several of its salient characteristics can be experienced or observed. Nike, for example, is more than its range of sportswear. Nike is part of the cult of American basketball as well as American athletics on a broad scale; it has its special logo; it has its special history, including its founders; its technologies (making shoes from recycled materials), and many other factors. When Nike operates in the market, it puts forward aspects of itself which together make up what we might call the 'identity' of Nike. This identity, consisting of various aspects of the company, makes it recognizable, not just by the customer, but also by its employees, partner companies, public authorities and competitors. Because conveying is about representing salient aspects of the company (including its products), when you buy a product, such as a pair of Nike shoes, although in physical terms you buy a pair of shoes only, the acquisition is based on more than just the shoes. The acquisition involves a perception of Nike as a company as well as the quality and price of the shoes. The success and pervasiveness of Nike's communication in this regard have made scholars define the Nike brand as an 'iconic brand' (Holt 2004).

Discourse as structures of things

'Representing' lies at the core of what is called 'discourse', which is the term we shall use from now on. Whereas 'representation' is a general and everyday term applied to individual aspects of a company, 'discourse' refers to a structured totality of the things that are communicated about a company.[1] When we say 'structured', it is to signify not only that several things related to the company are considered, but also that they make sense relative to one another. The various representations are assembled in such a way that they make sense in terms of their totality and in terms of the relations between its elements. The elements making up discourses can be structured in various ways to perform what we shall talk of as discursive structures. Later we will show how several discursive structures emerged as ethical dilemmas in the context of a dairy corporation.

So what can be said about the discourse of a company? To be sure, there are hundreds, or thousands, of things that make up a company. However, there are some things that tend to be more recurrent – and hence more noticeable – than others. To explore these more closely, we will work from the idea of *discursive structures*. By the term 'discursive structures', we mean the ways in which features of the company connect to one another in order to represent the company as a whole in people's minds. These are the things that we associate with that specific company, and which make up what we call its identity. When we read about a company, when it is mentioned in the media, or when we use its products or services, some things about it are more noticeable than others. Let us return to the Nike example, to see what things might be seen to make up its discursive structure. The first element constituting the discursive structure may be the stated *mission*[2] of the company, which is: 'To bring inspiration and innovation to every athlete in the world'.[3] While the common understanding of the word 'athlete' is that of someone participating at sports events, the word 'athlete' is specifically used in the mission formulation to suggest that anybody is or can be an athlete. Hence, the mission statement reflects release of potential in anybody's 'body'. Mission statements are generally written down to give a sense of direction for decisions in the company, while also providing an overall indication to outsiders about the values of the company.

A second element making up this structure may be the *leadership structure* of the company, by which we mean essentially two things. First, the positions of key persons in the company. Often this relates to top executives, but it may also include other prominent persons, such as important designers or software developers. Positions of key persons are important elements of the discursive structure because key persons are often seen to embody the company's culture[4] and the basis for strategic choices. A notable example here is given in Apple CEO Steve Jobs' keynote addresses at the annual MacWorld events in San Francisco, at which he evokes the Apple culture, as well as the novelty and performance of its products. In the case of Nike as another example, the founder, former CEO and now chairman of the board, Phil Knight, appears extensively in media, in advertising and in Nike internal communications. He appears as a central and strong leader who evokes the history of the company, as well as its current mission.

A third element that may make up a company's discursive structure is its *organizational composition*. The organizational composition includes company functions serving to group and support company activity. Most companies include standard functions, such as marketing, finance, personnel, R&D, to name a few. Moreover, many such functions operate similarly in different companies, using the same or similar working methods and computer software. Some functions, however, are conceived to distinguish a company from others, either in order to give it a competitive edge or to provide it with an identity different from other companies. Nike's discourse includes emphasis on its organizational functions dedicated to community work. There are, in fact, two functions: (1) the Nike Foundation is a Nike-supported non-governmental organization that extends aid to projects working to help disadvantaged teenage girls around the world; (2) Community Affairs extends funds to non-profit organizations that help kids get more physically active and involved in team sports.

A fourth example of a central element of the discursive structure is represented by the products of a company. For example, Nike shoes have been made from waste material or recycled shoes for many years, making them a positive force addressing environmental concerns of modern consumers. This may appeal to the more socially and environmentally aware segments of the population, including higher-income adults. The products relate closely to the *customer groups* of a company, although customers are physically outside the company. In the case of Nike, there is a 'structure' of customer groups. At the top of the pyramid we find top athletes representing largely 'symbolic customers' that other customers consciously or subconsciously want to emulate. Below that level we find a number of sponsored and non-sponsored active athletes who prefer the shoes for their specific qualities. There are also deals between professional, college, and high school athletic teams and the sports companies whereby the companies (sales people) will go to an athletic team and offer lower cost or free products if the team will use their products. Still, among the dominant customer groups in terms of numbers, we find a number of groups as different as urban low-income youngsters and middle class, middle age persons. Products are targeted, more or less specifically, to different customer groups.

The making of a dairy corporation and its changing discursive structure

To illustrate the elements that are conveyed by a company, we have analysed the emerging discursive structure of the Norwegian dairy cooperative TINE.[5] We explore how these structures develop over time and also identify how they take the form of discursive strategies as the corporation tries to cope with ethical dilemmas, mainly concerned with the problem of milk being both a source of nutrition and a potential health danger.

We will first look at the core asset of a dairy cooperative, namely milk itself. Milk is a symbol of life, a source of nutrition, and a product. This makes it a particularly interesting object of study with respect to ethics. The essence of milk is that it has strong connotations of health and hygiene. Much of the Norwegian national diet in the post-Second World War years was based on dairy products. In fact, the diet proved to be far more than just a diet. It also connected to national culture and perceptions of 'Man and Nature'. TINE has been the main carrier of this strong symbolism, using values related to milk and its several symbolic qualities to underpin its organizational culture.

So, what happens then, when milk is perceived to be a health hazard rather than being 'the source of life itself'? In post-Second World War years the belief was that the more milk and dairy products you consumed, the better it was, and the main concerns were related to logistics, costs, prices and hygiene. However, with research suggesting that milk fat causes heart disease, corporations such as TINE have had to review their products as well as the discourse around their products. What has happened in the case of the cooperative TINE is that its very identity of production has shifted from being a provider of health to being seen as a potential producer of risk. Although our study has mainly looked at written material spanning the last 37 years, we have also studied some scarce source material dating back more than a century, in addition to interviews with people in the company. What we found was that TINE has gone from being a functional organization, where the main concerns were how to serve their owners' (dairy producers) economic and political needs best, to a market orientation. With this new orientation, dilemmas of ethics have emerged.

What could we identify as a possible discursive structure of a dairy corporation? In order to come to grips with its discursive structure, we studied the annual reports of the corporation between 1970 and 2007 to understand how it communicated its performance. Over the 37 years, between 1970 and 2007, an adaptation of the discourse surrounding milk took place. The increasing diversification took place as milk came under attack from various actors in public life. Perhaps the most important organizational crisis that TINE has yet faced occurred in the late 90s. Prominent health spokespersons, practitioners and researchers emerged with public warnings against drinking too much milk, which had been highly recommended to reduce osteoporosis. We witnessed a reactive discursive strategic change in the annual reports. (Examples of this discursive transition will be shown under the section on TINE's strategies for handling ethical dilemmas.) For the first time in its history, TINE was now threatened by a perception that might, if fully developed, seriously harm the company's existence. Decreasing demand for milk has more or less been the order of the day for the last thirty years, but this attack on the a priori acceptance of milk as a unique source of nutrition represented the largest crisis in ideology that TINE had yet encountered.

TINE[6] was founded in 1881 as a dairy cooperative in Norway, and is today the major producer of dairy products in Norway with an annual turnover of approximately 1.6 billion US dollars and approximately 4400 staff. It dominates by far the Norwegian domestic market in terms of dairy products. Such a position is not unique to TINE and Norway. In 2001, approximately 93 per cent of the world's production of milk was consumed in the country of production (Pritchard 2001). TINE is also a major exporter of cheese (e.g. Jarlsberg cheese) to other countries, mainly the United States, Great Britain and Japan. In fact, in 2004 it was the largest single international exporter of cheese to the US.

When the corporation's predecessor was formed in the nineteenth century, its aims were dictated largely by the logistical necessity of local farmers to find a collective solution to the problem of transporting milk to their customers. Over time, the corporation and its activities have become woven into national questions of nutrition and politics, to the extent that today, TINE has to manoeuvre in a discursive public arena in addition to keeping up its functional operations.

From the middle of the nineteenth century, Europe experienced a sharp increase in the focus on hygiene, which derived, in part, from Pasteur's work on germ theories in France in the 1860s (Latour 1988). 'Pasteurization', the killing of pathogenic bacteria in fluids such as milk, was adopted as an important way of protecting the public from diseases. Additionally, there was a concurrent, although not entirely unrelated, focus on health. According to Latour (1988) industrialization took its toll on workers through hard work under harsh conditions. Amid a rapidly rising industrial activity, the general health of the population was degenerating, and medical journals in Europe began to focus on 'regeneration' of populations. At the same time, a demand emerged in industry for 'healthy men' in order to sustain production outputs (Latour 1988: 18).

The increase in focus on nutrition, health and hygiene prepared the ground for the mass consumption of milk. Milk, however, demands close attention and control to prevent lactic bacteria cultures from developing. At the same time milk is extracted in environments that are far from clean. Hence, the logistics of milk from early on has been subjected to constant refinement of methods of extraction, tapping, storage and transport in order to ensure that the milk is fit for human consumption. Dairy corporations such as TINE have, since their inception, not only ensured logistics, but also provided advice, training and control to ensure that standards of hygiene were kept. This is alluded to throughout the annual reports. In fact, a basic role for dairy corporations lies in facilitating the logistics imposed by the combined challenge of a required high production volume and the organic fragility of milk. Similarly, in a study of the American dairy industry, Dupuis (2002: 35) observes that milk, perceived as a perfect source of nutrition, led to tight links between industry, technology and science. The focus on technology and science has also made its mark on the organizational culture. One director said in an interview 'Listen, this has traditionally been a culture of straight pipes'. Another person interviewed was amused when he recalled that less than 20 years ago, administrative staff at the corporate headquarters in Oslo actually wore white technician coats.

In the case of Norway, milk is associated with hygiene, nature, and cultural identity. It is clear from our sources that TINE has been closely interwoven into Norwegian national culture over several decades. Some organization studies point to connections between national culture and organizational values. Trice and Beyer (1993) in particular show how ideologies arise from extra-organizational sources. The 2002 TINE annual report features various photographs of a male farmer, his wife, cattle, work on the farm, Norwegian scenery and the harsh climate of winter. The overall theme has a national romanticist flavour to it, which we find throughout other annual reports. The theme of Norwegian culture and TINE as an actor in the expression of nationalism comes out in several places.

For example, several reports have pictures of visits by the royal family to TINE dairies. At a culinary level, TINE has been displaying recipes on how to make variations of traditional Norwegian dishes (of course, using their products) on their internet site for years.

The element of national culture is by no means accidental. The cooperative that eventually became the TINE Corporation was founded as a dairy cooperative in 1881, at a time when there was a surge of nationalism and national romanticism in Norway that eventually led to the dissolution of the union with Sweden in 1905. National character and national autonomy were themes used in the playwright Henrik Ibsen's writings and other artistic artefacts from around the turn of the century. The national romanticism comes out clearly in paintings from the 1880s, with landscapes in warm colours and farmers in national costumes amid grazing cattle, and this imagery is mirrored throughout the annual reports of TINE. Nationalism in Norway is strongly linked to nature, something that comes out clearly in works of music, poetry and literature. Thus we see that TINE has maintained this very tight connection with developments in Norwegian society for more than a century. The very identity of the Corporation, as shown by text and pictures in the annual reports, is almost inextricably interwoven with national trends. This fact makes it particularly vulnerable to reactions from society, and its dilemmas extend beyond the need to survive as a commercial enterprise.

Cleanliness and ethics

Traditionally, milk has been closely connected to cleanliness. Its white colour is pervasive in the TINE discourse, drawing upon a number of associations. Cleanliness relates to high ethical standards. A social anthropologist, Mary Douglas (1966), studied rituals in social groups and suggested that rituals serve to separate cleanliness from dirt and how the distinction in turn serves as a mechanism of social cohesion. Social cohesion and institutional rules are created and maintained by reminding members of a society about what is considered proper and clean for that society. She quotes Lord Chesterfield, who defined dirt 'as being matter out of place'. Consistent with this definition, Douglas sees dirt as that which upsets the sense of coherent thought in a society and hence threatens to upset the social order. For example, if monks of various orders are in contact with women, they need to cleanse themselves through praying and repentance. Hence cleansing is a central element so that one can be brought back into the fold of 'the coherent'. Cleansing is a logical remedy to having become dirty, because dirt, according to Douglas, is associated with that which is found at the edges or the margins of society. Getting dirty should induce bad conscience while staying clean should guarantee good conscience (or avoiding bad conscience). In Western society, cleanliness tends to be associated with bright colours whereas dirt tends to be associated with dark colours. For example, myths and fairy tales have traditionally shown white and brightness as representing the good while black and darkness represent evil. Witches[7] for example, had dark hair and were dressed in black, whereas princesses had fair hair. Angels are white whereas the devil is dark. Hell is dark whereas heaven is bright. Thus we see that TINE has successfully made use of a pre-established cultural dichotomy between white (good/clean), and dark (evil/dirty).

Milk, as it is presented in the TINE discourse, symbolizes cleanliness. Cleanliness because it is white, but cleanliness also because it is seen to represent health and nature, which in the Norwegian context connects to snow, which of course is also white. The annual report from 1986, for example, shows a link between milk and health by featuring a photograph of a Norwegian female cross-country skiing team drinking milk. Milk is nature's own perfect food, to borrow from Dupuis' (2002) study of the role of milk in American society.

The connection milk–cleanliness–ethics is particularly important to corporations such as TINE. Cleanliness is synonymous with health, that which is good. Health is good for the nation, so the corporation that produces milk, and thus contributes to good health, is good for the nation. The connections between health, cleanliness, nation and corporation thus become interwoven and nested. The nesting takes place in the form of positive loops, where a positive value attached to one element triggers a positive value in another element. In this way, a positive mutual reinforcement circulates among the elements. TINE has made strong efforts to highlight the cleanliness related to milk production using images of their laboratories and technicians, while at the same time showing how clean the cows' stables are.

TINE has been a company (or cooperative) during a time when great societal changes have occurred. This has posed challenges to the corporate ideology and engendered various ethical dilemmas. The position of TINE as an almost monopolist actor in Norwegian dairy production makes such questions critical. While its market position cannot necessarily be challenged, at least not in the short run, its very prominence in the national market makes it a perfect target for discursive attacks, not just from competitors, but from other pressure groups and nutrition specialists. When one element of the discursive structure, and in particular the main element of milk, comes under attack, it has potentially serious consequences for the corporate identity, especially since it is linked to societal developments and attitudes.

TINE's discursive strategies for handling ethical dilemmas

TINE has employed several strategies over the last 37 years to adapt to market orientation. It has been under pressure for several reasons. We have previously mentioned milk fat and heart disease which have created ethical dilemmas for the corporation. We will describe how TINE has used four strategies to cope with these types of ethical dilemmas. We also propose a fifth strategy that we have identified in other business cases, which we did not find in TINE's repertoire.

Diversification

Companies, whose identity is built around core products or processes, may seek to diversify their activities so that their fate is not exclusively linked to their core products in case their core products might cause ethical problems. This is a strategy that seeks to avoid putting all of the company's proverbial eggs in one basket, and is particularly relevant when the main product or service puts the organization in a particularly vulnerable position. Diversification is a way of handling risk related to ethics. It diverts attention to a broader range of products and activities and reduces some of the negative attention towards the main product line.

The market orientation at TINE has seen a distinct diversification of the product range to cater to the increasingly diverse needs of an expanding number of customer groups. Forty years ago, there were basically two versions of milk; whole milk and fermented milk. Today the range of products has more than a dozen options, including, for example, the production of low-lactose milk for people with lactose intolerance. It is clear that the corporation talks and acts in a wider range of domains than it did previously. Its areas of expansion and diversification have altered its discursive structure over time. First, going after new consumer groups, such as the toddler market, in which TINE launched a number of products in 1999.[8] Second, by introducing functional foods and fresh instant dinners through the acquisition of Fjordland in 1994. Third, by developing new tastes and products, such as exotic tasting yoghurts in the 1980s and fruit juices in the 1990s. Fourth, by expanding production into foreign markets, such as setting up a Jarlsberg cheese plant in the USA in 2002.

These initiatives reflect a diversification of TINE's products serving to expand its discursive structure with new elements. One effect of diversification is to diminish the risk of being seriously hit by ethical ambiguities associated with wholemilk-based products. It means, for example, that when stakeholders focus on the harmful effects of milk, the criticism does not have to be absorbed by the entire range of products.

Countering

Countering may be seen as a means to defend one's actions based on evidence about one's actions. One example is when outside research institutes are contracted by a corporation to carry out research. Countering is largely a defensive strategy, attempting to thwart attacks on the organization from, say, pressure groups and competitors. Countering usually involves building the capacity to provide validated evidence. As mentioned, this means mounting scientific counter evidence showing that products, seen from another angle, are less harmful than critics allege. Countering may be done through a number of different mechanisms, including publicity, conferences and publications.

In the case of TINE, we identified several ways of countering. We have mentioned that the largest organizational crisis that TINE faced occurred in the 90s when prominent health spokespersons, practitioners and researchers emerged with public warnings about drinking too much milk which they argued was associated with osteoporosis. The argument was that Norwegians are among the largest consumers of milk in the world, and health spokespersons speculated about whether osteoporosis was related to consumption of too much calcium. We now witnessed a reactive discursive strategic change in the annual reports. This initially resulted in TINE first denouncing these charges (as found in the annual report of 1998) as 'unscientific'. An annual report reads

> The Board is worried about the effect of the biased presentation some of our central nutrition experts give of milk and dairy products. [...] The Board has a hard time understanding the negative critique that occurs from time to time and hopes for a better cooperative climate in the time to come.
>
> (Executive summary: 11–12)

Later reports showed that the fact had sunk into the organizational discourse, because the annual reports started using more space to show the public and farmers that they went a long way to work with the antagonists to find solutions to reducing the risk of osteoporosis, as we witness in the next annual report from 1999:

> TINE's research tasks related to nutrition and health are often conducted in cooperation with other environments, either it is within the agricultural cooperative, or other external groups. One example of such coordinated research projects through the year 1999 was the project called 'The significance of milk', where researchers from various institutions studied consummation of milk and its possible effects on diabetes and osteoporosis.
>
> (Annual report 1999: 31)

A web-based information service on dairy products was established in 2003 and co-financed by TINE. The service provides information on a number of issues related to dairy products. Rather than touch upon the question of heart disease, it offers a range of other research and consumer data on dairy products. For example, it may highlight an internationally published article on how milk helps with losing weight. As a discursive element, such a strategy is structural in the sense that the organization co-finances an external agency that serves its purpose. At the same time, the agency appears, in this case, as an autonomous agency, which lends it credibility as a countering device. In any event, it can be seen as a communicative strategy with the aim to defend the legitimacy of milk as a source of nutrition.

Repackaging

Repackaging means redefining practices, putting them in a context in which they can be criticized, but with more difficulty. For example, companies who outsource activities to poor countries may come under attack for 'selling out' employment. They may then repackage their intentions as a means of ensuring that the trademark remains as a national ownership. Repackaging is primarily a means of diverting attention, by changing the meaning of certain practices.

Milk as a nutritious substance was an a priori factor that was never questioned in the early stages of the history of TINE. As mentioned above, much of the Norwegian national diet in the post-Second World War years was based on dairy products. This gave TINE a central national role as a 'provider of health' during the reconstruction of the economy.

From around 1986, however, the potentially harmful qualities of milk came under increasing attack. From this time on we see that TINE began to emphasize the cow as a symbol closely linked to nature and also national identity. Although there was still a strong emphasis on the functional aspects, the annual reports that we studied shifted significantly towards a romanticization of milk and cows. This happened at a time when milk was slowly starting to lose ground in the market as the premium source of nutrition and milk was increasingly coming under attack. It forced TINE to shift their discursive strategy to focus strongly on the national importance as well as the historical importance milk had had for the building of a healthy society. For example, 1994 was the year where Norway arranged the winter Olympics. TINE was naturally interested in tying their product and logo to these important athletic events to enhance the perception of the strong ties of nationality and their importance in the national project. For example, the corporation ran advertisements where leading Norwegian athletes were pictured with milk moustaches, which later were included in the annual reports.

In this case, repackaging was done in relation to the corporation's main product, and significantly attributed a different image to the product than what had been done previously. Since the main product (milk) was a core discursive element, the repackaging of the product thus represented an alteration of TINE's overall discursive structure.

Structural decoupling

Structural decoupling means dissociating the organization from practices that are potentially harmful to the conscience of the organization. It may mean firing a person employed by the organization because of disreputable behaviour that reflects badly on the company. It may also mean sub-contracting activities with which the organization does not want to be associated. This is the tactics employed by Nike, for example, in having their sneakers produced by low-income workers in South East Asia. After researchers discovered that Nike and other similar companies paid abysmal wages to their workers, production in these places was largely sub-contracted so that the workers would not be seen as employed by Nike. Instead they would be on the payrolls of local and national sub-contractors whose practices Nike claimed not to be able to control, except through contracts. Following increased reactions from activist groups and research institutes, Nike realized that just decoupling was not enough, and then demanded that their sub-contractors adhered to basic labour laws as well as human rights. As Nike imposed their demands, they were able to counter criticism by developing their own information records of their practices.

TINE experienced a crisis of business ethics in 2005, which led to a decision to decouple, although in a different way from the Nike example. Having enjoyed an almost monopolistic position in the Norwegian market, it became increasingly threatened by competitor Synnøve Finden, a privately owned dairy company.

Competition focused on getting exclusive access to chains of food stores. In one case it transpired that TINE had paid – or offered to pay – the ICA food store chain[9] if they removed Synnøve Finden's cheese from their stores. Removing Synnøve Finden's cheese from store shelves would make sure that TINE cheese was the only brand available. When the story came out, it angered consumers as well as farmers and other stakeholders.

After having tried to cover up the real story for some days, TINE finally admitted to unethical behaviour, and fired its CEO to retain legitimacy with its stakeholders. This is a way of structural decoupling in the form of a discursive strategy because it sends a message that the CEO could be seen to be associated with the unethical behaviour. In a sense, the CEO was an element that could be disposed of so that the corporation could get off to a fresh start with its customers and society at large. In a discursive sense, the incident was all the more significant because the CEO had repeatedly claimed that TINE welcomed new players in their market niches. Under the title 'Faith is a fresh produce' we hear TINE, through its newly appointed CEO, voice the organizational crisis:

> In the spotlight of the media, politicians, consumers and our owners, the dairy producers, we in TINE have been through our roughest ordeal, maybe ever. [...] We still want to be represented in most refrigerators, and we will get there through healthy competition.
>
> (TINE Annual Report 2006: 4)

At the start of this crisis, TINE was a solid number two according to the most important company list from Synovate MMI.[10] It then dropped to number 25 in 2005, and worked its way up to number 11 in 2006. In August of 2007, TINE has managed to climb up to number 9. The magnitude of the crisis is demonstrated by the fact that TINE had been among the three most popular businesses in Norway for the ten years preceding this crisis.

Cover-up

Finally, we will propose a fifth discursive strategy, that of *cover-up*. This is the activity of purposely hiding certain practices or internal data from the wider public, including most of the people in the organization. One famous example is the 45-year cover-up by the American tobacco industry of their knowledge of the link between cigarettes and cancer. Their own confidential research reported in 1953 that tobacco was harmful to health. They then acted promptly by declaring that there was 'no proof' that smoking causes lung cancer. They were not taken to task before the late 1990s. A cover-up becomes possible when a few centrally placed actors control information that deceives not just the public, but also many of those working in the organization. Apart from the incident where TINE tried to cover up with respect to the ICA/Ahold crisis, we have not found signs of other cover-ups in our studies at TINE.

Conclusion

We have demonstrated how elements such as milk, health, research, market, politics and economy come together and form the corporation's discursive structure over time. In our case, we saw how these discursive elements shifted from being synonymous with health and a cornerstone of nutrition, to being perceived as a risk hazard and thus potentially unethical. We observed that the organization had to work to reorganize the elements of discourse. The discursive elements needed to be reassembled in a structure that made the activities again convey the message of health and purity. We found that TINE used four discursive strategies in coping with the challenges it faced; diversification, countering, repackaging and decoupling.

Notes

1 Our definition of discourse is derived from works by Laclau and Mouffe (2001) in sociology and from Heidegger (1927) in philosophy.
2 The Nike discourse is also subjected to critical scrutiny. See, for example, Klein (2000) or Knight and Greenberg (2002). Numerous organizations have spoken out against abusive and intolerable practices in factories manufacturing Nike products.
3 To be found on www.nike.com.
4 This is not always so. Founders tend to influence the culture of their companies, but generally company directors fail to influence the culture of the company.
5 http://www.jarlsberg.com
6 TINE has had several names from its origin, but has been the official name for the company since 2002.
7 From the classic movie, *The Wizard of Oz*, you had both good and evil witches. The good Witches (North and South) were dressed in bright, wonderful clothes, airy, 'clean', shiny golden hair,and even spoke with a pleasing voice, while the wicked witches of the East/West had dark hair, dressed in a dumpy black gown, and spoke in a gravelly voice that one expects from evil witches. (We are grateful to Bente Velapoldi for this comment.)
8 It should be noted that quite a few of the innovations of TINE are not merely a result of market demands, but also from necessity based on a huge overproduction of milk. Thus, the company is forced to find other markets for its products.
9 A part of the Ahold food retail corporation.
10 http://www.synovate.no

References

Douglas, M. (1966) *Purity and Danger*, London: Routledge.
DuPuis, M. (2002) *Nature's Perfect Food – How Milk became America's Drink*, New York: New York University Press.
Heidegger, M. (1927) *Being and Time*, Oxford: Blackwell.
Holt, D. B. (2004) *How Brands Become Icons: The Principles of Cultural Branding*, Boston, MA: Harvard Business School Press.
Klein, N. (2000) *NOLOGO*, London: Flamingo.
Knight, G. and Greenberg, J. (2002) 'Promotionalism and subpolitics: Nike and its labor critics', *Management Communication Quarterly*, 15(4): 541–570.

Laclau, E. and C. Mouffe (2001) *Hegemony and Socialist Strategy: towards a radical democratic politics* (2nd edn), London: Verso.

Latour, B. (1988) *The Pasteurization of France*, Cambridge, MA: Harvard University Press.

Pritchard, B. (2001) 'Current global trends in the dairy industry', unpublished manuscript, University of Sydney.

TINE, Annual Report (1998) Available online at www.tine.no/page?id=79.

—— Annual Report (1999) Available online at www.tine.no/page?id=79.

—— Annual Report (2004) Available online at www.tine.no/page?id=79.

Trice, H. M. and Beyer, J. M. (1993). *The Cultures of Work Organizations*, Englewood Cliffs, NJ: Prentice-Hall.

4 Does rule-based moral management work?

A case study in sexual harassment

Steve McKenna

There is a belief that if an organization invests in rule-based moral management it will become more ethical in its behaviour through the behaviour of organizational members. Ingredients of rule-based moral management include ethical audits, ethics training, whistle-blowing mechanisms, disciplinary procedures, codes of conduct, ethics programmes and officers, ethical decision-making systems and so on. There is also a belief that the moral climate of an organization can be detached from the moral climate of society, the moral climate of business and industry and from the moral sense of individuals. Indeed, in order to have any chance of moral management within organizations it is critical, perhaps, that this separation takes place. If behaviour in organizations is a reflection of the business system and the moral sense of individuals (and/or is related to society), organizational rule-based moral management is at best difficult and at worst untenable.

What is the nature of and inter-relationship between the moral climate of society, the business system and the moral sense of individuals then that may make this rule-based management of morals difficult? Firstly, it might be suggested that the moral discourse of a society is a changing landscape and what is, or is not, morally acceptable fluctuates. Secondly, it may not be possible for organizations to be moral, or act as moral agents, because as Rowland (2005) argues, organizations and individuals within them have to follow a script that is devoid of morality and emphasizes, above all else, the need for profit. Thirdly, as some writers have argued, in the postmodern world individual identity and the 'self' are fractured and fragmented, being pulled in many ways by many different discourses. Sennett (1998) has argued that this leads to a 'corrosion of character' because of a loss of community and the increasingly self-absorbed nature of the modern world. What all this may amount to is the lack of a moral compass that has diluted, perhaps, the notion of 'having a conscience'. Consequently, organizational rule-based moral management is attempting to enforce appropriate moral behaviour in an increasingly morally fragmented world.

Rule-based moral management is premised mainly on the idea that moral behaviour can be managed through rules and that despite the content of an individual's conscience with respect to behaviour, rules can achieve the desired end of morally acceptable behaviour in organizations. Thus, the idea is that rules encode or infuse individuals with knowledge about how to act, and failure to act in a morally acceptable way will bring some form of punishment. For example, a person who engages in behaviour that constitutes sexual harassment will know that there are penalties for doing so even though they may not have felt a conscience about their behaviour. This brings to mind Durkheim's dictum (1947): 'we must not say that an action shocks the common conscience because it is criminal, but rather that it is criminal because it shocks the common conscience'. These relationships between conscience and rules, moral management and moral behaviour are considered in this chapter through a story written by an organizational professional: Diane.

Diane

Diane is one of many managers and professionals who have contributed a story to an ongoing project collecting written narratives. Through executive education programmes, graduate courses and other fora, managers and professionals were asked if they would be willing to contribute a non-graded narrative on an organizational experience(s) that has been significant to them. Managers and professionals from parts of the Asia-Pacific, Europe and North America have contributed narratives for the database in English. At the time of writing her narrative, Diane was completing a postgraduate diploma in business administration. She was an IT professional, in her mid-30s, married and Australian.

In summary the chain of events that Diane narrates are as follows.

- She is hired by a small IT company (Compco[1]).
- She initially has a positive impression of the company.
- She volunteers for a project won in competition by the company in Thailand for the Thai government.
- This is the company's first business venture outside Australia.
- There is a delay in starting the project and the originally assigned project leader is replaced by his assistant, Peter.
- The team goes to Thailand.
- On arrival in Thailand, Peter and the other male members of the team embark on unethical and unprofessional behaviour (regularly sleeping with prostitutes, abusing Diane both physically and psychologically, abusing female Thai colleagues, failing to work on the project).
- The project fails and the team returns home.
- The home office is rife with sexual liaisons.
- The company is taken over.

There are many ways in which Diane's narrative can be analysed and in this chapter I am concerned with viewing it as a *living story* of Diane, one that has a life of its own and reflects a set of experiences she has had. In addition, Diane's narrative will be considered in a *realist* and *pragmatic* way. As a realist narrative, judgement is suspended and we assume that the narrator is offering useful knowledge about the workings of an organization. From this, pragmatic learning can be achieved that offers lessons that inform future action.

Compco's moral code

Within its broad code of business principles, Compco has a statement on *standard of conduct* and specific sections on dealing with employees and customers. The code of business principles is comprehensive in its coverage. On paper it appears impressive; for example, the statement on the standard of conduct is:

> We conduct our business with honesty, integrity and transparency. We respect the rights and interests of our employees. We also respect the interests of other stakeholders with whom we have relationships.

In relation to employees specifically the code of conduct states: 'No employee shall endure harassment, physical, mental or other form of abuse.'

According to the Institute of Business Ethics (IBE), an organization based in the UK, to be effective, a code of conduct should be based on a number of good practices (http://www.ibe.org.uk). These good practices include:

- that the code should be rooted in core ethical values;
- staff should all have a copy of the code;
- a mechanism should be available that enables breaches of the code to be reported in a confidential manner;
- ethical issues are included in corporate training programmes;
- setting up a board committee to monitor the effectiveness of the code;
- reporting on the code's use in the annual report;
- making conformity to the code part of a contract of employment;
- making the code available in languages used in the company;
- making the code available to business partners;
- reviewing the code in the light of changing business circumstances;
- ensuring senior executives 'walk the talk'.

The extent to which there was deep embeddedness of Compco's code of conduct was questionable. Furthermore, the good practice that the IBE encourages raises as many questions as it answers. For example, what are the 'core ethical values' that a code should be rooted in? How does being given a copy of the code lead to its effectiveness? What follows the reporting of a breach even if it is done confidentially? In what way should ethical issues be included in corporate training programmes, if such programmes exist? What if the company is small or medium sized with no governance structure? How is the effectiveness of a code to be monitored? How can a code be defined – and by whom – in such a way that it becomes part of the contract of employment? Perhaps, more importantly, how are practices that seem good theoretically able to be translated into ethical behaviour? A realist and pragmatic reading of Diane's narrative might throw some light on these issues, and indicate the gap that exists between the rhetoric of moral management and the 'reality'.

The narrative

Beginning

I take up Diane's narrative at the point where the team arrives in Bangkok. We know that this is a team on international assignment and from Diane's narrative we learn that the process of selection for the team and preparation for the assignment was at best haphazard and at worst non-existent. It certainly did not follow 'best practices' prescribed in the literature. Diane portrays Peter's (the team leader) intentions on arrival in Bangkok:

> Within two hours of our planes touching down, we were all gathered at Pat Pong. I was to learn that Peter, who had been there for about a month prior to our arrival, had had a choice. We could have lived in Sukimvit, which was about a 5 minute drive from the Thai government department in Klong Toey, or Silom, which was at best 30 minutes drive. Pat Pong, supposed sex capital of the world, was just off Silom Road, so, it was explained to me, there was no choice [...] Not one week later, I noted that all but one of our male colleagues was fully enticed by the lure of Pat Pong and we (the women in the team) were no longer needed. Within two weeks the units were crowded with visitors.

Appropriate preparation for this assignment in terms of team selection, team leader selection, pre-departure preparation and *in situ* support might have prevented these problems from developing. Additionally, clear rules and policies laying down acceptable behaviour might have helped. But would they? Is it not known that much goes on in organizations that is ethically questionable despite codes of ethics? Is it not the case that there is much that is unethical, or at least dubious about some men's behaviour when they are on business trips about which we know little, or simply accept? And, if it is simply accepted or tolerated, why is this so? Is it because such behaviour is innocuous, a form of coping and winding down? Also, what about the behaviour of some women on business trips and projects? Do women behave badly?

Middle

Diane narrates that Peter exercised control and power in other ways and used company funds to support 'recreational activities'. In her narrative Diane suggests that Peter was 'taken over' by the power he had and the opportunities that made themselves available to him for sexual gratification in Bangkok. The other males on the team followed suit. Gradually the space between outside of work behaviour and sexual harassment at work became blurred. Diane notes that 'despite the obvious rapport Joanne (the other female member of the team) and I had with the Thai women in the office, Peter decided that, as women, we would not be sufficiently respected, and were therefore, not permitted to attend any meetings'. Work, she recalls, became more and more difficult. There were no project plans, deadlines were built around social outings rather than client needs, goals were not being met. Peter became increasingly distanced, psychologically and physically, from the project, as did the other men on the team: 'from my perspective these guys had lost their grip on reality'.

Peter regularly reminded Diane and Joanne that Western women were 'fat and ugly'; that they were 'white and flabby'. Diane began to 'roll with the punches' and to endure the 'unreality' of her situation. She was subjected to increasingly blatant levels of harassment and 'although in a complete whirl, I knew that my immediate behaviour would be important, but how could I possibly behave so that this situation would diffuse?' On one occasion, when surrounded by the group of men on the team she had an instinct to slap Peter. She recounts, 'might I have slapped him? On closer analysis, I suspect that I had been in desperate need of a protective shield – something to protect my face, my privacy and my emotions'.

Diane felt that she was not in a position to leave the project. She did not report it, but she did write to her fiancé in Australia telling him about it. She was determined 'not to give my male colleagues the pleasure of destroying my life in Thailand'. At an Australian embassy function she found Peter on the balcony sobbing at the receipt of his divorce papers. Offering to take the rather drunk team leader back to their apartments she was sexually assaulted by him in the back of a taxi and responded by elbowing him in the nose. She had a meeting with the team's second in command about the incident, indicating that she had not yet determined what to do. Casey, Peter's lieutenant offered reasons for Peter's behaviour. She reported nothing but increasingly separated herself from the rest of the group and focused only on what little work she was allowed to do: 'for the rest of the project, I decided to avoid conflict by adopting an avoidance strategy. I remained quiet, happy to be excluded from the user meetings, happy to be in a cab earlier than everyone else and to stay later than everyone else'. Diane saw this as a way of getting back: 'I made sure that not one bit of my work could be seriously criticized and my vindictive payback was that I provided exactly what was asked for – nothing more, nothing less'.

Ending

'Given the project had no clear direction and knowing that quality of the deliverable was pitiful, this did not require all my energy and I could use what was left over to keep my wits about me'. Diane had decided to isolate herself from the situation and now observed how the men in the team treated female employees of the Thai client. They boasted of their nights with prostitutes, patted local female employees on the head and told them 'they were nearly as pretty as the girl they met last night'. Diane felt that, for the men on the team, the line between female colleague and prostitute was now completely blurred.

As the failed project came to a close, the Thai client eventually firing Compco, Diane was once more physically and verbally abused by Peter who indicated that 'what happens on tour, stays on tour', and that she should be careful what she said when they returned to Australia. On the team's return to Australia, the office was apparently riddled with sexual liaisons and affairs. Diane left the company 14 months after her return and it was shortly after sold to an overseas corporation. Diane never reported her experiences in Thailand.

Discussion

Many questions arise from reading Diane's narrative. Two questions seem particularly interesting: firstly, why did Diane not report the serious sexual harassment that took place; and, secondly, what possessed the males on the team to behave the way they did?

Why did Diane not report the serious harassment that took place?

What might have prevented Diane from reporting the harassment she experienced? Sexual harassment is a very persistent phenomenon. Carr *et al.* (2004) note that women do not report sexual harassment for a variety of reasons: fear of retaliation; fear of job loss; loss of promotion opportunities or because an individual wants to obtain a job reference. Some women do not report sexual harassment because they feel their complaint is not 'serious' enough, or that they may not be believed. Diane fits this framework and in her narrative she indicates that she did not report what went on because she felt she would not get home office support; she would lose her job; and she was intimidated. According to Carr *et al.* (2004):

> Women cope or react to their harassment experiences in a variety of ways. Some women leave their jobs. Some women silently endure for years. While we hold the expectation that women will report their experiences of non-sexual and sexual workplace harassment, data on the reporting of sexual harassment complaints indicates that very few experiences are reported. Instead of reporting, women cope with the harassment in whatever way possible.

Furthermore, responses to harassment tend to be conceptualized in a one-dimensional way, as either assertive or non-assertive. If a victim fails to act assertively it is supposed that it is the victim who is to blame if there is further harassment. Indeed, when Diane's narrative was shown to undergraduate students undertaking a degree in Human Resource Management (HRM) – of which 75 per cent were young women – the overwhelming response was that Diane is partly responsible for her problems because she did nothing to stop it. Such a view, however, is not only unfair it is simplistic.

Women cope behaviourally and psychologically with harassment. Avoidance of potentially abusive situations is an externally focused behavioural strategy and is one that Diane adopted. Assertiveness and reporting the harassment would also have been externally focused behavioural responses. Diane's coping strategy, particularly early on in the harassment was internally focused or psychological: denial – *'this is unreal'*; detachment – *'he's going through a divorce'*; endurance – *'I made sure that not one bit of my work could be seriously criticized and my vindictive payback was that I provided exactly what was asked for'*; reattribution – *'they were only messing around'*; self-blame – *'perhaps I was being quite unreasonable'*. It is clear that Diane adopted a range of coping mechanisms and this is consistent with research that indicates women have a number of reactions to the harassment experience. The outcomes of coping are also important and may lead to positive and negative discoveries and learning. In Diane's case she offers two points of learning. In the first she appears to reduce the sexual harassment she experienced to a form of conflict that could have been resolved through better mechanisms and processes, forgetting, it seems that Compco had a code of conduct.

> In subsequent teams, I have made an effort to ensure that the methods of conflict resolution are well known and easily utilized, particularly for individuals less likely to speak out. I concern myself that this may appear paranoid, but I have also observed that the very existence of such mechanisms often minimizes the need to use them.

Secondly, Diane 'learns' that she was partly, if not mainly to blame for not being more assertive despite the difficulties she had when on the project.

> For women, I did not take a stand. The fact that there was little support, even from disparaging women back home, does not alleviate the personal responsibility I feel to women in the world; this male-dominated industry and that organization. Further, I can bring myself to feel shame at my own self-pity, when I consider the plight of some others. I do not intend to belittle issues such as rape.

Compco had a code of conduct that included reference to sexual harassment in the workplace, yet it did not prevent Diane from being abused, or the abusers from abusing. It is not enough to expect that all sexually harassed women will simply report harassment. As Carr *et al.* note, 'when faced with a sexually harassing situation, targets first appraise whether or not the situation is stressful or threatening. Second, based on this appraisal, they decide how to cope with their harassment'. Furthermore, it is idealistic to expect harassment to disappear because of the existence of a code of conduct. In essence, a complex problem cannot be dealt with through the mere existence of, and superficial adherence to, codes of conduct. For example, I should like to address Diane's response to her experiences in relation to the extensive 'not text book recommendations' that Carr *et al.* make in their report, and which emphasized the complexity of successful approaches and methods for dealing with sexual harassment.

Organizational codes of conduct imply that dealing with harassment can be contained within the organization. However, the complex psychological, behavioural and social aspects of sexual harassment indicate that it must be dealt with more broadly. Carr *et al.* make recommendations that consider this complexity. Firstly, sexually harassed women or men should take the experience seriously and not allow its import to be minimized by others, or through self-blame; harassment is the abuse of power and authority by others. They ought to remember that sexual harassment will not go away if ignored. That doing things to feel good and be positive through the experience are important. Experiences of harassment should be documented in detail, including what happened, when and where. A target of harassment should ask for a performance evaluation that makes it difficult for the harasser 'to explain why they suddenly find you incompetent or your work not up to standard'. Harassed employees should talk to colleagues and former employees to discover if they have experienced sexual harassment. The process of reporting is often a long one and it needs persistence, support and commitment. Organizations, despite codes of conduct, may not make it easy to pursue complaints. Family and friends should be involved and realize that the issue is abuse of power and control and not sex.

Secondly, and generally, employers and human resource departments must have systems and a culture in place that deal with sexual harassment in detail. Furthermore, organizations should have in place not only policies, but programmes dealing with sexual harassment in employee orientation, training and so on. Where unions are present they need to be involved. Bystanders and co-workers, as with Diane, can join in, or be active witnesses to the harassment. Sexual harassment reporting may also involve lawyers, police, investigators, mediators and so on. Most of this structure and involvement was missing in Diane's case. Nevertheless, how comprehensive would it have needed to be for her situation to have been different? Would she have considered pursuing the issue worth doing? Would she have received unconditional, long-term support from her employer? Is the process manageable? In addition, if the issue became external to the organization, would she have been certain of justice? Surely, the variables involved in satisfactory conclusion are too many to be sure of justice.

What possessed the males on the team to behave the way they did?

Sexual harassment is generally accepted to be an abuse of power and authority. In Diane's narrative she was sexually harassed, Thai women in the client's office were harassed and the men on the project regularly entertained prostitutes. Certainly, there was an abuse of power and a willingness on the part of the men to engage openly in morally suspect behaviour. If the activities of the men on the project had been more closely monitored by the organization and its senior management in Australia perhaps the harassment and participation in dubious recreational activities would not have occurred. But, is it not also necessary to consider personal responsibility, and from where such personal responsibility might arise?

A number of theoretical approaches have been offered to explain sexual harassment. At one extreme is the notion that men are biologically driven to be sexual aggressors and that sexual harassment is merely an example of this in practice. Patriarchy suggests that the social, political and economic structure of societies operate to oppress women. Cultural explanations suggest that in order for sexual harassment to decline, male-dominated work cultures should be replaced by a more gender-neutral culture. Employers have an important part to play in ensuring these 'new' cultures become embedded. A discourse perspective emphasizes the importance of 'naming' harassment for what it is and ensuring that it is dealt with. Thus, it is always important to challenge harassment, however it is experienced.

What is the personal responsibility of men who are involved in harassment? The men in the Thai project clearly lacked acceptable norms of behaviour, but would training in different behaviour, coupled with close monitoring by the employer, work? Possibly: in this section, however, we discuss the idea that the men on the project behaved the way they did because they lacked a developed conscience.

Conscience

Jenkins (1955) notes that conscience concerns the character of the self and that the content of conscience contains important aspects that may be beyond the reach of systems of moral management in organizations.

> This content of conscience is obviously fluid and variable; it differs among individuals and cultures; it is a gradual accumulation and always subject to change. This content is largely conditioned by the circumstances of the individual life: it derives from family, friends, and society, such as school, church, the state; from temperament, personal interests, and biographical accidents.

For Jenkins, conscience is social but always subject to change. The extent to which an individual acts with a conscience and in accordance with conscience will be related to an individual's life experiences. For Fuss (1964) acting with a conscience is related to personal integrity which is derived from an individual's knowledge or belief about what is 'right' and 'wrong'. Thus, to behave unconscionably indicates a lack of personal integrity and a somewhat faulty process of conditioning.

Steven Rose (1999) seems to consider this aspect in his idea that the growth of conscience involves the gradual increase in impulse control; the incorporation of parental moral standards; the development of shame and guilt; the learning of the consciousness and practice of rules; and, the maturation of the sense of justice. In reviewing psychoanalytical and psychosocial approaches, cognitive theories and social learning theory, Rose (1999) suggests that conscience can now be understood in relation to empirical referents rather than only as a philosophical and theoretical concept. This may be the case; however, there are considerable problems with this approach, not least of which is the emphasis on the notion of 'internalization'. Conscience may indeed be related to the internalization of what society considers to be 'good' moral values, standards of behaviour and a sense of right and wrong; but in a morally fragmented society is it clear what is being internalized and how its development can be 'measured'? Is it not the case that what is 'right' and 'wrong' changes, or what we are internalizing is that there is no sense of right and wrong at all?

Rowland (2005) makes the point that it is not possible for corporations to be moral or moral agents given that their *raison d'être* is simply to make profit, and they have no tolerance for human motivation or values that contradict those of the corporation: the actors are simply required to follow closely the author's script. Under these circumstances it is somewhat paradoxical to have organizational members with well-developed consciences yet who have to behave in accordance with a script that shows no recognizable conscience. If individuals do not have well-developed internalized consciences concerning behaviour, as appears to have been the case with the men in Diane's narrative, can organizational rules and policies enforce appropriate behaviour?

Goodpaster argues that this is not possible exactly because conscience is concerned with moral commitment, not behaviour, and so we end up with organizations with 'virtual conscience'. Ethics and ethical behaviour are invoked but not institutionalized, and attempts at institutionalization result in systems that people believe can be 'so perfect that no one will need to be good'. Goodpaster (2000) is clear that systems for moral management, that would include policies, procedures and codes of ethics to deal with sexual harassment, are doomed to failure because conscience cannot be outsourced or automated. His solution to this problem, however, is to develop a 'corporate culture that institutionalizes ethical awareness' through the development of organizational reflectiveness, humility, anticipation and community involvement. Suggestions that Rowland (2005) might consider impossible given the very nature and purpose of the business system itself.

So where does this leave us with respect to the management of sexual harassment in organizations? This chapter has offered no direct answer to the question 'does rule-based moral management work?', but it has implied that, despite the proliferation of codes of ethics, rule-based moral management, at least with respect to sexual harassment, is not working. Sennett's (1998) idea that society is suffering from a 'corrosion of character' seems more pertinent than ever, and organizations are doomed to struggle with issues that are ultimately beyond the influence of organizational management. Perhaps this struggle is the best that can be achieved in an era when 'conscience' is only a caricature of its rhetorical self.

Notes

1 A pseudonym.

References

Boje, D. (2001) *Narrative Methods for Organizational and Communication Research*, London: Sage.

Carr, J., MacQuarrie, B., Huntley, A. and Welsh, S. (2004) 'Workplace harassment and violence report', Toronto: Centre for Research on Violence against Women and Children.

Czarniawska, B. (2004) *Narratives in Social Science Research*, London: Sage.

Dowling, P. J. and Welch, D. E. (2004) *International Human Resource Management*, London: Thomson.

Durkheim, E. (1947) *The Division of Labor in Society*, New York: Free Press.

Fuss, P. (1964) 'Conscience', *Ethics*, 74(2): 111–120.

Gayle Baugh, S. (1997) 'On the persistence of sexual harassment in the workplace', *Journal of Business Ethics*, 16(9): 27–36.

Gergen, K. J. (1991) *The Saturated Self: Dilemmas of Identity in Contemporary Life*, New York: Basic Books.

Goodpaster, K. E. (2000) 'Conscience and its counterfeits in organizational life: a new interpretation of the naturalistic fallacy', *Business Ethics Quarterly*, 10(1): 189–201.

Jenkins, I. (1955) 'The significance of conscience', *Ethics*, 65(4): 261–270.

Karakowsky, L., Carroll, A. B. and Buchholtz, A. K. (2005) *The Responsibilities of Business*, Scarborough: Thomson Nelson.

Rose, S. R. (1999) 'Towards the development of an internalized conscience: theoretical perspectives on socialisation', *Journal of Human Behavior in the Social Environment*, 2(3): 15–28.

Rospenda, K. M., Richman, J. A. and Nawyn, S. J. (1998) 'Doing power: the confluence of gender, race, and class in contrapower sexual harassment', *Gender and Society*, 12(1): 40–60.

Rowland, W. (2005) *Greed Inc*, Toronto: Thomas Allen.

Sennett, R. (1998) *The Corrosion of Character*, New York: Norton.

Uggen, C. and Blackstone, A. (2004) 'Sexual harassment as a gendered expression of power', *American Sociological Review*, 69(1): 64–92.

Williams, C. L., Giuffre, P. A. and Delinger, K. (1999) 'Sexuality in the workplace: organizational control, sexual harassment and the pursuit of pleasure', *Annual Review of Sociology*, 25: 73–93.

5 Challenges to leader integrity

How leaders deal with dilemmas of honesty

Steven L. Grover and Robert Moorman

The adage 'Honesty is the best policy' seems applicable to leaders in the business world. Some individuals undoubtedly wish they had lived by the motto, such as Martha Stewart, who did jail time for lying, not for insider trading. However, being honest in business is not clear and simple. In this chapter we explore leadership honesty and integrity, critically analysing some of the honesty dilemmas leaders face and theorizing about consequences of both honesty and dishonesty among leaders.

The purpose of this chapter is to explore some of the dilemmas that managers and other leaders face when trying to be honest. Leaders[1] with high levels of integrity or honesty tell the truth to the people around them, follow through on promises, and behave consistently across time. Followers perceive leaders' honesty, which engenders trust, and consequently a propensity to engage with, or to follow, the leader. In the first part of this chapter we will describe some different approaches to leader integrity.

How leader integrity works

Leadership scholars have created a number of different overlapping interpretations of integrity. Some have focused on honesty, while others have focused on consistency of behaviour, and still others examine integrity through a lens of morality.

Honesty

Honesty is an inclusive term referring to a propensity not to lie, cheat, or steal, making it a bit confusing when attempting to develop behavioural theory. For the purposes of this chapter and the leader integrity construct, we consider truthfulness under this category and the other unethical behaviours as part of morality.

Kouzes and Posner (2002) advocate truthfulness as essential to leadership, identifying it as the most desired trait in leaders by subordinates (Posner and Schmidt 1984). A reason for its importance is that followers seek ways to gain comfort in their decision to put their trust in their leaders. If followers believe their leaders are truthful, they can accept with confidence the credibility of their leaders' promises and trust that their leaders will lead them ethically and effectively.

There are many different ways to tell the truth or lie in business (Grover 2005). Behaviourally, lying is making a statement that one knows to be false. This definition presumes that the leader making the statement knows the truth, because if leaders make statements they discover to be incorrect later, they have not lied. There are endless permutations to lying, but scholars generally class lying behaviour as lies of deceit and lies of concealment (Bok 1978; Ekman 1985). Deceit is purposeful and direct, following the precepts of the definition given here, whereas concealment is a type of deception in which the perpetrator leads the victim to believe something that is known to be false. For example, when the subordinate asks whether the extra duties being added to the job are likely to benefit them in the context of a pay rise decision, the boss using concealment might agree that there may be benefits without saying that there would or would not be a pay rise. The boss knows that no pay rise will be coming, but leads the subordinate to believe that it is. Although management researchers have primarily investigated the deceit type of lying, this is probably out of an empirical convenience (Boles *et al.* 2000; Grover 1993; Grover and Hui 1994; Schweitzer *et al.* 2004). Both deceit and concealment are relevant to leader integrity: It makes little theoretical or practical difference to the follower whether they are directly or indirectly deceived.

Truth-telling type of honesty has a direct bearing on the follower relationship. Trust is the primary mechanism by which the follower relationship is affected by honesty. People are more likely to trust those who tell them the truth and, conversely, less likely to trust people who do not. Negotiation research illustrates this point. Boles and her colleagues (2000) found that people did not trust those who deceived them, avoided dealing with them in the future if possible, and offered retribution against them if it was not possible. Another study specifically analysing trust recovery found that trust could be recovered after untrustworthy behaviour, but it was very unlikely to be recovered following untrustworthy behaviour accompanied by direct deceit (Schweitzer *et al.* 2005). That study used a trust game that depended on parties giving a certain amount of money in early rounds in order to benefit both parties maximally. Untrustworthy behaviour involved giving a self-benefiting amount in early rounds. The trust could be restored if accompanied by an apologetic promise about the future. However, when that same behaviour was accompanied with a direct lie, trust was never recovered.

Truthful leaders can be trusted and should engage followers. Trust is usually defined as making oneself vulnerable to another but believing that one's interests will still be protected (Rousseau *et al.* 1998). People are generally less likely to make themselves vulnerable to a person who has not told them the truth because the same behaviour may happen in the future and a person's vulnerability could be punished (Mayer *et al.* 1995). The need for trust to motivate followership flows most naturally from a Leader–Member Exchange (LMX) theory (Graen and Uhl-Bien 1995) because there is a sense of exchange that is sometimes absent in transformational leadership in which leaders and followers raise one another to higher levels of motivation and morality (Burns 1978). The leader, for example, who makes promises, and whose promises come to fruition is likely to engender trust, or vulnerability, in followers in the future. Followers expect that the promises made today will be delivered in the future as part of an exchange. Leaders lacking this veracity cannot be trusted to deliver in the future. As in Schweitzer and colleagues' (2005) study, if the untrustworthy action were accompanied by direct deceit, then the antipathy should be even stronger. Truthful leaders therefore express a conscience that engenders trust and engages followers.

Consistency

The second element of leader integrity drawn from the leadership and trust literature is the notion of consistency. The first type of consistency is between words and deeds. Kouzes and Posner (1993) call this credibility, and it is expressed by colloquialisms like 'practise what you preach', 'walk the talk', 'do what you say you'll do'. The notion is that there is a consonance between what a person says and how the person behaves. For example, saying that quality is paramount and then approving the shipment of some products with minor defects violates the consistency between words and deeds. Hypocrisy is the opposite of credibility and is the impression that followers gather of leaders who do not demonstrate consistency of words and actions. This type of consistency is important to reputation because it demonstrates that the leader, and hence the organization, stand for something. They have ideals or principles that need to be upheld to provide a guidance and unity to their being.

Word–deed consistency is closely related to honesty because it shows that one is truthful about what one will do. However, it is subtly different from merely telling the truth. It is often easy to tell the truth, but difficult to follow through and act on the words that have come before. Things change or the audience of a message shifts, creating conflicts that make it easier to behave in a different way. Jansen and von Glinow (1985) call this internal conflict ethical ambivalence, and it has been shown in empirical studies that people will lie more under competing expectations (Grover 1993; Scott 2003). For example, a leader might tell a certain follower that he will support a project to be presented to a higher-ranking authority by supporting budgetary approval in a committee meeting with peers. Once the peers start criticizing the proposal, however, it may become easier to shift or withdraw one's support. Subordinates who discover leaders providing no support for projects they said they would support draw perceptions that the leader may not be consistent.

Most leaders behave inconsistently under certain circumstances. Consistency violations can be mitigated by explanations as described in the interactional justice literature (Bies *et al.* 1993; Bies and Moag 1986). Leaders can explain in a humane way why they are doing something different. In the example above the situation may need to be explained. Leader perceptions are not drawn in a snapshot, however. The perceptions of leaders that followers hold are created over time from the milieu of experiences with a leader and the many perceptions derived from knowing the leader. This experience over time gives rise to another type of consistency, that being the consistency of behaviour over time.

Time consistency

In addition to consistency between words and deeds, leaders' behaviour across time is another component of integrity. This sort of consistency has different connotations that have similar results of making the leader appear to be solid and have a direction, or a sense of purpose. Consistency suggests that the leader makes decisions in the same way across time and situations. While this concept is relatively easy for the closely involved worker to discern, it is potentially difficult to measure or perfectly describe. The concept is that in an isolated, abstract situation the leader would make the same decision repeatedly, given identical situations and purposes. However, identical situations rarely exist. Two subordinates might make requests that appear to be similar, but coming from different people might require different answers or decisions. The request for some additional training, for example, might be met with open arms by a relatively junior staff member, but considered with scrutiny when coming from a senior staff person who has a history of abusing opportunities. That measurement issue aside, some people make decisions more consistently than others. Most readers will be able to picture a leader they know who falls down on this characteristics, perhaps even seeming to make virtually random decisions. Some leaders have the characteristics of being easily distracted. For example, Maccoby (2000) describes narcissistic leaders, who are brilliant strategists but easily bored with the mundane and easily influenced by the constantly shifting environment of contemporary business life.

Decision-making consistency is a key component of procedural justice (Tyler 1989). A key feature of procedural fairness is that people expect different individuals to be treated the same, and they perceive it as unfair and distressing when people are treated differently. There are a host of organizational outcomes influenced by that fairness (Brockner and Wiesenfeld 1996; Colquitt *et al.* 2001), strongly suggesting that people will have a negative opinion of leaders who are not consistent in the way they make decisions. If favouritism, for example, is shown to some employees, that should diminish the leader's reputation.

The consistency of behaviour goes beyond just decision making. The person whose various actions move together with strategic purpose demonstrates consistency. As an example, the hotel general manager who stops to assist a client on the way through the lobby, then calls in extra staff to a swamped kitchen, and purchases a new machine to provide better housekeeping service has conducted a series of behaviours that might be seen as consistent under an excellent customer service strategy. In contrast, the inconsistent cost cutter who chastises an employee for excessive travel reimbursements, alters a budget to reduce costs, and then spends lavishly on a machine that seems sexy will appear inconsistent.

Consistency perceptions may come largely from the exceptional, salient circumstances or action. It is well known in human perception that people note exceptions as more salient (Fiske and Taylor 1991). The classic example is the bowl of white marbles, with just one red marble. The red marble is salient and noticed. One of the challenges of leadership, then, is that the exceptional behaviour is the one that is noted. Employees may pick up the one slip-up or the one single inconsistent action. Again, the longer term the relationship with individual perceivers, the less salient will be these exceptions. Managers build their credibility over time, and the salience of single actions loses power after some time. Once a reputation is established, we also know from social cognition that people abhor changing their perceptions (Fiske and Taylor 1991). In sum, the sequence and consistency of leader behaviour creates the platform from which followers form perceptions of the leader's honesty and integrity. A leader's honesty is demonstrated by a consistency between a leader's words and what the leader knows to be true. Similarly, a leader's integrity is demonstrated by a consistency between a leader's words and deeds and between a leader's deeds across time.

Ethics

Ethics constitutes a fourth element of leader integrity. Our bias is to examine the behaviours above as critical parts of leader integrity. A complete picture, however, requires some consideration of ethical framework. Bass and Steidlmeier (1999) have argued that true transformational leadership or 'authentic' leadership is grounded in a positive ethical framework. They draw largely on virtue ethics to claim that authentic leaders have real impact (Palanski and Yammarino 2007). One of the primary virtues of honesty focused on truth telling above. Another primary virtue rooted in a global historic ethic is being consistent with value systems. Behaving consistently with one's values should demonstrate this virtue to followers.

Becker (1998) used Ayn Rand's 'objectivism' philosophy to argue against, or at least beyond, virtue ethics. Consonant with the notion above of consistent behaviour, Becker suggested that 'integrity' should be considered primarily as acting out a set of behaviours that fits a set of ethics. This notion is similar to ethical egoism, in that it expects the manager to behave in a manner that benefits them. Becker goes on to say that managers demonstrating integrity behave according to a morally justifiable value system. True integrity in this case requires perfect consistency in the face of conflicting demands, which requires the actor to have a perfectly attuned view of what is right and wrong and supposes that there are no shades of grey, that moral relativism should not operate.

Bass and Steidlmeier (1999) suggest that authentic leadership goes beyond virtue ethics to embrace the Western philosophies of liberty, utility, and distributive justice. One element of leader integrity thus far ignored in our treatment is the notion of treating people fairly and equitably. The leader with integrity treats people consistently, which is an element of fairness noted above. Additionally, our informal appraisals of the subject with executives find that unethical leaders take credit for other people's work. The ethical leader in contrast recognizes the contributions of followers, or demonstrates and exercises a concern with the entire operation as opposed to advancing themself.

Any serious consideration of leader integrity that ties together individual and organizational levels demands a consideration of the ethical component of leadership. The potential trouble with excluding ethics is that the leader might have a value system that is out of sync with the values of potential followers. Hence, such a leader is unlikely to create a strong bond with followers or to be effective. The position we have adopted is close to Becker's (1998) in that we do not propose that the philosophy guiding the leader is 'good' per se. To place this in a context accessible to academics, the idea that 'research' is a good thing that university management departments should do may seem like a positive value to some academics, but not to others.

Challenges

Leaders face challenges to their integrity. We will explore challenges to the three bases of integrity: truthfulness and two types of consistency.

Leaders cannot always be truthful. There are limits to their truthfulness, conditions under which they cannot tell the truth and some times when the truth becomes not so. For example, leaders sometimes have to keep confidences in order to protect people or in order to protect the organization as part of their fiduciary responsibility. If the company plans to merge or to purchase a competitor, then it might be in the organization's morally legitimate interest to conceal these facts. The trouble is that there might be people who are relationally close to the leader who need to be deceived or at least with whom information cannot be shared. In general, this is a small ethical dilemma for most people. While honesty might be a virtue, philosophers, with the exception of Kant, rarely ascribe honesty as a strict moral precept, and most managers negotiate this moral maze as a routine part of their work.

Some lies have greater impact than others. Some are of no consequence to anyone and probably have little to do with their creator's moral identity or perceptions of that person as an ethically reflexive leader. The moral content of the act is likely to be measured with its impact or cost. If the lie, or the inconsistency, has a negative impact then the action will be judged more harshly by observers (Jones 1991).

The impact of leaders' actions is potentially amplified by virtue of their being a leader. The more spotlighted a leader becomes, the more impact seemingly inconsequential actions have on their reputations. The behaviour of our political leaders, for example, is placed under a microscope in the media, which highlights inconsistencies or dishonesties that may not be noticed in typical business leaders. The same is true in contemporary society, however, for our highest-ranking business leaders because they increasingly are gaining celebrity status.

We are led, therefore, to consider the perceptions of leaders. The interesting question for leaders and those who study them concerns how people perceive their integrity. A provocative declaration is that it does not matter how ethical/ unethical, consistent/inconsistent, honest/dishonest a leader is because the perceptions become the reality. Leadership researchers like the present authors theorize nevertheless that integrity will influence the propensity of people to follow. We submit that this propensity to follow a leader comes from within the follower and is based on the follower's perceptions of the leader (Graen and Uhl-Bien 1995). Therefore, the perception of leader integrity influences or controls the important outcomes, at least from a leader-theoretic point of view.

Let us consider some of the different situations in which leaders may not be able to be completely honest and consistent. For example, leaders may have to shade the truth in order to protect others in some instances. This is particularly true with thorny human resource difficulties. Discretion becomes particularly important when working with individual human resource issues because potential negative impact on individuals in poorly handled human resource cases is potentially devastating to the individuals involved. Human resource issues have heavy potential consequences because one is dealing with people's lives, or at least some of the elements of life that people hold dear, including the esteem that comes with roles, self-respect, livelihood and professional esteem.

Hiring, firing, and retraining are some of the primary potential contexts in which leader integrity will be tested. Both formal and informal leaders have information about who is going to be hired or promoted as well as how people are fitting in or meeting the challenges of new roles. This sort of performance and decision information can be harmful if given to the wrong people. For example, a long time employee of the organization was negotiating his exit from the workforce. Therefore, the formal leaders understood that he would soon be gone and that important changes would ensue to fill the void; however, the information could not be revealed even to the people closely involved because it could have jeopardized the negotiations and delayed the positive outcome.

The question then becomes one of how do managers or leaders deal with these situations in which they cannot be completely forthright? Senior managers note that dealing with this ethical ambivalence is learned over years and is somewhat of an art. Admittedly, managers sometimes have to say that there are certain confidences, or things that they cannot discuss. They probably need to do this in a way that is reassuring for the audience so that the followers can still believe that the leader knows where they are going and can lead them there. In addition, the ethical leader wants to do so in a way that continues consistency and fairness and the notion of promoting ethical values, even though complete transparent honesty is not possible.

All organizations have some secrets. These secrets range from the protected intellectual property of the organization (think of Coca-Cola's 'secret formula') to the financial operations of the organization to its competitive strategy. Ethical leaders deal with the secrets in ways that protect who they are meant to protect while maintaining the semblance of honesty, consistency, and morality. Accomplishing both is a paradoxical feat, which, again, may come down to a sense of artistry over the process. At some level people are all aware that there is sensitive, protected information that cannot be revealed. Leaders can capitalize on this understanding. Leaders who claim that they are not prepared to talk about an issue due to legal or other concerns, can be ultimately perceived as ethical if the secrets turn out to be actual secrets and if they turn out to be necessary. However, if it turns out that everyone else knows the secret anyway, or that indeed there was no reason for the secret, then it will tarnish the leader's reputation and make him or her appear less ethical.

We do not always make the same decisions given the same information and we do not always deliver exactly the same information in different contexts. Many reasons contribute to our human inconsistency: We forget things; we are distracted in a particular situation; we actually change our minds. There are, in sum, good reasons why we might endorse a programme one week and then decide the next week that it is not a good one. Interactional justice theorists, for example, suggest that the manner in which inconsistencies are dealt with is important, and sometimes more important than the issue of the inconsistency itself. Leaders can ameliorate any consequences of inconsistencies by providing reasons for other accounts when the differences emerge. For example, 'I know that I always say not to use water on wood, but this case is different'. Sometimes the seeming inconsistencies need to be explained or resolved. While it might appear inconsistent to provide different levels of a certain kind of funding to two seemingly similar departments, the leader might explain to people why the levels are different by providing good reasons.

Perceptual bias

In order to perceive something like the integrity of a leader, people gather information individually and then try to draw a schematic perception of the leader. This schematic perception is biased for a number of reasons. For example, our perceptions are fixed or at least influenced by our experience and the context. For leaders' integrity perceptions this suggests that if people believe that the leader or leaders usually tell the truth, then their trust in what the leaders tell them will tend to be upheld. When there are good reasons for such leaders having to lie, then followers are likely to realize this necessity, especially when the reasons are stated. The trust recovery literature addresses this in that people can give accounts for why they had to behave in a distrustful manner (Bies and Moag 1986).

Managers, leaders and everyone else in the world are capable of inconsistent behaviour. Again, there are reasons for being inconsistent, for example when a situation changes, leaders cannot follow through on their promises. While the reasons given may have an influence on how leaders are perceived, such as above, the pattern of behaviour is the central analysis. When leaders behave consistently most of the time, but occasionally deviate, perceivers will have a mental calculus that may set the rare inconsistencies aside. However, when leaders rarely behave consistently they will be perceived as lacking in integrity/honesty. It might be a good idea at this point for the reader to try to recall a leader who behaves inconsistently more often than consistently in order to get a point of focus on this issue. This consistency represents to followers the leader's integrity and therefore tells something about his or her conscience. A leader with a strong conscience will tend to behave consistently, because the situational demands of the moment interfere little with convictions.

A common perceptual bias is that people look for confirming information and discount disconfirming information (Fiske and Taylor 1991). This contributes to the creation, maintenance and changes in the ethical perceptions of leaders. First, confirming information will be sought, which suggests that initial impressions will be supported. The bias that followers hold about a person or even a position are normally difficult to unseat. If employees think that all bosses are unethical because the last one (or 10) was unethical, then the new, ethical leader has the proverbial long row to hoe. Those employees will highlight to one another the inconsistencies and half-truths that emerge from the leader. Given that we have argued that most people are sometimes inconsistent and even sometimes deceitful, preordained images are hard to unset due to the perceptual bias of looking for confirming information.

The same confirming information bias, however, stands leaders in good stead who hold long-term relationships with the people around them. If these people have developed perceptions of the leader as relatively honest and ethical, then the occasional ethical breech will be discounted, unless it is severe. The perceptual bias then seems to suggest that perceptions of leaders will become more stable over time, and in fact may become increasingly difficult to unseat over time. This characteristic of perceptions further suggests that looking at leader–follower relationships over time has a great deal of utility for researchers and practitioners.

Summary and conclusion

This chapter has drawn together a varied range of contemporary social science literature to demonstrate the difficulties of ethical leadership and created theory that suggests the construct of leader integrity is drawn from perceptions of leaders across time, and that those perceptions shift across the time span. The major contribution of the chapter is in identifying the following characteristics of the leader integrity construct.

1   The images of leader integrity are based on the perceived consistency of leader behaviour, including consistency in behaviour across time, consistency between words and deeds, and consistency with certain ethical principles including the need to treat people with dignity and respect.
2   The perceptions of the leader's behaviour across time is subject to perceptual bias, especially of not seeking disconfirming information once an image of the leader's integrity has been struck.
3   Maintaining perfect consistency is difficult or impossible for managers and therefore the manner in which they explain and otherwise recover is crucially important to restoring positive perceptions of their integrity.

Leading people is paradoxical. On the one hand, most would agree that honest leaders are perceived more positively and that they will attract and motivate followers. On the other hand, it is recognized that being transparently honest is difficult or impossible. Contemporary leadership theorists advocate integrity in various ways. Many, such as Kouzes and Posner (2002) or Avolio and Gardner

(2005) describe positive leadership as demonstrating and living one's values. Prescriptions abound to lead in ways that are consistent with values. Yet, as suggested in this chapter, honesty is fraught with difficulty, and people's perceptual bias may accentuate deviations from consistency. Leaders are like ships navigating a channel of ethically ambivalent waters, hoping neither to be swept away by the current of dishonesty nor crushed by rocks when honesty detracts them. Instead, leaders need to chart their own course at their own rate.

Notes

1 This chapter adopts the language of follower and leader while recognizing its limitations. Follower and leader are used as broad terms to refer to people who have a relationship in which one person attempts to influence the other. In many cases the terms will refer to superordinate/subordinate relationships. However, leaders and followers may not have formal roles that enact one person having an impact on the other; the roles may be extremely informal, in which case we expect mechanisms of leader integrity to apply just as if there were formal expectations placed on both parties.

References

Avolio, B. J. and Gardner, W. L. (2005) 'Authentic leadership development: Getting to the root of positive forms of leadership', *Leadership Quarterly*, 16: 315–338.

Bass, B. M. and Steidlmeier, P. (1999) 'Ethics, character and authentic transformational leadership behavior', *Leadership Quarterly*, 10(2): 181–217.

Becker, T. E. (1998) 'Integrity in organizations: Beyond honesty and conscientiousness', *Academy of Management Review*, 23(1): 154–161.

Bies, R. J. and Moag, J. (1986) 'Interactional justice: Communication criteria of fairness', in Lewicki, R., Sheppard, B. and Bazerman, M. (eds), *Research on Negotiation in Organizations*, Greenwich, CT: JAI Press.

Bies, R. J., Martin, C. and Brockner, J. (1993) 'Just laid off but still a "good citizen"? Only if the process is fair', *Employee Responsibilities and Rights Journal*, 6: 227–238.

Bok, S. (1978) *Lying: Moral Choice in Public and Private Life*. Hassocks, UK: Harvester Press.

Boles, T. L., Croson, R. T. A. and Murnighan, J. K. (2000) 'Deception and retribution in repeated ultimatum bargaining', *Organizational Behavior and Human Decision Processes*, 83(2): 235–259.

Brockner, J. and Wiesenfeld, B. M. (1996) 'An integrative framework for explaining reactions to decisions: Interactive effects of outcomes and procedures', *Psychological Bulletin*, 120(2): 198–208.

Burns, J. M. (1978) *Leadership*, New York: Harper & Row.

Colquitt, J. A., Conlon, D. E., Wesson, M. J., Porter, C. O. L. H. and Ng, K. Y. (2001) 'Justice at the millennium: A meta-analytic review of 25 years of organizational justice research', *Journal of Applied Psychology*, 86(3): 425–445.

Ekman, P. (1985) *Telling Lies: Clues to Deceit in the Marketplace, Politics, and Marriage*, New York: W. W. Norton.

Fiske, S. T. and Taylor, S. E. (1991) *Social Cognition*, New York: McGraw-Hill.

Graen, G. B. and Uhl-Bien, M. (1995) 'Relationship-based approach to leadership: Development of leader–member exchange (LMX) theory of leadership over 25 years: Applying a multi-level multi-domain perspective', *Leadership Quarterly*, 6(2): 219–247.

Grover, S. L. (1993) 'Why professionals lie: The impact of professional role conflict on reporting accuracy', *Organizational Behavior and Human Decision Processes*, 55: 251–272.

—— (2005) 'The truth, the whole truth, and nothing but the truth: The causes and management of workplace lying', *Academy of Management Executive*, 19(2): 148–157.

Grover, S. L. and Hui, C. (1994) 'The influence of role conflict, role strength, and reward contingencies on lying behavior', *Journal of Business Ethics*, 13: 295–303.

Jansen, E. and von Glinow, M. A. (1985) 'Ethical ambivalence and organizational reward systems', *Academy of Management Review*, 10(4): 814–822.

Jones, T. M. (1991) 'Ethical decision making by individuals in organizations: An issue contingent model', *Academy of Management Review*, 16(2): 366–395.

Kouzes, J. M. and Posner, B. Z. (1993) *Credibility: How Leaders Gain and Lose It, Why People Demand It* (1st edn), San Francisco: Jossey-Bass.

—— (2002) *The Leadership Challenge* (3rd edn), San Francisco: Jossey-Bass.

Maccoby, M. (2000) 'Narcissistic leaders: the incredible pros, the inevitable cons', *Harvard Business Review*, 69–77.

Mayer, R. C., Davis, J. H. and Schoorman, F. D. (1995) 'An integration model of organizational trust', *Academy of Management Review*, 20(3): 709–734.

Palanski, M. E. and Yammarino, F. J. (2007) 'Integrity and leadership: Clearing the conceptual confusion', *European Management Journal*, 25: 171–184.

Posner, B. Z. and Schmidt, W. H. (1984) 'Values and the American manager: An update', *California Management Review*, 26(3): 202–216.

Rousseau, D. M., Sitkin, S. B., Burt, R. S. and Camerer, C. (1998) 'Not so different after all: A cross-discipline view of trust', *Academy of Management Review*, 23: 393–404.

Schweitzer, M. E., Hershey, J. C. and Bradlow, E. T. (2005) 'Promises and lies: Restoring violated trust'. Unpublished manuscript, University of Pennsylvania.

Schweitzer, M. E., Ordonez, L. and Douma, B. (2004) 'The role of goal setting in motivating unethical behavior', *Academy of Management Journal*, 47(3): 422–432.

Scott, E. D. (2003) 'Plane truth: A qualitative study of employee dishonesty in the airline industry', *Journal of Business Ethics*, 42(4): 321–337.

Tyler, T. R. (1989) 'The psychology of procedural justice: A test of the group value model', *Journal of Personality and Social Psychology*, 57(5): 830–838.

6 Transparency tricks

Corporate accountability through visibility

Christina Garsten and Monica Lindh de Montoya

Introduction: transparency – a tale of our times

Transparency is today one of the hype buzzwords in nearly every realm of social life. In corporate boardrooms, in financial trading rooms as well as in government offices, transparency is now a goal and 'a must'. The notion of transparency also influences working life: companies promote the use of the open-floor office organization (where people do not have separate, closed offices), they make employees' calendars available to colleagues by posting them on servers, and promote diverse technical means whereby employees can exchange information. We also insist upon transparency in family relationships and in our love life. Parents should be forthright with their children and spouses should have no secrets from one another.

The notion seems to have rubbed off on fashion, design and entertainment as well. Transparent materials are often used in furniture, products and buildings. Clothing is becoming increasingly thin or transparent, tight and revealing. Some products, such as storage boxes and electronics, are manufactured in clear plastic so that one can see their contents or inner mechanisms. Public and commercial buildings tend to use more glass, allowing in light and public observation. Home design is beginning to integrate the kitchen, once the private part of the house, with living rooms. Restaurants may even bring their kitchens out into the open among the customers and the chef steps into the limelight to practise his art. Transparency has also been utilized in the media as a selling point for a number of years; for example, successful films may make a second film explaining how they made the first film, and celebrities of different kinds are expected to share their lives and feelings in the media. 'What you see is what you get', seems to be the idea.[1]

While calls for openness and transparency permeate our lives in all sectors, nowhere are voices as loud as in the economic sector. The misrepresentation of accounts in large public companies has outraged the public and led to attempts to prosecute those responsible and to further attempts to improve regulation and accountability. Transparency has become ever more highlighted in connection with the globalization of markets as a way to strengthen the dynamics of global capitalism and to reveal and control the everyday workings of local and global economies (Sanders 2003: 148–149). Transparency also has a central position in the operations of many international organizations, such as the United Nations, the European Union, the World Bank, the World Trade Organization and numerous non-governmental organizations (e.g. Clamers 1997; Kopits and Craig 1998; Kratz 1999; Marceau and Pedersen 1999). It is discussed as a key element in relation to 'good governance' and democratic procedures in public affairs (Hood and Heald 2006); and it is considered a central aspect of corporate governance.

A central concern in corporate governance is to limit information asymmetries between central actors, such as corporate managers, stockholders, holders of different positions in corporations and boards, as well as stakeholders more widely. In the context of corporate governance, transparency usually goes under the heading of 'disclosure' (e.g. Lowenstein 1996). Despite what one might think, given its present heyday, transparency in corporate governance is no newborn. It pre-dates the twentieth century by far, and has gradually been institutionalized with growing obligations and regulations on posting of accounts and disclosure of stock value and the like. In the twentieth century, obligations of corporations to disclose information about themselves tightened with the audit and accounting reforms that followed a series of corporate scandals from the 1980s and onwards. The increased complexity of financial markets, with a growing number and differentiation of groups and niches in trading, also contributed to this development (Jönsson 1988). Overall, the inside flow of information within corporations was being more closely scrutinized.

Corporate codes of governance were at this time seen as voluntary ways of addressing information asymmetries and generally taking on a greater degree of corporate social responsibility. Transparency is often promoted under the general heading of 'corporate social responsibility' (CSR). During the last three decades, we have seen a tremendous expansion of interest in this area and in organizations whose mission is to promote it (Boli and Thomas 2006). Generally, the focus of CSR has moved beyond a concern with health and safety in the workplace to encompass a wide array of external and social factors, including human rights and corruption (Power 2007). As Michael Power has stated, 'Indeed, CSR now seems to take as its object the entire ethical character of the organization and its governance' (2007: 133). An assemblage of ideas and practices, soft norms, standards and codes of conduct, as well as certification and audit procedures targeting the 'social' are being put in place alongside conventional management systems, practices, and rules. Instrumental in pushing for CSR are the media and non-governmental organizations (NGOs) (see the chapter by Spar and La Mure in this volume). Media and NGOs are forcing organizations to think 'outside in' (Jackson 2004). These measures are, in our view, part of a neo-liberal turn in regulation and governance, according to which soft, market-based and voluntary forms of regulation are preferable to legally binding and state imposed systems of rules. In this context, 'soft' norms and standards (e.g. Mörth 2004), i.e. rules that are non-binding and entail no legal sanctioning, are introduced as a means to enhance transparency of corporate processes and to contribute to greater accountability.

In addition to attempting to implement notions like corporate citizenship or CSR tools and standards, corporations are making increasing use of 'morality tests' in the recruitment of new employees. Even if corporations have long been taking care to attract and select the right individuals for their companies with the aid of a variety of tests and experts, we now see the proliferation of specific morality tests as part of the procedure. Such tests are meant to diminish misconduct of various kinds in companies and may be part of quality programmes. The tests are proposed to have a specific value in the financial sector, which is seen as particularly exposed to moral misconduct. (We may recall Barings Bank and more recently the Carnegie Bank examples.) Morality tests are a common procedure in many American companies and spreading rapidly to other countries.

The placing of transparency on the corporate agenda reflects a concern for points of reference for ethics and norms in a volatile economic and political environment. It may also reflect a concern with global social and environmental risk scenarios. Transparency in corporate processes and decision-making may establish trust and reduce elements of risk. Engaging with transparency may be a way for management to re-position the corporation as a reflexive and ethical actor in the global market. Engaging with transparency may even provide new market opportunities in the positioning of the transnational corporation as a socially responsible actor – a 'corporate citizen'.[2]

The practices and tools intended to promote transparency have contributed to the emergence of new ethics and politics of governance. The norms and values of these new forms of governance are positioned as voluntary and self-regulatory and therefore something that individuals and organizations alike take on by volition. Such voluntary forms of governance may express a sincere will of corporations to be accountable for their actions and to contribute something worthwhile to the world. It, however, may also offer a means for corporations to be absolved from a bad conscience simply by adhering to formalized and ritualized procedures (Garsten 2003). There is thus a sense in which transparency tools and practices may be examples of a 'formalised accountability' (Power 1997).

Transparency is a tricky notion. It is often used to promote trust, and trust is partly what makes a corporation exist. Without trust, there are no customers, no suppliers, no investors, no employees and probably no corporation. Transparency depends for its workings on human beings, how we reason about what is to be transparent, and what is not. This is where we tend to run into challenges. To understand the tricks played with transparency in corporate settings, we need to understand the social dimension of organizational processes. Words like transparency will acquire a range of contingent meanings; existing meanings may be stretched in novel and unpredictable directions when used by different actors with differing interests and when introduced into new areas of operation (see Williams 1976; see also Shore and Wright 2000). Exactly how and by whom transparency is to be defined and put into action is seldom clear. The abstract character of the concept renders it open to negotiation. What is to be revealed and what is to be hidden is often an issue of debate and conflict. While transparency is widely canvassed as a key to better management and governance, it is more often preached than practised, and more often referred to than defined (Hood and Heald 2006: 3).

This chapter deals with transparency as performative practice and the ethical dilemmas involved. It discusses the ideals attached to notions of transparency, how they may play out in the context of corporations as CSR standards and codes of conduct as well as in managerial narratives. We suggest that the assumptions and practices of transparency bring with them ethical dilemmas in that transparency is always a matter of negotiation, articulation and of position. It is by nature social and contested. Transparency may just as well contribute to openness, visibility and accountability, as it may lead the way towards more closure, opacity and irresponsibility. It all boils down to a matter of ethical reflexivity.

Making things visible

Balancing the hidden and the visible is an integral part of social life. Already as small children, we learn to play with visibility and opacity. We play peek-a-boo, then hide and seek. We learn the importance of telling the truth, but discover that social fibs are both tolerated and sometimes necessary. As we grow older, we learn what information to withhold from parents, teachers, employers and colleagues. However, we also learn that belonging to a group is largely a matter of sharing information, secrets and of 'being in the know'. We also gradually learn the art of self-presentation and impression management. On the other hand, there are aspects of our lives we learn to make more visible, through CVs and résumés, through photographs and film recordings, and through the life histories we tell friends and colleagues. Our friends and colleagues also help us do the job through the mechanisms of anecdote and gossip. In general, then, transparency goes hand in hand with the established doctrine that social affairs in general should be conducted with a high degree of frankness, openness, and candour (Hood 2006: 6).

Much of the potential and power of transparency tools and practices in organizational life is related to transparency being a mechanism for revelation, disclosure and visibilization. We may also see transparency in corporations as something communicated and constructed – or not – from the moment of its birth. The pioneers of a company determine the level of public and private information in practice and it is then communicated to succeeding generations of workers. In this way, the hidden and the transparent become communal work, not just the responsibility of management. Furthermore, they become closely linked to the image and brand of the company, a linkage that is also continuously worked on. The employees of a company are taught when to share, as well as to hold on to, information, when to copy sheets of paper and email communication to colleagues and when not to, in what situations it is appropriate to forward important information and so on. Not least, the technologies of performance evaluation, at the individual as well as the collective level, remind us that what is valuable is also visible and measurable. An important part of organizational life consists of handling information in a way that balances secrecy and confidentiality with openness and sharing. When information is not handled the 'proper' way, consequences can be embarrassing, and even cause conflicts.

Entrepreneurial business activity depends on elements of secrecy and confidentiality – be it in business concept, product design, or company strategy and organization. Information on new products is rigorously kept secret from competitors during the early stages of research and development. Leaking information about suppliers, production prices, labour arrangements and new products may rob companies of their competitive edge. Prospective employees often need to sign contracts prohibiting them from revealing information about key aspects of the company without prior approval. Sometimes these constraints continue for one or two years after the person leaves the company. Control over information is a significant aspect of organizational activity and may become even more so as demands for transparency grow.

To a certain degree, the public's opinion as to the transparency of a company – be it in economic accountability or social accountability as reflected in procurement and labour policies – is an important part of the company's image and brand identity, and of its reputation. Companies with well-known brands, such as Nike, Levi's, and Starbucks, can no longer afford to take the risk of being seen as opaque and secretive. It has become imperative to build a certain degree of openness and disclosure into their management systems as well as into their practices of social responsibility. The brand signals the position of the corporation in the landscape of social responsibility, almost as much as it signals energy, style, or taste.

Clearly then, a corporation is designed to reveal, but also to conceal. Knowing what to reveal and what to conceal and when to do so is of utmost importance. The will to reveal – to make visible and transparent that which is invisible and opaque – is central to the organizing process. The norms of corporate transparency are often at odds with other equally important norms of commercial confidentiality, which may outweigh transparency claims. In addition, individuals in an organization may demand openness that contradicts socially established notions of personal integrity (see also Hood 2006: 20, on counter transparency doctrines). From this perspective, organizational boundaries are also boundaries between what is visible and what is hidden. Organizational boundaries are often taken to be congruent with spatial location, membership or discourse. Current transformations in organizational design suggest that we may have to rethink the conventional nature of organizational boundaries to one that takes into account the management of knowledge and information – there may be 'boundaries of secrecy' and 'boundaries of discretion' (as suggested by Hernes and Paulsen 2003:3), as well as 'boundaries of transparency'.

Transparency is also closely linked to organizational power and control. Jeremy Bentham's notion of the Panopticon, which appeared in 1791, has been influential in understanding modern forms of organizational power. Seeing, and being seen, have been intricately linked to discussions on the nature of power and ways of exercising control. Bentham's basic idea was that, through careful architectural design of a new type of prison, every single prisoner could constantly be observed by the prison guards. The design would allow the guards to observe without the prisoners being aware of it, thus creating a 'sentiment of an invisible omniscience'. The awareness of being seen would also contribute to the self-disciplining of prisoners. Since they had no idea when they were being watched, they would internalize the presence of the 'all-seeing eye'. Optimism around this new panoptic design was high. Bentham himself declared: 'I do really take it for an indisputable truth, and a truth that is one of the corner-stones of political science – the more strictly we are watched, the better we behave' (1995: 277). The model was intended to be widely used in schools, hospitals and factories where people needed to be managed and, to some extent, controlled. The self-disciplining implications meant that control, hypothetically at least, could be made more efficient and cost-effective. This utopian vision of the power of seeing was never a great success in reality, at least not in the shape of the Panopticon. Nevertheless, early management theorists, planners and policy makers, as well as academic scholars (most notably Michel Foucault) picked up the ideas and they continue to influence organizational life.[3] Whether we like it or not, it would be difficult to conceive of an organization without some degree of control of its members, be it through direct visibility (such as direct supervision, open space office landscapes) or through indirect forms of visibility (such as cell phones, open access calendars, emailing). Seeing, and being seen, is a central aspect of the organized world.

Articulating ethical dilemmas

In organizations, mobilization around ideas of transparency ideally makes managers more attuned to ethical considerations in decision-making. Transparency provides a platform and a conceptual tool around which they may organize reflections around dilemmas attached to openness and visibility. But it may just as well offer a way out from responsibility or liability for mishaps. For example, by providing information on risks associated with some corporate undertaking before the event may not so much be a way to protect the public as it is to transfer liability or responsibility to others (Power 2004). As with all acts of communication, disclosure and dissemination in the name of transparency may leave audiences unaware that there has been any communication, or leave them unable to grasp the relevance or significance of the communication. Engaging with transparency is thus, largely, a matter of communication and of being able to articulate that which one wishes to display.

Communication makes up a vital aspect of organizational life. As part of a larger research project on corporate social responsibility, one of the authors of this chapter, Christina Garsten, attended conferences in different places around the world with the intent to follow discussions among various types of organizations concerning CSR issues. One such conference, organized by the American business association BSR (Business for Social Responsibility), took place in Miami in 2002. An entire session at this conference was devoted to the discussion of 'corporate transparency' and how to communicate potentially harmful information across organizational boundaries.[4] Christina attended this session as one of the participants, notebook and pen in hand. As she entered, she observed that the seating was arranged according to the 'fishbowl concept'. The invited panellists, five representatives of different organizations, were seated on high chairs at the centre of a number of concentric circles of seats. The audience thus constituted the periphery of the fishbowl, so to speak. The moderator opened the discussion by stating, 'If you want to talk about transparency – this is the place!' She then went on to outline her view on transparency. In her view, this implied a broad understanding of the term, such as access to information, being able to respond to the concerns of stakeholders or employees, and replying when somebody is critical or just curious. 'Transparency also involves a process of verification, providing information to a broader audience', she continued. One of the participants, a male business leader in his early forties, then presented his case, and opened by stating:

> Transparency is about communication, about telling the full story in order to offset conspiracy theories among our customers. It is about opening up our books to show what we are doing, to build trust. Facts are friendly. Transparency is so much more than a single document.

To him, transparency starts within the corporation and the individual manager and moves outwards. It is the responsibility of management to decide what to reveal and what not to reveal. However, this does not necessarily mean that managers can be content and relaxed about taking the easy way out. Even that which is difficult, painful or embarrassing, should be made transparent. However, it remains an issue for the individual manager as part of his or her critical ethical reasoning.

Another participant, a male NGO representative, underlined that business leaders have a responsibility to report to those who have legitimate interests: 'Stakeholders have a right to know. Transparency builds good relationships with stakeholders'. In his view, transparency should ideally be pushed from the outside in, from stakeholders of the company onto corporate management. The outside society is in a better position to demand what should be known and what need not be known than the managers themselves. His view thus differed considerably from that of the previous speaker.

A third participant, a man who had set up his own CSR consultancy in the aftermath of an environmental crisis caused by the company at which he was employed, had his own view on transparency:

> Transparency is about telling what makes us uneasy. It goes beyond what you would want to know. Basically, we should demand from companies what we demand from our children – that they tell when they did wrong, that they are honest. Transparency is a personal thing.

The moderator asked him what it was that made him come to this position on transparency. He confided that he was working in a managerial position at a corporation in the chemical sector when it became known that the production facilities were leaking hazardous chemicals into the groundwater in the local community. Some local activists had pushed to disclose the information, partly by making use of local media. It came to a stage in which it was impossible for the company to ignore it.

After long and troublesome discussions, and a great deal of disagreement, senior management and the board decided to go public on the whole affair and not only to disclose the information the citizens and the activists were demanding, but to tell 'the full story'. The full story in this case meant revealing all the information they had on the incident, from the first day they knew that something went wrong. They also decided to offer voluntarily compensation to citizens for their sufferings. In this way, they reasoned, they could, if things went well, eventually gain back the trust of the local community.

He went on to discuss his own feelings of anger, guilt and relief throughout the process. He told about the ethical dilemma among managers in trying to evaluate the potential consequences of different responses to the public. What was the right thing to do, and from whose perspective? Who were they loyal to: their stakeholders or their colleagues? How much should be disclosed? In the end, opting for a full disclosure meant they could direct attention away from further details, assigning blame, assessing delay, digging into history, and focus instead on the future.

Working through the process of going public, dealing with people's reactions, and coming to terms with the implications of his company's business, he eventually decided to quit the company and set up his own consultancy. His idea was to offer assistance to corporations on corporate social and environmental responsibilities and to train them to implement tools and procedures to prevent anything like this happening again. That is what he was doing at the conference.

This last speaker's view on transparency was, in a sense, more comprehensive than the two other panellists' views. He saw transparency as both stemming from individual ethical reflection and as coming from the outside, from the stakeholders' need and right to know. In his perception of transparency, he combined an outside-in right to transparency with an inside-out responsibility.[5]

Following these accounts were a number of other short narratives of ethical dilemmas experienced in corporate activities. They all centred on the problem of deciding how much to reveal to the public and how much not to reveal. Questions about loyalty, integrity and honesty were raised and personal accounts of the feelings these processes brought about were given. The narratives discussed during the session turned into a sort of 'confessional tales' that were powerful in their personalized and authentic nature.

Visibility and accountability

Transparency is present in corporations not only through the narratives told by managers and others but also in the many auditing and assessment procedures at work in CSR standards, labelling programmes and codes of conduct. CSR standards such as SA 8000 or the new ISO 26000 represent efforts to show the infusion of ethical concerns into corporate management systems. They are essentially vessels for the communication of the social accountability of business. In a sense, they are windows through which to observe corporate prioritizing.

While adherence to CSR standards may attract consumers looking for ways to reduce adverse social or environmental impacts through their purchasing choices, they have also led to some confusion and scepticism. Without investigation by an independent third party, consumers may not be certain that the company's assertions guarantee that it lives up to its aspirations and claims. This concern with credibility and impartiality has led to the formation of both private and public organizations providing third-party certification and verification, what Power (1997) has referred to as an 'audit explosion'.

If used conscientiously, CSR standards can be a useful source of information, primarily on the conditions under which clothes, food or other goods have been produced. Much of the work on certification and verification is to help make sure that stakeholders get the information they need in an understandable form. In this sense, complex processes are made legible and rendered visible, indeed transparent, through the use of standards and accompanying procedures.

However, labels do more than just provide information. They are technologies of right and wrong, indicating which organizations are taking social responsibility seriously and which are not. They are a proxy for the degree to which organizations are responsive to the normative demands placed on them by stakeholders. As such, they can do a tremendously important job of informing and revealing priorities and actions taken. The difficulties arise when the check-up procedures start to resemble more 'box-ticking exercises' than serious assessments. In interviews with managers, it has surfaced that sometimes there is neither time nor resources to follow up on a lead suggesting that a subcontractor is breaching workers' rights; even if confronted with facts, management may decide not to deal with an issue at the time, since it might jeopardize the expansion of business in the region. Alternatively, the issues may be understood as having to do with different cultures and values rather than with universal human rights or workers' rights and may conveniently be left unaddressed.

Yet another problem arises when standards, as proxies, are mistaken for 'reality' (Power 2007: 177). Standards are rules that stipulate a normative direction. They do not necessarily correspond to the state of affairs to which they aspire. Furthermore, while narratives of transparency may be complex in character, standards are by nature reductive, since they are meant to further measurability, comparability and auditability. In the process of working through forms and tables, through a series of meetings and conversations, these proxies may be regarded as the things they stand for. In the process, the critical distance between goal and reality, between vision and current state of affairs, is lost. Transparency becomes a mere exercise of legitimation.

What do these narratives and technologies of transparency tell us about the relation of transparency to accountability? As traditionally understood in a liberal democratic society, accountability means both answerability and redress. It denotes modalities of oversight and constraint on the exercise of power and the capacity of citizens to keep in check those in power through mechanisms compelling them to give reasons for their actions. Then, when performance is deemed unsatisfactory, to sanction them by media-enabled protests, legal challenges, withdrawal of electoral support or as in the case of corporations, consumer boycotts (see Mason 2006: 3; Flinders 2001: 9–15). There is a dual nature to accountability that speaks both of the answerability ('responsiveness') (Pellizzoni 2004) and redress (sanctions).

To make organizational processes transparent, depending on relevance, timing, and other factors, can be taken as a sign of answerability, of a responsive accountability. It suggests that the organization and its management are willing to communicate on main aspects to interested stakeholders. Especially if done voluntarily, without having been forced to open up to scrutiny, it suggests an invitation for the outside world to have a look inside. This element of voluntarism, or of volition, has been described by Ann Florini (2003) as a central component of transparency:

> Transparency means deliberately revealing one's actions so that outsiders can scrutinize them. This element of volition makes the growing acceptance of transparency much more than a resigned surrender to the technologically facilitated intrusiveness of the information age. It is a choice, a potential standard for the way powerful institutions [as well as individuals (authors' addition)] ought to behave.

However, tools and techniques for revealing organizational procedures and decisions, priorities and strategies, as well as tools and techniques used in assessing, auditing and evaluating, may sometimes be coercive (see Strathern 2000b on 'the tyranny of transparency'). Demands for disclosure may come under the label of voluntariness and volition, but may entail undesired consequences if not answered. Organizations that refuse to disclose, for example, conditions of work in an outsourced production facility would most probably be found guilty, regardless of their guilt or innocence. The best strategy is often to precede any demands on transparency, as in the case above, and to welcome and invite evaluations and assessments, and other forms of exposure.

There is also a sense in which the call for transparency, as a means to maintain and restore trust, might serve to undermine the very trust it was meant to support. As Ghosh and Tsoukas (1997: 835) have it:

> The information society which promises to deliver the ideal of transparency undermines the trust that is necessary for an expert system to function effectively.

Concerns with transparency, if excessive, may lead to a sense of insecurity and distrust of people in power or of expert systems. The ongoing search for information, for hidden facts, for opaque decision-making, may lead to a heightened sense of insecurity and discomfort. In a sense, not only is there never an end to what you may find if you try hard, but there is also a chance that you may well find that which you are looking for.

Practising transparency is never simply a matter of following rules. It is shaped and reshaped in small and inconspicuous ways – or through very obvious ways. The practice of transparency is an ongoing process of articulation and of visibilization and since transparency is never a neutral concept, but normatively charged by the different interests, priorities and values of people using the concept, it is bound to lead to ethical dilemmas. Some degree of ethical reflexivity necessarily goes with the notion of transparency. Exactly how this plays out depends on one's relation to the issue at hand. Who is in a position to see what is demanded? Who can decide what information to reveal and what to shadow? Whose priorities should guide the information to be disclosed and what is to remain hidden from view? The call for transparency is like a play of veils (Garsten and Lindh de Montoya 2008c), involving just as much revelation and openness as veiling and closure.

Concluding notes: transparency and ethical reflexivity

Transparency has become an important tool for organizations and individuals to be more accountable. The particular strength of this concept is that it has the capacity to move across organizational, social and political contexts, to disentangle itself from the particularities of local context and to re-entangle with new actors in new contexts and situations. It is an idea that travels (see Hannerz 1992; Czarniawska and Sevón 2005). In addition, its abstractness and visionary character facilitates its use across social contexts, organizations, countries and cultural boundaries of any sort. The 'transparency doctrine' promotes communication by providing a language and a set of tools for organizing.

Transparency, and the discursive structure of which it is a part, are performative. It sets into motion particular ideas and actions that may be consequential for organizational processes. It provides a point of direction among and for parties that may represent very different interests. It may also work as a motivational force with the capacity to influence and mobilize people in certain ways. It prescribes and encourages certain types of behaviour, often supported by various types of practices, such as those of evaluation, reward and sanctions, and like any discursive element, it can be used in different ways. All new configurations of doing and being, all new demands and practices, come into the social worlds of organizations with their own agendas, and tend to be used to further those agendas, or to circumvent rules. The financial scandals at Enron, for example, did not occur because of a lack of regulation, but rather because of ingenious new ways – both technically (such as special purpose entities and synthetic leases) and socially based – of working around existing regulation in order to present a different picture to the public (see Brinkmann and Simms in this volume).

Every new attempt to enhance transparency will inevitably lead to new and creative ways of circumventing and avoiding transparency. There will always be an 'aspiration gap' (Cyert and March 1963) in relation to transparency efforts. The higher we set the standard, the more likely it is that we fail to reach it. Managers and other organizational members can be expected both to create and to face ever-new inventions towards, as well as resistance against, the goal of making things visible, legible and manageable. However, the fact that all processes geared towards transparency are situated in social context and mediated by certain tools and technologies remains a fundamental challenge in achieving transparency. There is always a social being, if not several, behind every narrative of transparency. The question is whose narrative is being told? On whose agenda is it defined? What happens to ideals of transparency when they are translated into CSR standards and labels?

It is clear that transparency may – somewhat paradoxically – never be defined and accomplished, but that is not the problem nor is it especially interesting. What transparency means and accomplishes exactly is of less importance than what organizational processes it sets in motion. As Rose (1999: 29) phrases it:

> It is not so much a question of what a word or a text 'means' – of the meanings of terms such as 'community', 'culture', 'citizen' and the like – but of analysing the way a word or a book functions in connection with other things; what it makes possible, the surfaces, networks and circuits around which it flows, the affects and passions that it mobilizes and through which it mobilizes.

By analogy, it is what transparency makes possible and what it mobilizes that is important. Does it encourage discussions around openness, visibility, clarity and the like or does it close them off? Does engaging with transparency mean that a greater degree of accountability is achieved or are we left with 'box-ticking accountability'? Do transparency narratives assist in articulating and sorting out ethical dilemmas or do they assist in avoiding them altogether? Can calls for transparency actually cause dilemmas?

The dominant version of transparency being pursued and put into practice in audit society today is built on 'trust in numbers' (Porter 1995). However, these practices, as seen in benchmarking, rating and ranking, may in fact be working against the development of an ethical reflexivity in organizational life. While the technologies of transparency are based on recognition of the merits of rationality, rules and organization, ethical reflexivity is, on the other hand, based on an individual capacity for intersubjective and reflexive reasoning and engagement with others.

Thus, while transparency as a technology may well be exercised at the level of organization, ethical reflexivity needs to be internalized by individuals. Such reflexivity, however, may have a hard time at the organizational level, since the processes of institutionalization and routinization at the very heart of organizing may work against the critical distance needed for moral judgement (see Arendt 1996: 121). Ethical reflexivity presupposes the critical agency of individuals and does not go well with habit, routine, bureaucratic rules or standards – which may shield the individual from thinking critically. To this end, transparency is no simple cure-all, but rests for its accomplishment entirely on the human capacity for critical reflection.

Notes

1 See Garsten and Lindh de Montoya (2008a) for a discussion of transparency as an organizational vision at large.
2 The concept of 'corporate citizenship' suggests that the corporation is seen as deeply embedded in social structures with accompanying rights and duties – an acknowledgement of the social and political nature of financial affairs (see Granovetter, 1985). The notion of 'corporate citizenship' is morally strong, connoting a responsibility to the public, in contrast to the established view that the only responsibility of the firm is to make a profit.
3 The idea of the Panopticon is widely known through the work of Michel Foucault (in particular *Discipline and Punish* (1977)). Foucault viewed Panopticon as a political technology with wide applicability and far-reaching consequences. The idea was central in his discussions of modern disciplinary societies and tendencies for close observation and forms of control. Perhaps more important than merely seeing and observing was surveillance. Surveillance has long been coupled with institutions such as factories, hospital inspections, school examinations and military reviews (Graeber 2001: 95). It is also central to contemporary corporate practices.
4 See also Garsten and Lindh de Montoya (2008b).
5 For a more comprehensive view of the different directions in which transparency can work, see Heald (2006).

Reference

Arendt, H. (1996) *Love and Saint Augustine*, edited by J. V. Scott and J. C. Stark, Chicago, IL: University of Chicago Press.

Bentham, J. (1995), 'Panopticon', in M. Bozovic (ed.), *The Panopticon Writings*, London: Verso.

Boli, J. and Thomas, G. (eds) (2006 (1999)) *Constructing World Culture*. Stanford: Stanford University Press.

Clamers, M. (ed.) (1997) *Developing Arms Transparency*, Bradford: Bradford University Press.

Cyert, R. and March, J. G. (1963) *A Behavioral Theory of the Firm*, Stanford: Stanford University Press.

Czarniawska, B. and Sevón, G. (2005) *Global Ideas. How Ideas, Objects and Practices Travel in the Global Economy*, Malmö: Liber & Copenhagen Business School Press.

Flinders, M. V. (2001) *The Politics of Accountability in the Modern State*, Ashgate: Aldershot.

Florini, A. (2003) *The Coming Democracy*, Washington: Island Press.

Foucault, M. (1977) *Discipline and Punish: The Birth of the Prison*, translated by Alan Sheridan, New York: Pantheon Books.

Garsten, C. (2003) 'The cosmopolitan organization: An essay on corporate accountability', *Global Networks* 3(3): 355–370.

Garsten, C. and Lindh de Montoya, M. (eds) (2008a) *Transparency in a New Global Order: Unveiling Organizational Visions*, London: Edward Elgar Publishing.

—— (2008b) 'The naked corporation: Visualization, veiling, and the ethico-politics of organizational transparency', in C. Garsten, and M. Lindh de Montoya (eds) (2008) *Transparency in a New Global Order: Unveiling Organizational Visions*, London: Edward Elgar Publishing.

—— (2008c) 'In retrospect: The play of shadows', in C. Garsten, and M. Lindh de Montoya (eds) (2008) *Transparency in a New Global Order: Unveiling Organizational Visions*, London: Edward Elgar Publishing.

Ghosh, P. G. and Tsoukas, H. (1997) 'The tyranny of light – The temptations and the paradoxes of the information society', *Futures* 29(9): 827–843(17).

Graeber, D. (2001) *Toward an Anthropological Theory of Value: The False Coin of Our Own Dreams*, New York: Palgrave.

Granovetter, M. (1985) 'Economic action and social structure: The problem of embeddedness', *American Journal of Sociology*, 91(3), November: 481–510.

Hannerz, U. (1992) *Cultural Complexity*, New York: Columbia University Press.

Heald, D. (2006) 'Varieties of transparency', in C. Hood and D. Heald *Transparency: The Key to Better Governance?*, Oxford: Oxford University Press.

Hernes, T. and Paulsen, N. (2003) 'Introduction: Boundaries and organization', in N. Paulsen and T. Hernes (eds) *Managing Boundaries in Organizations: Multiple Perspectives*, Basingstoke: Palgrave Macmillan.

Hood, C. (2006) 'Transparency in historical perspective', in Hood, C. and Heald, D. (eds) (2006) *Transparency: The Key to Better Governance?*, Oxford: Oxford University Press.

Hood, C. and Heald, D. (eds) (2006) *Transparency: The Key to Better Governance?*, Oxford: Oxford University Press.

Jackson, I. and Nelson, J. (eds) (2006) *Profits with Principles: Seven strategies for delivering value with values*, New York: Doubleday

Jönsson, S. (1988) *Accounting Regulation and Elite Structures*, Chichester: Wiley.

Kopits, G. and Craig, J. (1998) *Transparency in Government Operations*, Washington, DC: International Monetary Fund.

Kratz, C. (1999) 'Transparency and the European Union', *Cultural Values* 3(4): 387–92.

Lowenstein, L. (1996) 'Financial transparency and corporate governance: You manage what you can measure', *Columbia Law Review* 96(5): 1335–1362.

Marceau, G. and Pedersen, P. N. (1999) 'Is the WTO open and transparent? A discussion of the relationship of the WTO with non-governmental organizations and civil society's claims for more transparency and public participation', *Journal of World Trade* 33(1): 5–49.

Mason, M. R. (2006) *The New Accountability: Environmental Responsibility Across Borders*, London: Earthscan.

Mörth, U. (ed.) (2004) *Soft Law in Governance and Regulation*, London: Edward Elgar Publishing.

Pellizzoni, L. (2004) 'Responsibility and environmental governance', *Environmental Politics*, 13(3): 541–565.

Porter, T. M. (1995) *Trust in Numbers: the Pursuit of Objectivity in Science and Public Life*, Princeton, NJ: Princeton University Press.

Power, M. (1997) *The Audit Society: Rituals of Verification*, Oxford: Oxford University Press.

—— (2004) *The Risk Management of Everything: Rethinking the Politics of Uncertainty*, London: Demos. Available online at http://www.demos.co.uk/publications/riskmanagementofeverythingcatalogue (accessed 28 October 2007).

—— (2007) *Organized Uncertainty: Designing a World of Risk Management*, Oxford: Oxford University Press.

Rose, N. (1999) *Powers of Freedom: Reframing Political Thought*, Cambridge: Cambridge University Press.

Sanders, T. (2003) 'Invisible hands and visible goods: Revealed and concealed economies in millennial Tanzania', in H. G. West and T. Sanders (eds) *Transparency and Conspiracy: Ethnographies of Suspicion in the New World Order*, Durham, NC: Duke University Press.

Shore, C. and Wright, S. (2000) 'Coercive accountability: The rise of audit culture in higher education', in M. Strathern (ed.) *Audit Cultures: Anthropological Studies in Accountability, Ethics and the Academy*, London: Routledge, pp. 57–89.

—— (2000b) 'The tyranny of transparency', *British Educational Research Journal*, 26(3): 309–321.

Williams, R. (1976) *Keywords*. London: Fontana.

7 The power of activism

Assessing the impact of NGOs on global business

Debora L. Spar and Lane T. La Mure

Introduction

Recent decades have witnessed the proliferation of non-governmental organizations (NGOs) and the emergence of activism across a wide variety of issues.[1] NGOs and activists represent an increasingly important constituency in a firm's non-market environment on topics ranging from human rights to labour conditions. Surprisingly, however, scholars have only recently begun to consider seriously the interaction between NGOs and firms. As an early step in an emerging research programme, we explore the different ways in which firms manage NGO pressure, noting instances of pre-emption, capitulation and resistance. Through a consideration of three case studies – Unocal, Nike and Novartis – we evaluate a series of preliminary hypotheses about the economic and non-economic factors that drive variation in firms' responses to NGO activism. We conclude with a discussion of our findings and some implications for managers.

In 1995, a group of Burmese and American graduate students at the University of Wisconsin at Madison created the Free Burma Coalition (FBC), a non-governmental organization (NGO) comprising a diverse mix of high school, university, environmental, human rights, religious, labour and grass-roots organizations. Reacting to the Burmese military government's atrocious human rights record and disdain for democracy, the Coalition sought to cut the flow of foreign currency provided by multinational investors and strengthen the country's prospects for democratic leadership. In pursuit of these objectives, the FBC targeted firms that sourced or produced goods in Burma with peaceful protests, consumer boycotts, shareholder activism, and federal and state lawsuits. In one instance, activists handed out flyers in front of Kenneth Cole's New York City store, pressuring the company to eliminate its production facilities in Burma. In another case, the FBC posted a condemnation of Sara Lee Corporation on its website, prompting the company to halt its manufacturing practices in the country.

By 2002, at least 30 firms – including Adidas, Costco, Wal-Mart and Levi Strauss – had bowed to FBC pressure and shuttered their Burmese operations. A handful of companies, however, such as Unocal, Suzuki and France's Total, vowed to remain. Despite embarrassing public protests and an ongoing barrage of lawsuits and related forms of activism, these firms elected to maintain, even to augment, their businesses in Burma.

Such a broad discrepancy raises an interesting puzzle: What accounts for the variation in how firms respond to activist pressure? Why do some firms take extremely proactive measures, engaging activist groups and anticipating their protests, while others stand defiant? Why do some firms capitulate to NGO demands while others refuse? In this chapter, we explore the different ways in which firms respond to activism. Specifically, we ask why firms choose one of three strategies – pre-emption, capitulation, or resistance – and what determines their response. Our analysis is more exploratory than definitive; designed to advance hypotheses in this area rather than test them. Still, drawing on existing studies and empirical cases, we suggest that the interaction between firms and NGOs can be systematically understood and even predicted. Firms respond differently to NGOs because they have different opportunities and constraints, different kinds of costs and different modes of weighing them. Much of this analysis can be contained within a standard, albeit modified, framework of profit maximization and cost-benefit calculation. Some, however, demands a new kind of calculus, one that integrates non-financial concerns and the personal preferences of key decision makers.

The remainder of this chapter proceeds in four parts. The following sections review the existing literature on NGOs and firms and lay out our working hypotheses about the causal factors that drive variation in firms' management of NGO activism. We then explore these hypotheses across three case studies: Novartis in the pharmaceutical industry, Nike in the footwear and apparel industry and Unocal in the oil and natural gas industry. We conclude with a discussion of our results and suggestions for future research.

The business of NGOs

Although they are often described as a distinctly modern (or even postmodern) phenomenon, NGOs are in fact rather old. If we define NGOs as non-profit groups that combine resource mobilization, information provision and activism to advocate changes in certain issue areas, then NGOs have been a figure of the global economy for over four hundred years, starting with the Rosicrucian Order, an Egyptian educational organization founded in the sixteenth century.[2] In their more current incarnations, NGOs run the gamut from small-scale, grass-roots groups such as Earth First! to large and professionally managed institutions like Amnesty International and the World Wide Fund for Nature. What distinguishes this often-motley collection is largely a list of what its members are not: not government, not business, not for profit or political office. Instead, NGOs and activists tend to organize primarily around ideas; around a collective commitment to some shared belief or principle.[3] Operating independently of any government, NGOs target both public and private entities, using whatever tools they can muster to secure their desired goal.

In their earliest days, NGOs tended to form around distinct and well-defined problems – around societal issues that were either being ignored or sponsored by more formal authorities. In the 1770s, for example, opponents of slavery slowly began to gather in groups to voice their opposition to a larger audience. In 1775, Quaker activists founded the Pennsylvania Society for Promoting the Abolition of Slavery, dedicated to liberating enslaved blacks and crusading against slavery more generally. They were followed a decade later by the British Society for Effecting the Abolition of the Slave Trade, which sought an end to the transatlantic slave trade.[4] Born of religious roots and motivated by belief in a higher, unwritten law, these groups rapidly became political players on both the national and international scenes, exchanging information, petitioning for anti-slavery legislation and popularizing the realities of the slave trade in books and pamphlets.[5] In short stead, and propelled no doubt by rapid-fire improvements in transportation and communication technologies, groups rallied around other, similarly principled causes: footbinding in China, female circumcision in Kenya, working conditions for children, the rights of women and immigrant groups.[6] Like their predecessors in the anti-slavery movement, these new organizations took their protests to the public and the streets, using conviction to combat existing practice and law.

As these groups gained prominence and won victories (minimum age legislation, for instance, and women's right to vote), they were joined by the subtle offspring of their own success. These new groups were also principled and politically active, but now targeted firms rather than states. When they wanted change, these organizations went to merchants or the market, using buying power to supplement political pressure.

This shift in emphasis is critical for understanding the current state of firm–NGO interaction. In the earliest days of NGO activity, protesters targeted the obvious source of power: if they wanted to end slavery or child labour, for example, they pressured the governments that presided over, or at least permitted, such practices. This dynamic of activism is eminently reasonable and continues today but it has also been joined, increasingly and importantly, by pressure directed at non-state actors and particularly at multinational corporations. Arguably, this shift isn't even all that recent – protestors in colonial America, after all, boycotted British imports after Parliament passed the Stamp Act in 1765 and early abolitionists organized boycotts of goods produced by slaves.[7] However, as corporations have gained prominence in the global economy, they have become more and more the direct target of activism – of boycotts, consumer protest and shareholder rebellion.

Consider three recent high profile campaigns. In the case of Burma, national dissidents have chosen to focus their ire, not directly at the country's ruling junta, but instead at the multinational corporations that arguably allow this junta to remain in power. In Indonesia, labour activists have sought to improve local working conditions by applying pressure on the brand-name apparel firms doing business in the country. When Global Witness wanted to stop the plague of violence in Sierra Leone, they campaigned, not against the country's warlords per se, but rather against the so-called 'dirty diamonds' that were funding their reign. In all of these cases, Western activists have targeted Western corporations as agents of change. Instead of taking their protests directly to the offending states or governments and instead of lobbying their own governments to engage in the time-worn process of diplomacy, they are taking their protests to the streets, and to the market, trying to persuade corporations to do the work once reserved for governments.[8]

The logic is infallible. In places like Burma, Indonesia and Sierra Leone, corporations such as Gap or De Beers can wield a disproportionate amount of economic influence, an influence made even larger in recent years by the relative decline of both foreign aid and official lending. If economic influence can be translated into political pull, then the best way to change a country's laws or practice may well be through the corporations that invest there. A similar logic applies even within countries like the United States, where, for example, animal rights activists and environmentalists have long realized the power of targeting firms directly, rather than (or at least in addition to) trying to affect the regulation that surrounds them.

On closer examination, the causal chain runs as follows: an NGO identifies a problem that it and its supporters feel passionately about redressing. In an effort to gain maximum impact from their finite resources, they select a target with the greatest potential to affect the problem at hand and the greatest susceptibility to external pressure. In many cases – natural gas firms in Burma, apparel makers in Indonesia, diamond brokers in Sierra Leone – this target is a firm rather than a state; a market player with purported political clout. Target in hand, the NGO then strives to communicate the link between its issue and the chosen firm (or firms). By making the issue public and connecting it with a well recognized, usually well heeled, organization the NGO effectively attaches a tangible target to a broader cause. It does not just inform people about violence in Sierra Leone, for example, it tells them that their engagement ring could be contributing to the ongoing war and violence. It does not just warn of the evils of child labour, but also suggests that a new pair of jeans may be part of the problem. Through a wide range of tactics and media – letter-writing campaigns, picketing, shareholder resolutions, boycotts and the like – NGOs deliver a powerful causal message: that there is a problem, and that the firm or firms in question can address this problem by altering their corporate behaviour. What is critical to realize, though, is that the causal mechanism relies on the threat of financial harm. Essentially, NGOs use consumer and public pressure to damage the firm. The targeted firm, in turn, tries to limit the damage by bringing its behavior in line with the NGO's mandate – the diamond merchant refuses to buy stones from Sierra Leone; the energy giant pulls out of Burma; the apparel manufacturer buys jeans outside Indonesia. Implicit in this process are three key turning points. First, the NGO must be able to threaten the firm with significant harm. Second, the firm must respond to this threat by changing its business practice. Third, the change must serve to advance the NGO's goals. In this process, the firm effectively acts as a conduit, the means by which outside actors try to achieve non-market objectives.

Ultimately, the most important question about this NGO–firm dynamic is whether it works: are firms good vehicles for the pursuit of principled goals? If diamond merchants stop buying gemstones in Sierra Leone, does the violence in that country get better or worse? When US firms pull out of Burma, do they weaken the ruling junta or strengthen its resolve? Arguably, NGOs have not yet fully grappled with these questions, or with the tools they can employ to gauge their own effectiveness.[9] For present purposes, however, what concern us most are the first and second pieces of this puzzle. Can NGOs really harm firms through their tactics of picketing, letter writing and such? Why do firms respond so differently to the threats that NGOs pose?

Concerning harm, the existing literature is intriguing though far from conclusive. Most concerns the financial impact of well-defined boycott campaigns and indicates a slight measurable effect. Pruitt and Friedman, for example, find that boycott announcements exert a negative impact on shareholder wealth, reducing average firm market value by $120 million.[10] Pruitt *et al.* reach a similar conclusion in an event study of 16 union-sponsored boycotts.[11] In a broader study that considers both boycotts and threats to boycott, however, Koku *et al.* reach the opposite conclusion, finding that boycotts and threats actually *increased* the value of target firms by an average of 0.66 per cent. The authors attribute this counter-intuitive finding to the possibility that boycotts could motivate firms to engage in active damage control or anti-boycott measures. For instance, when gun owners organized a boycott of Estée Lauder products to protest the firm's commitment to handgun control, gun control advocates encouraged like-minded consumers to buy Estée Lauder cosmetics in response.[12]

More generally, some scholars have been able to link protest to a decline in firm value, at least as measured by share price. In an empirical investigation of the 1999 Seattle WTO talks, for example, Epstein and Schnietz find that while a portfolio of Fortune 500 firms suffered a 1.9 percent decline in equity value as a result of the failed trade talks, firms that were perceived as being abusive to labour or the environment (from the mining, logging, oil, toy and apparel sectors) suffered a 2.7 per cent loss. The scholars thus conclude that 'investors penalized firms in labor and environmentally "abusive" industries because they were members of the industries under direct attack by Seattle's protestors, not simply because they were multinational firms'.[13] Konar and Cohen offer a related finding, suggesting that even firms operating within the law may suffer from behaving in an environmentally irresponsible manner. In a study of environmental performance among firms in the S&P 500, the authors find a strong correlation between 'good' environmental performance and relatively higher intangible asset values.[14]

The most widely researched case, however, considers the impact of activism on firms operating in apartheid South Africa.[15] Between 1971 and 1994, a diverse group of international activists sought to bring pressure on the South African regime by targeting Western firms doing business in that country. In a high profile, highly principled media campaign, NGOs and their supporters called for multinationals either to withdraw from South Africa or to accede to standards of behaviour (the Sullivan Principles) that far exceeded those embedded in South African law. Many firms left, some stayed, many complied with the principles while others ignored them. Did all this pressure damage those who resisted it? The record is unclear. In a study of divestment announcements and legislative sanctions, for example, Teoh *et al.* find little effect on firm value, concluding that 'the announcement of legislative or shareholder pressure had *no* discernible effect on the valuations of banks and corporations with South African operations or on the South African financial markets'[16] (emphasis in original). Meznar *et al.* reach the opposite conclusion, suggesting that firms announcing the withdrawal of operations from the country suffered an average 5.5 per cent *decline* in stock price.[17] And Patten, who considers the market reaction to firms' adoption of the Sullivan Principles, simply finds that non-signing firms experienced significantly higher trading volumes than signing firms on the announcement date.[18] At a minimum, then, the evidence suggests that even the highest-profile activism may have but a minimal effect on what firms purportedly value most: their share price.[19]

Yet, despite the limited measurable impact of activism, a growing body of work suggests that firms do in fact take activism seriously, and that many of them respond to the pressures that they face. Hamilton, for example, evaluates hazardous waste processing firms and finds that their managers explicitly choose expansion sites in communities with low voter turnout, calculating that citizens from these areas will be less likely to engage in environmental campaigns.[20] Similarly, Maxwell *et al.* find that firms in states with vibrant environmental groups are more likely to adopt voluntary emission controls.[21]

We are left, therefore, with the puzzle laid out above: if firms cannot discern a measurable cost of activism, why do they respond to it at all; and why is there such wide variation in what should be a fairly consistent pattern of response?

A calculus of response

Theoretically, firms and their managers should respond to NGO pressure in a predictable and reasonably consistent manner. If firms behave as rational, profit-maximizing agents, their first and overriding concern will be creating and maintaining value for their shareholders, a value manifest most loudly in the firm's stock price. When faced with a barrage of outside criticism or demands, these firms should therefore run through their usual cost–benefit calculus, weighing the benefits of compliance with its estimated costs. How much, for example, would it cost a chemical plant to install the scrubbers or filters demanded by the protesters at the gate? Would the installation of these tools please the firm's shareholders or anger them? Would investors reward the firm for its foresightedness or punish it for wasted expense? Such calculations are difficult but not impossible to produce. If firms engage in them, we should see evidence of this reasoning in their collective response to activism. Firms should accede more rapidly and completely to demands that are cheap to address. They should pay more attention to expensive protests and ignore those without significant impact. In a world of multiplying boycotts and shareholder resolutions, firms should simply treat activism as another cost of doing business, one that demands a rational and well-calculated response. We suggest that three variables are particularly important in this regard: transaction costs, brand impact and competitive position.

First, managers evaluate the transaction costs associated with capitulating to NGO demands. How costly is it for the firm to abandon existing investment, create new facilities or switch production methods? For firms with significant transaction costs, compliance with NGO pressure may prove prohibitive or infeasible, especially if the NGO demands geographic relocation or a significant change in production methods. Managers also consider the costs associated with securing new inputs. In many cases, NGOs demand that firms source inputs from either a different region or a different set of suppliers. In cases where a firm cannot shift sourcing without significantly damaging its competitive position (oil and gas, for example, or other natural resources), we would expect managers to opt for resistance. In general, we expect the probability of resistance to increase along with capital intensity and high transaction costs: the more capital that a firm utilizes in a particular project, and the more difficult it is to switch, the more likely the firm is to choose the path of resistance. Clearly, this probability will vary strongly along industry lines.

Second, managers consider the firm's brand and the extent to which public protest is likely to shift consumer preference. As noted, NGOs often seek to impose costs on a firm by highlighting the negative aspects of its operation – the environmental impact of its production process, for example, or poor working conditions in its plants. To sharpen their point, NGOs frequently target the otherwise positive image that a firm may have spent decades nurturing. The stronger and cleaner this image, ironically, the more enticing the target. Accordingly, the greater the importance of brand to a firm, the more susceptible its managers are to activist pressure and the more likely they are to capitulate.[22] This tendency will be particularly pronounced in industries such as footwear or apparel, where brand is often the central feature distinguishing one corporation's products from another.

Finally, managers evaluate the firm's competitive position, weighing both the negative effects of NGO activism and the possibility of capturing strategic advantage. Odd as it may seem, capitulation in certain cases may bring competitive reward. When the Earth Island Institute, a small environmental group, targeted tuna firms for harming dolphins in the harvesting process, Starkist implemented new procedures and branded its tuna as 'dolphin free', differentiating itself from other producers.[23] Reebok moved quickly in 1996 to answer critics' claims that soccer balls were being stitched by children, and BP (British Petroleum) sought to assuage environmentalist concerns about global warming by voluntarily reducing its emissions of greenhouse gases.[24] Both anecdotal and limited statistical evidence lead us to hypothesize that firms situated in industries characterized by strong competition and high brand recognition are more likely to capitulate than firms in less competitive, non-branded industries.[25] Moreover, firms engage in these calculations and behaviours even when they cannot gauge the precise results of their response.[26]

This brings us to the last hypothesis. If managers relied exclusively on cost–benefit analyses, then resistance would almost certainly be their dominant response, for the costs of activism and the benefits of capitulation are exceedingly difficult to isolate and weigh. Yet, as noted, firms do capitulate to NGO demands and sometimes even pre-empt them. Managers respond to external critics when a strict cost–benefit analysis might suggest doing otherwise, and they are responding, it appears, with increased frequency.[27] To explain this behaviour we need to move beyond strictly economic models to consider the personal motives and beliefs that can also motivate managerial decisions.[28]

We begin with the obvious but often neglected proposition that managers have lives beyond the firm. They raise families, reside in communities and participate in social events. They have different social and educational backgrounds, diverse belief structures and moral systems. To a large extent, of course, custom (and academic models) dictate that managers leave these belief systems at the office door. Yet they don't always. Managerial preference can make a significant difference, particularly at the highest levels. In some cases, managers may actually sympathize with an NGO's cause, even if they do not necessarily agree with the group's tactics. They may want to save dolphins, preserve trees, or prevent eight-year-olds from labouring in their overseas factories. Such desires are perfectly rational, although not in the sense presumed by rational actor models. They may be difficult to calculate and impossible to isolate in a large empirical study, but they are important nevertheless. When corporations are run by particularly charismatic CEOs or dominated (both managerially and financially) by a particular individual or family, the sway of personal preference becomes especially strong. Simply put, strong CEOs or tightly held firms may choose to respond to NGO demands even if, from a strict cost–benefit perspective, they don't have to.

In the cases that follow, we explore how three different firms from three very different industries have responded to outbursts of activism. While we allow for a full range of variation across the dependent variable, our case selection is not meant to be scientific: these firms may be outliers and their responses could be highly idiosyncratic. Given the relative lack of empirical work in this field, however, and the inherent difficulty of ascribing either cause or effect to this kind of response, case studies seem the best window into the complex dynamic at play here; a way, at least, to probe how corporations view NGO attacks and why they respond so differently.[29]

Unocal in Burma[30]

In early 1993 the Unocal Corporation, a $7.8 billion US oil and gas firm, entered an investment consortium to develop the Yadana natural gas field, a deposit of over 5 trillion cubic feet of reserves in the Andaman Sea, 43 miles off Burma's coast. The $1.2 billion project involved the construction of a 416-mile pipeline to transport natural gas from the offshore gas field across the southern panhandle of Burma and into Thailand. Once onshore, gas from the pipeline would flow into both Thailand and Burma, providing both of these countries with much needed energy.

Economically, the project was a great boon for Unocal, a medium-sized oil and gas firm that had been struggling in the 1990s to compete against better-heeled rivals. With Yadana, Unocal stood to reap over $110 million in annual revenue as well as a strategic toehold in the booming Asian market. Politically, however, Yadana was marked by its strong links to the SLORC (State Law and

Order Restoration Council), a brutal junta that had ruled Burma since 1988.[31] In its violent ascent to power, the SLORC had killed several thousand citizens and imposed its own brand of authoritarian control, closing universities, banning public gatherings and enforcing strict curfews. Military rulers suspended basic rights, including due process, freedom of speech, press, association and religion, and engaged in unprecedented repression, relying on tactics such as the arbitrary seizure of property, forced labour, extrajudicial execution, kidnapping and torture. Since 1990, they had also confined Aung San Suu Kyi, the Nobel Prize winner and charismatic leader of the country's leading opposition party, to house arrest, forbidding her from meeting with supporters or even visiting her dying husband. Such behaviour made Burma a pariah on the international scene and drew the ire of a large and well-connected activist movement.

Despite this environment, though, Unocal had eagerly embraced the Yadana project in 1994, joining with the SLORC, Thailand's national energy company and the French energy giant, Total. Unocal committed approximately $340 million to construct the pipeline and joined Total in implementing a three-year, $6 million socioeconomic development programme designed to provide health care, educational facilities and agricultural projects to the area's 35,000 local inhabitants. The consortium began construction in 1996, employing two thousand local workers at higher than prevailing market wages to construct the pipeline's 39-mile land route through Burma. Throughout Unocal's involvement in the project, the company's board of directors conducted periodic reviews, concluding that 'from moral, ethical, economic and human development perspectives, the Yadana project represents a significant opportunity to bring sustainable, long-term benefits to the people of Myanmar' (Garcia 1996). The consortium completed the project in mid-1998 and commercial production commenced in early 2000.

No amount of development spending, though, could divert activists' attention from the Yadana pipeline, and protests to the contrary did little to limit Unocal's involvement with the SLORC. During the initial phase of construction, anti-SLORC rebels killed five Burmese members of a Yadana survey team, and subsequent attacks on Total's base camp reportedly injured another six project workers. In response, and purportedly to prevent further attack, the SLORC deployed 4,000 troops along the pipeline route. These troops, according to activists and other observers, were subsequently involved in atrocious violations of human rights, forcing villagers to serve as unpaid labourers and subjecting the local population to arbitrary killings, beatings, rape and theft.[32]

As word of these atrocities slipped back to the West, a firestorm of controversy arose. It quickly coalesced around the Wisconsin-based Free Burma Coalition (FBC) and soon constituted one of the largest student movements in the world. Modelled after the anti-apartheid movement in South Africa, the FBC served as an umbrella organization for groups seeking to stem the flow of foreign currency to the SLORC and end the junta's rule. Through grass-roots networks and the internet, the Coalition spread like wildfire, with active chapters on more than 100 US college campuses and in over 25 countries.[33]

While the FBC pressured all foreign firms sourcing or producing goods in

Burma, it focused much of its protest at Unocal, the country's largest US investor. Beginning with peaceful protests and publicized consumer boycotts, the FBC then moved to more direct action, urging members to send mutilated credit cards to the company's CEO and chaining themselves to trucks and storage tanks at Unocal's California shipping terminal. Activists also introduced shareholder resolutions seeking a variety of changes, including a report on the firm's Burma operations (1994), a proposal to consider activist organizations when making investment decisions (1995) and a report on the costs of doing business in Burma (1997–1999). While none of the resolutions passed, a resolution at Unocal's 2002 shareholders meeting calling for the adoption of the International Labor Organization's code of conduct on workplace human rights received a record 31 per cent of the vote. Finally, the Coalition also lobbied for federal sanctions as well as state and local selective purchasing laws. By early 1997, the US government had imposed economic sanctions on Burma and 13 cities, including New York City and San Francisco and the state of Massachusetts had passed laws barring government agencies from purchasing goods or services from any company with operations in the country.[34]

In addition to steady and widespread pressure from the FBC, Unocal also encountered a number of legal challenges related to the Yadana project. Two separate lawsuits in US courts alleged that the company's use of SLORC security forces had led to the systematic destruction and relocation of villages, the widespread use of forced labour and a series of human rights atrocities, including murder and rape. The suits sought an undisclosed amount in monetary damages and an injunction against Unocal's participation in the pipeline project. While a federal judge in the case dismissed the claims against the SLORC and Burma's state-owned oil and gas company, he allowed the suit against Unocal to proceed.

Unocal mounted a vigorous legal defence, calling the allegations 'absolutely false'[35] and the lawsuits 'irresponsible, and frivolous'.[36] The company used satellite photography to argue that no villages had been destroyed or relocated and claimed that all pipeline workers were paid above market wages, as formalized under signed agreements. In September 2000, a US District Court granted summary judgment to Unocal under both cases and ordered the plaintiffs to pay the firm's court costs. The Court ruled that while Unocal officials were aware of the alleged human rights abuses, they did not actively engage the government to commit them, nor did they control the military's decision to employ slave labour.[37] In response, the plaintiffs appealed the District Court decision and in September 2002 the US Ninth Circuit Court of Appeals reversed the lower court's dismissal, finding adequate evidence to support the claim that 'Unocal gave practical assistance to the Myanmar military in subjecting plaintiffs to forced labor'.[38] At the same time, activists filed state law claims in the Los Angeles Superior Court where Unocal was to face trial in February 2003.

The Unocal Corporation has thus been fighting a concerted activist campaign for nearly 10 years. Though tactics on both sides have changed over time, their conflict remains at a standstill: Unocal has refused to pull out of Burma and the activists have refused to back down. Initially, Unocal's only concession was to agree to meet with representatives of the activist groups. Relations were far from cordial, however, and the company explicitly and unequivocally vowed to continue in Yadana. In a 1995 meeting with activists, for example, the company's president, John Imle, was blunt: 'Let's be reasonable about this', he stated. 'What I'm saying is that if you threaten the pipeline, there's going to be more military. If forced labor goes hand-in-glove with the military, yes, there will be more forced labor. For every threat to the pipeline, there will be a reaction'.[39] Unocal also publicly seized the offensive, suggesting that activists had been engaged in a disinformation campaign against the company: 'Over the past five years, activist groups who oppose the military government of Myanmar have not been willing to limit the debate to the merits of engagement or isolation. Instead, these groups have resorted to spreading false and hurtful allegations about Unocal and the Yadana natural gas project'.[40]

As protests continued, Unocal coupled its public denouncements with a vigorous public relations campaign. In 1997, Unocal sponsored site visits for European, Asian and American reporters, two non-governmental organizations, several US Congress members, and State Department officials. Throughout, Imle argued that the firm's protests to the SLORC had actually reduced human rights abuses in the country, with the government agreeing to curb the use of forced labour on certain infrastructure projects.[41] Unocal also employed two consultants in 1998 to visit the Yadana project and survey the human rights conditions. At the conclusion of a five-day review, the consultants re-affirmed Unocal's positive social, economic and public health impact on the region's population and found 'clear evidence that neither the project operator nor Unocal has any involvement in human rights violations'.[42]

Admittedly, the firm did eventually make some small concessions to the activists' complaints. In April 2000, Unocal hired its first Director of Corporate Responsibility, charging him with implementing the firm's new commitment 'to improve the lives of people wherever we work'.[43] A year later, it engaged the Center for Corporate Citizenship at Boston College to conduct a self-assessment of the firm's corporate responsibility and established an internal Corporate Responsibility Steering Team. Finally, Unocal claimed to seek a limited dialogue with NGOs. In 2002, the firm released 'Human Rights and Unocal: A Discussion Paper', in which it sought 'a dialogue with international corporations, humanitarian and human rights groups, and other non-governmental organizations (NGOs) in order to clarify the challenges faced by multinational companies and others doing business in societies with very different cultural and political systems'.[44]

As of 2002, Unocal remained Burma's single largest US investor and had no public plans to withdraw operations from the country. At the same time, NGO and activist groups continued to pressure the company through lawsuits, boycotts, protests, shareholder resolutions and related tactics, while in Burma, the ruling junta maintained a firm grip on power through repression and human rights abuses. In mid-2002, with foreign exchange reserves dwindling, annual inflation exceeding 50 per cent and foreign investors pulling out at a rapid rate, the economy stood on the brink of collapse.

It is not clear, therefore, whether the activists or the corporation 'won'. What is obvious, though, is that, despite years of pressure and opposition, Unocal has not capitulated to the activists' demands.

Nike[45]

Founded in 1972, Nike is one of the world's most popular and well-known brands. Its sneakers grace the feet of Michael Jordan and Tiger Woods, and its advertisements bear the endorsement of these superstars. Known for its street appeal and can-do attitude, Nike is also famous for its radical system of mass production, a system that eschews in-house manufacturing in favour of a global network of contract suppliers. Conceived originally, by CEO Phil Knight, Nike's production network allows the firm to search constantly for the lowest-cost shoes, and to siphon off the resultant savings into sales and marketing campaigns. The results of this system are dramatic, giving Nike both a cost advantage over its rivals and a well-honed, high-profile brand image.

Between 1972 and 1998, this strategy worked phenomenally well. Nike became the largest seller of athletic footwear and apparel in the world, with fiscal 1998 revenues of approximately $9.5 billion and net income of nearly $400 million.[46] The firm was a darling of Wall Street and in the media world, where its Just Do It campaign garnered rave reviews. By the early 1990s, however, vulnerability in Nike's low-cost, high-profile strategy was becoming evident. Nike, it appeared, was a nearly ideal target for activist attacks – a perfect symbol of low-wage labour, and a symbol so prominent that attack was easy. Once the activists targeted the firm, they showed no sign of letting go.

Problems began to appear in 1991 when labour activist Jeff Ballinger produced a report for the Asian-American Free Labor Institute (AAFLI) on working conditions and wage levels at Indonesian factories. Involved in labour politics since high school, Ballinger believed that foreign companies often exploited low-wage, politically repressed labour pools. Subsequent work with the AAFLI substantiated this belief, suggesting that foreign firms routinely violated Indonesian labour laws, paid below subsistence wages, mistreated workers, assigned excessive overtime, ignored health and safety conditions, and obstructed worker efforts to unionize or seek representation. When a wave of labour unrest accompanied Nike's entrance into Indonesia in 1991, Ballinger seized an opportunity to focus media attention on the unsuspecting firm.

Following a 'one country–one company' strategy, Ballinger suspected that he could capitalize on Nike's brand name to drive public outrage about labour conditions in overseas factories. In 1992 he published an article in *Harper's Magazine*, famously comparing Michael Jordan's Nike endorsement contract to an Indonesian factory worker's pay stub and noting that it would take the worker 44,492 years to earn Jordan's pay. The comparison was jolting and quickly drew the attention that Ballinger had anticipated. Shortly after the *Harper's* piece, Nike's hometown newspaper, the Portland *Oregonian*, ran lengthy articles criticizing the firm's operations in Indonesia. Then protestors appeared at the 1992 Barcelona Olympics, decrying Nike's exploitation of factory workers.

Initially, Nike responded with resistance, arguing that it could not be held accountable for conditions in factories that it did not own. As one Nike spokeswoman put it, 'We're about sports, not manufacturing 101'.[47] Similarly, when asked about labour violations in Nike's contracting factories, the firm's general manager in Jakarta stated 'I don't know that I need to know'.[48] In 1992, Nike did adopt a Code of Conduct that addressed labour issues such as safety standards, environmental regulation and worker insurance.[49] Notably, however, the firm remained adamant on the subject of wages, arguing that low wages were a crucial element of a country's path to growth.[50]

Opposition continued to mount. In 1993, Ballinger founded Press for Change, an NGO dedicated to raising awareness of labor conditions and wages in Nike's overseas plants. A wave of media attention soon followed, with harsh criticism of the company's practices appearing on major US television networks and in national publications such as the *New Republic,* the *New York Times, Rolling Stone*, and the *Los Angeles Times*. In April 1996, a related campaign against the apparel industry revealed that a line of clothing sponsored by Kathie Lee Gifford, a popular talk show host, had been manufactured by children in Honduras. Almost immediately thereafter, Gifford appeared sobbing on the screen, pledging an end to the use of child labour in factories manufacturing her line. More negative publicity followed in July, when *Life* magazine published a photo of a 12-year-old Pakistani boy stitching Nike soccer balls.[51] Activists continued to pressure Nike throughout 1997, launching rallies and chanting 'Just Don't Do It' at Niketown retail store openings across the country. Students on college campuses became equally animated, protesting Nike endorsement arrangements with their schools. Then the sports media joined the fray, using press conferences and related events to raise labour issues with Nike sponsors like Michael Jordan and football hero Jerry Rice. Even *Doonesbury*, the popular comic strip, became involved, parodying Nike and its labour practices for a full week.[52]

However, Nike, in its critics' eyes at least, did little to respond. Early in 1997, the firm hired Andrew Young, the civil rights leader and former mayor of Atlanta, to evaluate its overseas operations. With authority 'to go anywhere, see anything, and talk with anybody', Young gave Nike a generally favourable report, which the firm was quick to publicize.[53] The activists responded by attacking once again, contending that Young had neglected the wage issue, relied on Nike translators and spent only ten days with workers in a few factories.

It was not until May 1998, in the face of weak consumer demand, retail oversupply and steady NGO activism, that Nike changed course. In a speech before the National Press Club, Phil Knight admitted that 'the Nike product has become synonymous with slave wages, forced overtime, and arbitrary abuse. I truly believe the American consumer doesn't want to buy products made under abusive conditions'.[54] Knight subsequently announced a number of reforms, including raising the minimum ages of sneaker and apparel workers to 18 and 16, respectively, adopting US clean air regulations in all of its factories, expanding monitoring and educational programmes, and offering microloans to workers. Knight's speech marked a turning point in Nike's NGO management strategy, signalling a movement from resistance to engagement and capitulation.

Shortly after Knight's speech, Nike became significantly more involved in both formal and informal attempts to address labour conditions abroad. In 1996, the firm had joined the Apparel Industry Partnership (AIP), a coalition of corporate, activist, labour and religious groups working with the Clinton Administration to address conditions in overseas factories. When the AIP began to fracture over issues of monitoring and enforcement in 1998, Nike took an active role in forming the Fair Labor Association (FLA), an entity designed to audit, monitor and enforce working conditions in member factories around the world. By 2002, over 21 NGOs, 170 colleges, 982 university licensee companies and several firms had signed on to the FLA's Code of Conduct, agreeing only to hire workers who were 15 years of age, paid at the legal minimum age, and working less than 60 hours a week.[55]

Reform efforts continued throughout 1999, with Nike launching educational and training programmes for its contractors' factory managers and assigning 1,000 production employees to the maintenance of labour standards. In April 1999, the company donated $7.7 million to create the Global Alliance for Workers and Communities, a non-profit organization dedicated to labour issues; and in 2001 it published its first corporate responsibility report, complete with a worker-friendly conclusion from Phil Knight: 'The performance of Nike and every other global company in the 21st century', he predicted, 'will be measured as much by our impact on quality of life as it is by revenue growth and profit margins'.[56]

Novartis

In March 1996, two of Switzerland's oldest pharmaceutical companies, Ciba-Geigy and Sandoz, merged to form Novartis, which instantly became one of the world's largest life sciences firms. With products such as CIBA Vision contact lenses and Gerber baby food already in its stable, the new company was explicitly committed to the emerging biotechnology industry and planned to innovate across three related areas: health care, agribusiness and nutrition. Led by its new CEO, Dr Daniel Vasella, Novartis was an approximately $100 billion firm by 2001 with 74,000 employees and operations in 140 countries.

Novartis's early years coincided with a period of extraordinary growth in the pharmaceutical sector. Between 1980 and 2001, the industry grew in value by 700 per cent, while research and development spending rose from $2 billion to an estimated $30.5 billion.[57] While much of this research came from the traditional fields of medicine and chemistry, an increasing – and critical – portion was also driven by developments in the emerging field of genomics, wherein scientists could map, sequence and analyse the basic building blocks of life. Like others in the industry, Vasella knew that genomics held a revolutionary potential for the pharmaceutical industry. For, if scientists could identify the specific genetic markers for disease, then life science companies could begin to address disease, and perhaps even cure or prevent it at the genetic level.

By the time Vasella took the helm of Novartis, genetically-based treatments were still in their infancy. Scientists had largely mapped the human genome, they had isolated several key genetic markers, but they had only built cures for a handful of diseases. Already, though, activists had targeted the nascent industry, accusing firms such as Monsanto and ADM of preparing to unleash a horde of genetically modified organisms and food products upon an unsuspecting world. In the United States, and even more so in Europe, broad-based NGOs took to the streets, decrying the potential economic, environmental and health risks that could result from the unfettered introduction of genetically modified products.

At the same time, even traditional aspects of the pharmaceutical industry were coming under attack. For decades, multinational giants such as Pfizer and Merck had suffered accusations that their prices were too high and their patents too tight; they had battled lawsuits around the unforeseen side effects of some drugs; and they had witnessed a constant stream of criticism around the diseases they did, or did not, target in their research. Although the battles were occasionally bloody, the firms were also extremely adroit at fighting them and managed to maintain profit levels that were consistently above the Fortune 500 average. In the 1990s, however, the spread of AIDS to the developing world had let loose a howl of protest. With nearly 39 million afflicted in Africa, Asia and Latin America, and over 3 million dying annually from the disease, activists charged the pharmaceutical firms with greed that bordered on murder. Led by groups such as ACT UP, the Health GAP Coalition and South Africa's Treatment Access Campaign, a growing and vocal body of NGOs charged that traditional patent and pricing policies were denying millions of poor people the life-saving treatments they so desperately needed. The catechism of complaint was straightforward: first, that the majority of research by pharmaceutical companies still benefited the developed world, with only 10 per cent of research and development spending directed at diseases that represented 90 per cent of the world's afflictions.[58] Second, that intellectual property rights – the legal core of the pharmaceutical sector – essentially prevented developing countries from gaining access to developed-country drugs or producing these drugs on their own. Third, that the price of these drugs, and particularly AIDS drugs, was simply too high for poor and afflicted countries. In 2002, for example, the standard AIDS 'cocktail' cost roughly $10,000 to $15,000 per year. Average annual per capita income in Africa, by contrast, ranged from $450 to $8,900.

Such criticism was hard to ignore. As an Oxfam briefing paper described it: 'The juxtaposition of images of terrible human suffering caused by disease alongside high-tech treatments offered to the rich represents a growing reputation risk to companies in a world of instant communication'.[59] Accordingly, by the late 1990s, the pharmaceutical sector had conceded on a number of fronts, lowering prices for AIDS drugs in poor countries and even allowing, in a handful of cases, for the generic production of patented drugs. Merck, a major producer of some of the most potent AIDS-fighting compounds, was arguably a leader on this front, followed by firms such as Abbott Laboratories, Bristol-Meyers Squibb and GlaxoSmithKline.

Novartis's position in this entourage was curious. For despite the company's stature in both the traditional pharmaceutical and biotechnology spheres, it was not directly involved in either the genetic engineering or the AIDS controversies. It had no AIDS treatment in its stock of products and only started to move into the GMO area. Still, the company moved vigorously to meet the activists' complaints, even while these complaints were not aimed specifically at Novartis. How they did this, and *why* they did this reveal some interesting insights into what might be termed pre-emptive capitulation.

First, in August 1999, Novartis established a code of conduct that pledged the firm to 'act the same way that a mature, responsible and conscientious citizen would act in the community'.[60] In addition, and in a greater break with industry practice, the firm committed to a transparent, ongoing dialogue with NGOs, activist groups and related stakeholders. As part of this process, the company collaborated in April of 2001 with the UNED Forum, a British NGO, to create a framework for dialogue with different stakeholders. In explaining this move, the company contended that 'A stable social and political framework is essential for the long-term sustainability of Novartis' businesses, hence, out of enlightened self interest, Novartis is working together with leading public and private organizations to improve the health of people living in the developing world'.[61]

At around the same time, Novartis also took steps to implement a corporate social responsibility programme. First, in 2000, the firm committed itself to the Global Compact, an initiative sponsored by United Nations Secretary General Kofi Annan. According to John Ruggie, former UN Assistant Secretary General, Novartis was a front-runner of the 50 firms involved, embracing the principle behind the Compact and working actively towards its objective of integrating human rights, environmental and labour concerns into business decision-making.[62] The company also established an internal foundation to support AIDS orphans in Tanzania and community development projects in Sri Lanka and pledged $30 million to the World Health Organization's leprosy-fighting project.[63] In 2001, it also agreed to provide Coartem, an anti-malaria drug, at cost to patients in the developing world.

Why did Novartis make these moves? Part of the answer seems to lie, as we might expect, in a straightforward calculus of cost. Unlike many of its competitors, the firm had not been singled out for activist attack – but it had seen the cost that attacks imposed on other firms and decided to move before these costs arose. Similarly, Novartis seems to have reasoned that the benefits of compliance were real and likely to affect the firm in a positive way. Such reasoning is evident in its public explanation of the Coartem decision: according to the company's website, this 'was a carefully considered decision on the part of Novartis in weighing its economic responsibilities to shareholders with its societal responsibilities. Intangible benefits – such as reputation, credibility and, ultimately, sustainability – counterbalance any potential loss of revenues'.[64] Similar sentiments were echoed by Urs Baerlocher, head of legal and general affairs, who suggested that 'Reputation is one of the most valuable assets of a company. It is not only closely linked to economic performance, but even more to employee behavior...'.[65] In an industry like pharmaceuticals, where the spotlight of public opinion is bright and increasingly powerful, it made economic sense for the company to move in advance of activist attack; to grab the potential benefits of reputation and pre-emption before the costs of protest were imposed.

Will Novartis pay a price for bowing to outside pressures it never really faced? Will shareholders tire of concessions to invisible stakeholders? Perhaps. But the Basel-based firm is blessed with relatively patient owners: 78 per cent of its shareholders are Swiss nationals and many of its US shares are held by long-term institutional owners.[66] As of December 2002, Novartis's stock had outperformed the S&P 500 by nearly 33 per cent.

Conclusions: probing the power to persuade

In the broader sweep of time, the interaction between firms and activist groups stands out as a recent phenomenon. Activist groups are themselves a creation of the modern global economy and their selection of firms as targets for influence is newer still. Will the business–NGO dynamic grow in importance over time? Will it become a significant lever of change in the international arena? It is too early to tell. What is clearer, though, is that NGOs are increasingly focusing their powers of persuasion on firms and that firms, in turn, have become increasingly responsive.

This response, however, is not consistent across either industries or individual firms. As our case studies indicate, some firms respond more vigorously to activist attacks than others; some work with the activists, others against them. As a first approximation, we suggest that part of this variation may be explained by a slight twist on standard models of profit maximization: when the costs of compliance are low or the benefits high, firms are more likely to concede. We see this calculus at work across several dimensions, including transaction costs, brand image and competitive positioning.

Higher transaction costs, for example, push firms towards the path of resistance. In cases such as Unocal, where capitulation to NGO demands will almost certainly burden the firm with significant switching costs, resistance serves as an economically rational response. That may be why companies in the natural resource industries tend both to be targeted by activist groups and to resist their demands.[67] It may also explain why Novartis has been less aggressive in responding to criticism of its GMO business where switching costs are high and activist demands not yet that heated. By contrast, in industries such as footwear, where switching costs are low, capitulation is less expensive and more frequent. Nike, for instance, faced relatively few transaction costs in its eventual decision to capitulate to NGO pressure. With a vast network of contract suppliers, the firm (and its competitors) could easily require that manufacturers meet higher production standards or, if necessary, quickly shift production from one locale to another. As NGO pressure mounted, capitulation thus became a dominant strategy for the firm.

Brand identity appears to affect firm decision-making in a similar way: simply put, the greater value a firm places on its brand, the more susceptible its managers will be to activist pressures. This tendency is particularly pronounced in industries such as footwear or apparel, where brand often acts as the central feature distinguishing one corporation's products from another. We see in the Nike case, therefore, how sustained external pressure eventually threatened the company's most important asset – its name. As activists continued to target the firm and associate its products with unpopular images (child labour, poverty, exploitation) the costs of resistance began to outweigh the benefits. Once again, capitulation became a rational, profit-maximizing response. Similarly, throughout its pre-emption campaign, Novartis recognized the potential link between social responsibility and brand image. A reputation as an upstanding corporate citizen would differentiate the firm from others in the pharmaceutical industry and reduce the likelihood of NGO criticism. Similar motivations surround BP Amoco's decision to seize the mantle of environmental responsibility in 1997, a move described by one senior executive as 'a cold, hard way of getting competitive advantage by taking a distinctive position'.[68] For Unocal, by contrast, the risk of damaging the brand virtually disappeared in 1997, after the firm divested its line of US gas stations to concentrate on exploration and production. In doing so, Unocal eliminated a central target for criticism and reinforced its resistance strategy.

Finally, standard models of profit maximization can also be applied to the subtle relationship that binds capitulation to competition. Odd as it may sound, firms can occasionally differentiate themselves by conceding first – being the first in their industry to accede to NGO demands. Particularly in industries dominated by intense competition and high brand recognition and in industries where all firms are subject to the same kind of activist attack – any individual firm can break from the pack by moving first. Such considerations may explain why Reebok, Nike's long-standing competitor in the footwear industry, has chosen to align itself with humanitarian concerns, and why Shell, after years of dodging activist attack, has recently redefined itself as dedicated to meeting 'the energy needs of society in ways that are economically, socially and environmentally viable'.[69] It is not clear that such early movement will always work: Starkist, for example, never recouped financial reward from its dolphin-free strategy, since Van Camp and Bumble Bee, the firm's major competitors, quickly announced identical policies. Yet in a business arena increasingly crowded with external constraints, concession may still make economic sense. Indeed, if firms suspect that the activists may eventually succeed in imposing their demands upon an industry (as happened, for example, in the environmental realm) then pure strategy may dictate moving first.

Lest one conclude that all concessions are marked by cost–benefit calculations, however, it is useful to consider the case of Novartis, and of companies such as Levi Strauss, Timberland and Patagonia that have pursued similar strategies of pre-emption. In these cases, response to activist demands cannot be explained by simple reference to profits. It is not clear, for example, that Novartis has sold more drugs than its less socially minded competitors; that Patagonia raincoats are the preferred outerwear of activist sympathizers; or that consumers appreciate Levi's aggressive attack on child labour. Even if these outcomes did occur, there is little to suggest that the outcomes themselves motivated the behaviour. In other words, the firms did not 'do good' just in the hope of 'doing well'. Instead, managers at the top seem to have had a strong commitment to the goals expressed by their potential critics, goals that they were willing to internalize within the corporate structure. Top management at Patagonia, for example, has been dedicated to environmental preservation through financial contributions and employee activities since the firm's inception. Would managers have been able to pursue these goals at great cost to the firm? Almost certainly not. Might they also have been affected by the desire to avoid personal embarrassment or gain recognition among certain social groups? Perhaps. What is important to note, however, is that neither of these motives fits directly with standard profit-maximizing models. They are instead more personal motives, drivers that can only be located within the individuals that manage and direct firms.

The research implications of these personal motives are profound. For, if firm strategy is determined even in part by individual preference, then standard models of rational profit maximization may need to be tweaked in a rather unwieldy direction. Add in the revisions to cost–benefit analysis described above, and the research agenda becomes even more complex. For essentially, we are suggesting that the emergence of activist groups and activist pressures has forced firms to make decisions in new ways, factoring in variables that once could be ignored: the costs and benefits of capitulation versus compliance; the competitive dynamics of concession; the personal beliefs and preferences of top management. Few of these factors exist in traditional studies of firm behaviour and many of them require new modes of analysis.

In this chapter, we have only scratched the surface of what could well be a new area of serious research. Our hypotheses suggest that there are identifiable patterns across the field of firm–NGO interaction, patterns that could be tested and elaborated by systematic research. For example, it should be possible to quantify more precisely the costs that NGO activism imposes on particular firms or industries. What happens to the share price of targeted firms over time? Do prices go down when activists attack and up when corporations concede? Are there significant variations across industry, with some (such as branded consumer goods) responding more vigorously on both sides of the dynamic? Admittedly, the natural variation in share prices will make it difficult to identify the specific effect of activist attack, but studies such as Epstein and Schnietz (2002) and Koku *et al.* (1997) suggest that such relationships can indeed be captured empirically. Likewise, large-N studies should help us to pinpoint variation in firm response, demonstrating the conditions under which firms are most likely to concede to external pressure. These conditions could then be linked to the costs of concession, which are themselves not all that difficult to quantify.

Far more difficult, of course, will be identifying, much less quantifying, the personal motives that occasionally drive firm behaviour. These variables defy quantification and do not lend themselves easily to large-scale inquiry. Even so, there are systematic ways in which the personal element can be explored. Case studies are an obvious vehicle, as are public accounts that repeatedly link corporate activity to a high-profile CEO. As these links are drawn, they can be analysed across time and industry sectors, showing whether the behaviour of a particular firm is more likely attributable to competitive or personal motives. Further studies can also then begin to probe the effects of personal choice, especially when it leads to pre-emptive concession. Do firms 'pay the price' in an empirical sense for following the principles of their leader; or are there tangible financial rewards as well?

None of these questions is easy to answer and the research agenda that accompanies them is admittedly large. But as NGOs became a bigger part of the global arena, as external pressures mount and corporations face an evolving mix of stakeholders, so too must researchers begin to analyse – empirically, systematically, and theoretically – this changing set of relationships.

Notes

1 This chapter is a reprint of D. L. Spar and L. T. La Mure (2003) 'The power of activism: Assessing the impact of NGOs on global business', *California Management Review*, 45(3):78–101. Permission granted.

2 According to Skjelsbaek, the Order assumed the characteristics of a modern NGO around AD 1694. Kjell Skjelsbaek (1971) 'The growth of international nongovernmental organizations in the twentieth century', *International Organization*, 25(3): 420–442.

3 Margaret E. Keck and Kathryn Sikkink (1998) *Activists Beyond Borders: Advocacy Networks in International Politics*, Ithaca, NY: Cornell University Press.

4 Ann Florini and P. J. Simmons (2000) 'What the world needs now?' in *The Third Force: The Rise of Transnational Civil Society*, Washington, DC: Carnegie Endowment for International Peace.

5 Like modern human rights groups, abolitionists often engaged in 'information politics', providing the public with factual accounts of the brutality underlying the slave trade. In 1839, abolitionist activists Theodore Weld and Angelina and Sarah Grimke published *American Slavery As It Is: Testimony of a Thousand Witnesses*, a compilation of dramatic individual testimonials. The book 'became the handbook of the anti-slavery cause, selling over 100,000 copies in its first year and continuing to sell year after year' (Keck and Sikkink p. 45).

6 Opposition to this practice was the source of considerable NGO activity, manifest in such groups as the London Missionary Society, the Antifootbinding Society, and Mrs. Little's Natural Foot Society. For more on footbinding and protest against it, see Keck and Sikkink, pp. 39–78.

7 See Monroe Friedman (1999) *Consumer Boycotts: Effecting Change Through the Marketplace and the Media*, New York: Routledge and Keck and Sikkink, p. 45.

8 For more on the rise of NGOs and the shift in their operating behaviour, see Susan Ariel Aaronson (2001) *Taking Trade to the Streets: The Lost History of Public Efforts to Shape Globalization*, Ann Arbor, MI: University of Michigan Press.

9 For more on the broader effectiveness of NGOs and the problems inherent in measuring their effectiveness, see Debora Spar and James Dail (2002) 'Of measurement and mission: Accounting for performance in non-governmental organizations', *Chicago Journal of International Law*, 3(1), Spring: 171–181; and Alan F. Fowler (1996) 'Assessing NGO performance: Difficulties, dilemmas, and a way ahead' in Michael Edwards and David Hulme (eds) *Beyond the Magic Bullet: NGO Accountability and Performance in the Post-Cold War World*, West Hartford, CT: Kumarian Press.

10 Stephen Pruitt and Monroe Friedman (1986) 'Determining the effectiveness of consumer boycotts: A stock price analysis of their impact on corporate targets', *Journal*

of Consumer Policy, 9: 375–387. For a thorough review of the boycott literature, see Friedman 1999.

11 Pruitt and Friedman 1986.

12 Paul Koku, Aigbe Akhigbe and Thomas Springer (1997) 'The impact of financial boycotts and threats of boycott', *Journal of Business Research*, 40: 15–20.

13 Marc Epstein and Karen Schnietz (2002) 'Measuring the cost of environmental and labor protests to globalization: An event study of the failed 1999 Seattle WTO talks', *The International Trade Journal*, 16(2): 19.

14 Shameek Konar and Mark Cohen (2001) 'Does the market value environmental performance?' *The Review of Economics and Statistics*, 83(2): 281–289.

15 For a thorough review of the South Africa case, see Prakash Sethi and Oliver Williams (2001) *Economic Imperatives and Ethical Values in Global Business: The South African Experience and International Codes Today*, Notre Dame, IN: University of Notre Dame Press.

16 Siew Hong Teoh, Ivo Welch and C. Paul Wazzan (1999) 'The effects of socially activist investment policies on the financial markets: Evidence from the South African boycott', *Journal of Business*, 72(1): 35–89.

17 Martin Meznar, Douglas Nigh, and Chuck Kwok (1994) 'Effect of announcements of withdrawal from South Africa on stockholder wealth', *The Academy of Management Journal*, 37(6): 1633–1648.

18 Dennis Patten (1990) 'The market reaction to social responsibility disclosures: The case of the Sullivan principles signings', *Accounting, Organizations and Society*, 15(6): 575–587.

19 The contradictory findings in the research on South Africa and the empirical work on boycotts reflect a broader trend in the literature on corporate social performance (CSP) and corporate financial performance (CFP). Despite more than 25 years of research, scholars continue to disagree on the nature of the relationship between the two. In a consideration of the extant research, Griffin and Mahon review a number of articles and suggest that methodological inconsistencies have led to numerous divergent findings. See Jennifer Griffin and John Mahon (1997) 'The corporate social performance and corporate financial performance debate: Twenty-five years of incomparable research', *Business & Society*, 36(1): 5–31. In a review of Griffin and Mahon, Roman *et al.* offer a more optimistic assessment, concluding that 'the vast majority of studies support the idea that, at the very least, good social performance does not lead to poor financial performance. Indeed, most of the studies reviewed indicate a positive correlation between CSP and CFP'. See Ronald Roman, Sefa Hayibor and Bradley Agle (1999) 'The relationship between social and financial performance: Repainting a portrait', *Business & Society*, 38(1): 109–125. Notably, however, scholars continue to disagree on the definition of, and relationship between, both concepts.

20 See James T. Hamilton (1993) 'Politics and social costs: Estimating the impact of collective action on hazardous waste facilities', *Rand Journal of Economics*, 24(1), Spring: 101–125; and Hamilton (1995) 'Pollution as news: Media and stock market reactions to the toxics release inventory data', *Journal of Environmental Economics and Management*, 28, January: 98–113.

21 J. Maxwell, T. Lyon and S. Hackett (2000) 'Self-regulation and social welfare: The political economy of corporate environmentalism', *Journal of Law and Economics*, 43(2): 583–617. For a study of how both corporations and states have adopted higher environmental standards as a result of consumer activism, see David Vogel (1995) *Trading Up: Consumer and Environmental Regulation in a Global Economy*, Cambridge: Harvard University Press.

22 For more on brands and the vulnerability they create, see Naomi Klein (1999) *No Logo*, New York: Picador.

23 Van Camp and Bumble Bee, the firm's major competitors, made similar pledges only hours after Starkist's public announcement of its policy change. See Richard H. K. Vietor and Forest Reinhardt, 'Starkist (A)', Harvard Business School Case 9-794-128 (1995) and Vietor and Reinhardt, 'Starkist (B)', Harvard Business School Case 9-794-139 (1995).

24 See Forest Reinhardt and Emily Richman (2000) 'Global climate change and BP Amoco', Harvard Business School Case 9-700-106.

25 David Baron (1995) 'Integrated strategy: Market and nonmarket components', *California Management Review*, 37(2): 47–65; Baron (2001) 'Private politics, corporate social responsibility, and integrated strategy', *Journal of Economics & Management Strategy*, 10, Spring: 7–45; Baron (2001) 'Private politics', Mimeo, Stanford University; Timothy Feddersen and Thomas Gilligan (2001) 'Saints and markets: Activists and the supply of credence goods', *Journal of Economics & Management Strategy*, 10, Spring: 149–171.

26 See Forest L. Reinhardt (2000) *Down to Earth: Applying Business Principles to Environmental Management*, Boston: Harvard Business School Press.

27 See Baron (1995).

28 For a fascinating discussion of why the profit-maximizing model may itself be incorrect or inappropriate, see Henry Mintzberg, Robert Simons and Kunal Basu (2002) 'Beyond selfishness', *Sloan Management Review*, Fall: 67 – 74.

29 As King, Keohane and Verba note, 'One of the often overlooked advantages of the in-depth case study method is that the development of good causal hypotheses is complementary to good description rather than competitive with it. Framing a case study around an explanatory question may lead to more focused and relevant description, even if the study is ultimately thwarted in its attempt to provide even a single valid causal inference'. Gary King, Robert Keohane and Sidney Verba (1994), *Designing Social Inquiry*, Princeton, NJ: Princeton University Press, p. 45.

30 This sections draws from, substantially revises and updates portions of Debora Spar, 'The Burma pipeline', Harvard Business School Case 9-798-078 (2000).

31 The junta changed its name to the State Peace and Development Council (SPDC) in 1997.

32 Earth Rights International, 'Total denial continues', (2000), available at www.earth-rights.org.

33 See www.freeburmacoalition.org and Kirstin Grimsley, 'Activists press Burma campaign: More companies agree that labor conditions are oppressive', *Washington Post*, January 5, 2002, p. E01.

34 In 2000, a unanimous US Supreme Court ruled the Massachusetts law and related state legislation unconstitutional, citing interference with the President's authority to make US foreign policy. See Erika Moritsugu (2002) 'The winding course of the Massachusetts Burma Law: Subfederal sanctions in a historical context', *The George Washington International Law Review*, 34(2): 435–482.

35 'Human rights and Unocal: A discussion paper', Unocal, 2002. Accessed at www.unocal.com.

36 'Unocal statement in response to press release from law offices of Cristobol Bonifaz', Unocal, September 3, 1996. Available at www.unocal.com.

37 See William Branigin, 'Claim against Unocal rejected', *Washington Post*, September 8, 2000, p. E10.

38 *Wall Street Journal*, 19 September 2002.

39 www.irn.org/burma/unocal.html. Accessed January 1998. In a December 1997 interview with the authors, Imle admitted to having made the statement but suggested that it had been taken out of context in an off-the-record discussion with activists.

40 'Human rights and Unocal: A discussion paper', Unocal, 2002.

41 Imle, interview with the author, 1997.

42 Unocal, 2002.
43 Corporate responsibility at Unocal: A progress report, 2000–2001, Unocal Corporation, 2001. Available at www.unocal.com.
44 Unocal, 2002.
45 This sections draws from, substantially revised and updated portions of Debora Spar, 2000. 'Hitting the Wall: Nike and International Labor Practices', Harvard Business School Case 9-700-047, 2000.
46 Nike, 2002 Annual Report.
47 Baron, 'Private politics, corporate social responsibility, and integrated strategy'.
48 Spar, 'Hitting the Wall', p. 5.
49 For more on corporate codes of conduct, see Ans Kolk, Rob van Tulder and Carlijn Welters (1999) 'International codes of conduct and corporate social responsibility: Can transnational corporations regulate themselves?' *Transnational Corporations*, 8(1): 143–180; Kolk and van Tulder (2002) 'Child labor and multinational conduct: A comparison of international business and stakeholder codes', *Journal of Business Ethics*, 36: 291–301; Kolk and van Tulder (2002) 'The effectiveness of self-regulation: Corporate codes of conduct and child labour', *European Management Journal*, 20(3): 260–271; and van Tulder and Kolk (2001) 'Multinationality and corporate ethics: Codes of ethics in the sporting goods industry', *Journal of International Business*, 32(2): 267–283.
50 Baron, David, 'Private politics'. As Knight noted, 'When we started in Japan, factory labor there was making $4 a day, which is basically what is being paid in Indonesia and being so strongly criticized today. Nobody today is saying, "The poor Japanese." We watched it happen all over again in Taiwan and Korea, and now it's going to Southeast Asia' (p. 7).
51 Subsequent reports revealed that the photo had been staged.
52 One critic likened being featured in the comic strip to 'getting in Jay Leno's monologue. It means your perceived flaws have reached a critical mass, and everyone feels free to pick on you' (quoted in Spar, 'Hitting the Wall', p. 7).
53 Andrew Young, Report: The Nike code of conduct. (Atlanta: Goodworks International, LLC, 1997).
54 Quoted in John H. Cushman, Jr. (1998) 'Nike to step forward on plant conditions', *San Diego Union-Tribune*, 13 May 1998, p. A1.
55 Baron, 'Private politics'.
56 Nike, Corporate Responsibility Report 2001. Accessed at www.nikebiz.com. Despite Nike's new policies, a number of NGOs remain dissatisfied over the issue of wages, factory conditions and worker unionization. In a review of changes in factory conditions since Knight's speech, Connor concludes that 'The promises made by Phillip Knight in his May 1988 speech were an attempt by the company to switch media focus to issues it was willing to address while avoiding the key problems of subsistence wages, forced overtime and suppression of workers' right to freedom of association. The projects Knight announced have been of little benefit to Nike workers. Some have helped only a tiny minority, or else have no relevance to Nike factories at all'. See Timothy Connor (2001) Still waiting for Nike to Do It: Nike's labor practices in the three years since CEO Phil Knight's speech to the National Press Club, San Francisco: Global Exchange, p. 5. See also Connor (2000), 'Like cutting bamboo: Nike and Indonesian workers' right to freedom of association', Community Aid Abroad, Briefing Paper no. 27, Australia: Oxfam; Connor, We are not machines (2000) San Francisco: Global Exchange; and 'Wearing thin: The state of pay in the fashion industry' (United Kingdom: Labour Behind the Label, 2001).
57 PhRMA Annual Report (PhRMA, 2001) pp. 8, 13; and 'Beyond philanthropy: The pharmaceutical industry, corporate social responsibility and the developing world' (Oxfam International, VSO and Save the Children, 2002) p. 7. Available at www.oxfam.org.
58 Oxfam, 'Beyond philanthropy', p. 8.

59 'Dare to lead: Public health and company wealth'. Oxfam Policy Paper, Oxfam International, April 2000, p. 3. Oxfam recognized an opportunity to provoke company response: 'Oxfam believes that pharmaceutical companies face a major reputation risk if they do not do more to promote access to life-saving drugs in the developing world. This is particularly important at a time of unprecedented scrutiny of the industry's record in this field. The withdrawal of public support could lead the industry to suffer the same problems of staff recruitment and retention suffered by companies charged with complicity in human rights abuses or environmental damage. Perhaps more significantly, it carries with it the real threat of more stringent government regulation' (p. 4).
60 Corporate citizenship at Novartis. Novartis, 2001, p. 36. Available at www.novartis.com.
61 Annual Report 2001, Novartis, 2002. Available at www.novartis.com.
62 Personal conversation with author, December 2002.
63 Corporate Citizenship at Novartis, p. 19; and Novartis, Annual Report 2001, p. 35.
64 Corporate Citizenship at Novartis, p. 33.
65 Corporate Citizenship at Novartis, p. 6.
66 Data from novartis.com, www.adr.com and yahoo.com. Confirmed with Novartis Investor Relations, January 2003.
67 Examples include NGO campaigns against ExxonMobil and Royal-Dutch Shell.
68 Quoted in Forest Reinhardt, 'Global climate change and BP Amoco', Harvard Business School case 9–700–106, 2000, p. 8.
69 Full text available at www.shell.com.

8　Thoughts and second thoughts about Enron ethics

Ronald R. Sims and Johannes Brinkmann

Introduction

This chapter[1] provides a brief look at the Enron Corporation debacle. In particular, the chapter discusses the business ethics background and leadership mechanisms that contributed to Enron's collapse and eventual bankruptcy. Through a systematic analysis of the organizational culture at Enron (following Schein's frame of reference) it highlights how the company's culture resulted in a series of ethical missteps by its employees. The chapter concludes with a typology of moral culture types and transitions to help us better understand how the Enron debacle came to fruition and as a way to make sense of future ethical debacles which will undoubtedly become known.

Today, when most people hear the word 'Enron' they think of corruption on a colossal scale – a company where a handful of highly paid executives were able to pocket millions of dollars while carelessly eroding the life savings of thousands of unwitting employees. Not long ago, Enron was a great business success soaring to a market capitalization in excess of $60 billion and ranking seventh on the *Fortune* 500 list. Enron was an adviser to the US Government, backed by the world's biggest banks and rated by the top analysts. It was frequently voted one of the most admired companies and one of the best companies to work for. Enron had been heralded as a paragon of corporate responsibility and ethics – successful, driven, focused, philanthropic and environmentally responsible. Enron appeared to represent the best a twenty-first-century organization had to offer, economically *and* ethically.

Enron looked like an excellent corporate citizen, with all the corporate social responsibility (CSR) and business ethics tools and status symbols in place. Enron also had a cut-throat corporate culture in which pushing the envelope was routine, failure led to departure, and a *new* catchword '*Enron Ethics*' (an ironic expression which is used now and then, see, e.g., the headings of Tracinski 2002 or Berenbeim in *Executive action* no. 15, Feb. 2002) – the ultimate contradiction between words and deeds, between a deceiving glossy facade and a rotten structure behind, like a definite goodbye to naive business ethics. Enron ethics means (still ironically) that business ethics is a question of organizational 'deep' culture rather than of cultural artifacts like ethics codes, ethics officers and the like. With this as a backdrop, the chapter describes and discusses how executives at Enron in practice created an organizational culture that put the bottom line ahead of ethical behaviour and doing what is right. The chapter systematically uses Schein's (1985) five primary mechanisms available to leaders to create and reinforce aspects of culture (i.e. attention focusing, reaction to crises, role modelling, rewards allocation and criteria for hiring and firing) to analyse the company's culture and leadership that contributed to its ethical demise and filing for bankruptcy. It is our contention that with such a point of departure one will be better prepared for a necessary discussion in our field of how to prevent an 'instrumentalization' of ethics and CSR for mere facade purposes that was prevalent at Enron.

The history and culture of Enron

Enron was formed in 1986 from the merger of natural gas pipeline companies Houston Natural Gas and Internorth, and in the following 15 years, the company diversified to provide products and services related to natural gas, electricity and communications. The company built its success on natural gas pipelines, energy production and an innovative energy trading business.

Enron was creative in its financial arrangements, entering into numerous partnerships with a variety of entities. The purpose of some of the partnerships and their related-party transactions was to transfer certain assets, their associated borrowing, and their profits, or more often losses, to the partnerships. This allowed Enron, with the approval of its auditor Arthur Andersen, to keep losses off its income statement and debt off its balance sheet. Many of the partnerships were organized by Enron executives, some of whom invested in them with guaranteed returns. Negotiations with the partnerships were thus not at arm's length, with Chief Financial Officer Andrew Fastow both representing Enron and participating through limited partnerships in deals with Enron. Fastow and several lower-level employees 'were enriched, in the aggregate, by tens of millions of dollars they should never have received' (Special Report 2002).

Enron's board had approved Fastow's partnership (but not the participation of other employees) even though, in some cases, they created a conflict of interest. The problem as suggested in the previous paragraph was that in some of the partnerships Fastow was both a manager for Enron and an investor in an outside entity that engaged in financial transactions, such as the buying and selling of assets, with Enron. The rules of the Financial Accounting Standards Board (FASB), an organization that sets guidelines for accounting practices, are that if an outside investor puts in 3 per cent or more of the capital in a partnership, the corporation, even if it provides the other 97 per cent, does not have to declare the partnership as a subsidiary. Therefore, assets and debt in the partnership can be withheld from the corporation's balance sheet. Using this device, Enron was able to hide losses and debt totalling hundreds of millions of dollars (Emshwiller and Smith 2002).

The partnerships allowed Enron to keep substantial losses off its financial statements. From the third quarter of 2000 through the third quarter of 2001 Enron reported a before-tax profit of $1.5 billion, but if certain partnerships referred to as Raptors had been consolidated into its financial statement, its earnings would have been $429 million. Although Enron stated that the partnership protected the company from risk, the risk was actually borne by Enron through guarantees to the Raptors. As Enron's share price declined in 2001 the Raptors' ability to protect Enron's earnings disappeared, CEO Jeffrey Skilling resigned abruptly in August 2001, while proclaiming that Enron was in good health.

Enron's bright picture clouded in October 2001 when Enron announced a $544 million after-tax charge against earnings related to the transactions of some partnerships. A month later the company said it was revising its financial statements from 1997 to 2001 to reduce net income by more than $1 billion. The restatements of earnings included the consolidation of a number of partnerships that had been used to keep debt and earnings fluctuations off Enron's financial statements. Fastow was asked to leave the company on October 23, and the Securities and Exchange Commission began an investigation. Revelation of the hidden losses destroyed any remaining confidence in the company, and its share price continued its decline from its peak of $81.39 on January 25, 2001, to less than a dollar in December 2001. Enron filed for Chapter 11 bankruptcy on December 2.[2]

The company's demise was a financial scandal on an epic scale – one that relied on the complicity of a huge array of Enron executives, lawyers, financial advisers, banks and perhaps even the White House. The consequences for employees were staggering: 20,000 jobs and two billion dollars in retirement funds and pensions evaporated when Enron went belly-up. Meanwhile, the executives at the top had cashed in their stock options before the company hit bottom. Since then these same executives have faced multi-billion dollar lawsuits from their former employees, many of whom lost their entire life savings.

The culture at Enron

As Enron's products and services evolved over its history, so did the company's culture. In this newly deregulated and innovative forum, Enron embraced a culture that rewarded 'cleverness'. Deregulation opened the industry up to experimentation and the culture at Enron was one that expected employees to explore this new playing field to the utmost. Pushing the limits was considered a survival skill.

Enron's former President and Chief Executive Officer (CEO) Jeffrey Skilling actively cultivated a culture that would push limits – 'Do it right, do it now and do it better' was his motto. He encouraged employees to be independent, innovative and aggressive. The Harvard Business Review Case Study *Enron's Transformation* (Bartlett and Glinska 2001) contains employee quotations such as 'you were expected to perform to a standard that was continually being raised', 'the only thing that mattered was adding value', or 'it was all about an atmosphere of deliberately breaking the rules' (Bartlett and Glinska 2001). A culture that admires innovation and unchecked ambition and publicly punishes poor performance can produce tremendous returns in the short run. However, in the long run, achieving additional value by constantly 'upping the ante' becomes progressively more difficult. Employees are forced to stretch the rules ever further until the limits of ethical conduct are easily overlooked in the pursuit of the next big success (see Sims 2003; Sims and Brinkmann 2002).

Enron's spectacular success, and the positive scrutiny the company was receiving from the business press and the financial analysts, only added fuel to the company's competitive culture. The business community rewarded Enron for its cleverness (and even its ethicality) and Enron's executives felt driven by this reputation to sustain the explosive growth of the late 1990s, even when they logically knew that it was not possible. A negative earnings outlook would have been a red flag to investors, indicating Enron was not as successful as it appeared. If investors' concerns drove down the stock price due to excessive selling, credit agencies would be forced to downgrade Enron's credit rating. Trading partners would lose faith in the company, trade elsewhere, and Enron's ability to generate quality earnings and cash flows would suffer. In order to avoid such a scenario at all costs, Enron entered into a deceiving web of partnerships and employed increasingly questionable accounting methods to maintain its investment-grade status. Enron executives probably felt that they were doing the right thing for their organization.

In a success culture like Enron's such behaviour represented a way of least resistance. Enron employees with a self-image of being the best and the brightest and being extremely clever did not make business deals that fail. Therefore booking earnings before they are realized were 'early' rather than wrong. The culture at Enron was quickly eroding the ethical boundaries of its employees.

The culture of cleverness at Enron started as a pursuit of excellence that devolved into the appearance of excellence as executives worked to develop clever ways of preserving Enron's infallible facade of success (i.e. the partnerships mentioned earlier). Although Enron maintained that top officials in the company reviewed the dealings with potential conflicts of interest, Enron later claimed that Fastow earned over $30 million from Enron with his companies. At some point in the bending of ethical guidelines for the good of the company, Enron's executives also began to bend the rules for personal gain. Once a culture's ethical boundaries are breached, thresholds of more extreme ethical compromises become lower.

In the end, Enron's executives could not 'rob Peter to pay Paul'. Even if the Enron culture permitted acts of insignificant rule bending, it was the sum of incremental ethical transgressions that produced the business catastrophe. Although Enron's executives had believed that everything would work successfully in the long run, the questionable partnerships left the company extremely vulnerable when financial troubles came to light. As partnerships began to fail with increasing regularity, Enron was liable for millions of dollars it had not anticipated losing. Promises became due and Enron did not have the ability to follow through on its financial obligations.[3] The very results Enron had sought to prevent – falling stock prices, lack of consumer and financial market confidence – came about as a direct result of leadership decisions that had been driven by Enron's culture. The company culture of individualism, innovation and aggressive cleverness left Enron without compassionate, responsible leadership. Enron's Board of Directors was slow to step up and fill the void; and individual Enron employees for the first time realized all of the ramifications of a culture with leaders that eschew the boundaries of ethical behavior.

What else can we learn about how the Enron executives moulded a corporate culture that resulted in unethical behavior and the collapse of the company? The next section of this chapter offers some answers to this question through the following illustration of how Schein's organization culture approach can lead to a better understanding of the Enron case.

Leadership mechanisms and organizational culture at Enron

When organizational leaders like those at Enron encourage rule breaking and foster an intimidating, aggressive environment, it is not surprising that the ethical boundaries of an organization erode away to nothing. Schein (1985) has focused on leadership as *the* critical component of the organization's culture because leaders can create, reinforce or change the organization's culture. This applies not the least to an organization's ethical climate (Sims 2003; Trevino *et al.* 2000; Sims and Brinkmann 2002). According to Schein (1985), there are five primary mechanisms that a leader can use to influence an organization's culture: attention, reaction to crises, role modelling, allocation of rewards and criteria for selection and dismissal. Schein's assumption is that these five criteria reinforce and encourage behavioural and cultural norms within an organization. This section of the chapter can be read as an illustration of Schein's assumptions. The Enron executives used the five mechanisms to reinforce a culture that was morally flexible, opening the door to ethics degeneration, lying, cheating and stealing.

Attention

The first of the mechanisms mentioned by Schein (1985) is attention. The issues that capture the attention of the leader (i.e. what is criticized, praised or asked about) will also capture the attention of the greater organization and will become the focus of the employees. If the leaders of the organization focus on the bottom line, employees believe that financial success is the leading value to consider. In such a context, rules and morality are merely obstacles, impediments along the way to bottom-line financial success (Sims 2003).

One former executive of Enron described Jeffrey Skilling as a leader driven by the almighty dollar. 'Skilling would say all that matters is money. You buy loyalty with money' (Zellner 2002). Enron executives' attention was clearly focused on profits, power, greed and influence. They wanted their employees to focus on today's bottom line. Skilling communicated his priorities to his employees overtly, in both word and deed. Consistently clear signals showed employees what was important to leadership – 'Profits at all costs' (Tracinski 2002). Another quote from a former Enron employee: 'there were no rules for people, even in our personal lives. Everything was about the company and everything was supposed to be on the edge – sex, money, all of it' (Broughton 2002). In her testimony before the House Subcommittee, Sherron Watkins described Enron as a 'very arrogant place, with a feeling of invincibility'. Still another Enron employee noted about the company's environment that 'it was all about creating an atmosphere of deliberately breaking the rules. For example, our official vacation policy was that you could take as much as you wanted whenever you wanted as long as you delivered your results. It drove the human resource department crazy' (Bartlett and Glinska 2001).

As Stern (1992) has suggested, if the organization's leaders seem to care only about the short-term bottom line, employees quickly get the message too. How else could employees read the Enron culture than being focused on short-term when their CEO (Ken Lay) both blessed the relaxation of conflict-of-interest rules designed to protect Enron from the very self-dealings that brought the company down and participated in board meetings allowing the creation of the off-balance sheet partnerships that were part of those transactions?

Reaction to crises

The second leadership method mentioned by Schein (1985) refers to a leader's reaction to a crisis situation. Schein asserts that a crisis tests what the leader values and brings these values to the surface. With each impending crisis, leaders have an opportunity to communicate throughout the organization what the company's values are. Enron was facing a crisis of how to sustain a phenomenal growth rate. Leaders reacted by defending a culture that valued profitability, even when it was at the expense of everything else. The off-balance sheet partnerships were tremendously risky. However, since normal growth of the stock price would have fallen short of expectations anyway, the only thing to do was to try to meet the unrealistic target profitability expectations. In such a case, an accident was waiting to happen.

Once the Enron situation became known, the reaction from the Enron executives was telling. The executives were busy shifting the blame and pointing fingers. Both Kenneth Lay and his wife proclaimed his innocence. Lay claimed to have been unaware of the sweetheart deals, which were entirely the brainchild of Skilling and Fastow. Watkins also blamed them for the debacle, while shifting any blame from her. Jeffrey Skilling even went as far as telling an incredulous Congress that despite his Harvard Business School degree and business experience he neither knew of, nor would understand the intricacies of the Enron accounting deals. (On the other hand, Skilling also was quoted on CNN saying 'if he knew then what he knows now – he *still* would not do anything differently'.) Even before the issues came to light, it appears that Skilling was willing to abandon the company to save his own skin as evidenced by his mysterious resignation in August 2001 and giving only the 'personal reasons' explanation for his sudden departure (and he still sold significant amounts of company stock at a premium). Both Kenneth Lay and Sherron Watkins also sold stock before prices began to dramatically plummet (Kenneth Lay claiming that he had some personal debts to pay off, Sherron Watkins referring to the September 11 terrorist attacks. Watkins also sold stock at the same time when she was making allegations of deceptive accounting practices).

'I take the Fifth' (US Congressional Hearing, 2002) – this was the response Kenneth Lay gave to the Senate Commerce Committee when asked to explain Enron's failure. Although all but one of Enron's officers (curiously Skilling) invoked the Fifth Amendment right to not self-incriminate, the story has played out much like that of the Salomon Brothers and John Gutfreund fiasco in the early 1990s. Document shredding and lies, both overt and those of omission, have become the preferred strategy for Enron's management (Brown and Sender 2002). These bold acts from Enron leadership show a poor reaction to crisis.

Willet and Always (2002) noted that 'the mantra at Enron seemed to be that ethical wrongdoing is to be hidden at any cost; deny, play the dupe, claim ignorance ("the ostrich instruction") lie, quit'. It appears that the truth and its consequences were not a part of the Enron culture.

Role modelling (how leaders behave)

Schein's third mechanism is the example leaders set for the acceptability of unethical behavior within an organization. Actions speak louder than words – therefore role-modelling behavior is a very powerful tool that leaders have to develop and influence corporate culture.

Through role modelling, teaching and coaching, leaders reinforce the values that support the organizational culture. Employees often emulate leaders' behaviour and look to the leaders for cues to appropriate behaviour. Many companies are encouraging employees to be more entrepreneurial – that is, to take more initiative and be more innovative in their jobs. The Scientific Foundation reports a study that showed that managers who want to change the organization's culture to a more entrepreneurial one must 'walk the talk'. In other words, they must demonstrate the entrepreneurial behaviours themselves (Pearce *et al.* 1997). This is the case with any cultural value. Employees observe the behaviour of leaders to find out what is valued in the organization. Perhaps, this was the most significant shortcoming of Enron executives.

According to the values statement in Enron's Code of Ethics and its annual report, the company maintains strong commitments to communication, respect, integrity and excellence. However, there is little evidence that supports management modelling of these values. For instance, while the first pillar of the values statement addresses an obligation to communicate, Sherron Watkins claims (quoted from the Hearing transcripts):

> I continued to ask questions and seek answers, primarily from former coworkers in the Global Finance Group or in the business units that had hedged assets with Raptor. I never heard reassuring explanations. I was not comfortable confronting either Mr. Skilling or Mr. Fastow with my concerns. To do so, I believe, would have been a job-terminating move.
>
> (US Congressional Hearings 2002)

Enron leaders' primary message about their values was sent through their own actions. They broke the law as they concentrated on financial measures and use of the creative partnerships described earlier in this chapter. The executives not only condoned such unethical behaviour, they initiated it and were rewarded for it. It also sent a message to employees that full and complete disclosure is not a requirement, or even recommended. If the company achieved short-term benefits by hiding information, it was acceptable.

Enron's leaders also ignored, then denied serious problems with their business transactions and were more concerned about their personal financial rewards than those of the company. For example, when the company's stock price began to drop as the problems were becoming public, the company was transitioning from one investment programme to another.

Another example is the executives' lack of integrity in communicating to the employees and investors. They maintained that the company was financially stable and that many of their emerging problems really were not too serious, even though they knew the truth and were making financial decisions to protect their personal gains (i.e. selling their own stocks).

Allocation of rewards

The behaviour of people rewarded with pay increases or promotions signals to others what is necessary to succeed in an organization – this is what Schein calls the 'allocation of rewards mechanism'. To ensure that values are accepted, leaders should reward behaviour that is consistent with the values (and actual rewards count obviously more than promised rewards, cf. Sims and Brinkmann 2002).

The reward system created by a leader indicates what is prized and expected in the organization. This view is in line with a basic management doctrine. When an instance of ethical achievement occurs – for instance, when someone acts with integrity and honor – the organization's leaders must reward it. Such an effort sends as clear a message to the rest of the organization as when an organization rewards an employee who acts unethically (e.g. Larimer 1997). Enron's reward system established a 'win-at-all-costs' focus. The company's leadership promoted and retained only those employees that produced consistently, with little regard to ethics. Skilling singled out one of his vice presidents, Louise Kitchen, for her results-oriented approach to Enron's online business. Kitchen had started the company's internet-based trading business even though Skilling repeatedly turned down her requests to begin such a programme. Kitchen ignored the former CEO's decision and instead used already-allocated funds to pull the new network together. As a former Enron vice president who attended the meeting described it best: 'The moral of this story is: break the rules, you can cheat, you can lie, but as long as you make money, it's all right' (quoted from Schwartz 2002).

The company's compensation structure contributed to an unethical work culture, too – by promoting self-interest above any other interest. As a consequence, the team approach once used by Enron associates deteriorated. Performance reviews were public events and poor performance was ridiculed. The strongest performing units even went as far as to 'ignore' company policy – granting unlimited vacation time as noted earlier as long as the work was done, ignoring Human Resources' complaints (Bartlett and Glinska 2001).

Extremely high bonuses were doled out to executives who behaved in desirable ways (e.g. in the form of stock options) which in turn incited executives to keep the stock price up at any cost (Lardner 2002). Annual bonuses were as high as $1 million for traders, and for executives they were even higher). Additionally, the executives at Enron played favourites, inviting top performers to spend weekend vacations with the executive staff. The best workers (determined through day-to-day bottom-line results) received staggering incentives and exorbitant bonuses. One example of this was Car Day. On this day, an array of lavish sports cars arrived for the most successful employees (Broughton 2002). Overall, Enron's reward system rewarded individuals who embraced Enron's aggressive, individualistic culture and were based on short-term profits and financial measures.

Criteria of selection and dismissal (how leaders hire and fire employees)

Schein's (1985) last mechanism by which a leader shapes a corporate culture, describes how a leader's decisions about whom to recruit or dismiss signals a leader's values to all of his employees. The selection of newcomers to an organization is a powerful way by which a leader reinforces culture. Leaders often unconsciously look for individuals who are similar to current organizational members in terms of values and assumptions. Some companies hire individuals on the recommendation of a current employee. This tends to perpetuate the culture because the new employees typically hold similar values. Promotion-from-within policies also serve to reinforce organizational culture.

Ken Lay placed an immediate focus on hiring the best and smartest people, those who would thrive in a competitive environment. Skilling shared Lay's philosophy. Skilling hired only Ivy-league graduates with a hunger for money that matched his and embodied the beliefs that he was trying to instil: aggressiveness, greed, a will to win at all costs and an appreciation for circumventing the rules. Skilling did everything he could to surround himself with individuals who had similar values and assumptions and fitted into the Enron culture.

The way a company fires an employee and the rationale behind the firing also communicates the culture. Some companies deal with poor performers by trying to find them a place within the organization where they can perform better and still contribute. Other companies seem to operate under the philosophy that those who cannot perform are out quickly (Sims and Brinkmann 2002).

Enron carried out an annual 'rank and yank' policy where the bottom fifteen to twenty per cent of producers were let go or fired after a formal evaluation process. Associates graded their peers, which caused a great amount of distrust and paranoia among employees. Enron's employee reviews added to the competition by reviewing job performance in a public forum and sending the bottom 5 per cent to the redeployment office – dubbed the 'office of shame' (Frey and Rosin 2002).

The company's corporate culture was ruthless, a nightmare brew of Ayn Rand and Social Darwinism. Employees were ranked on their work performance by their colleagues on a scale of one to five; a full ten per cent of the workforce was required to be slotted in the 'five' ranking and fired every year. At the same time the corporation was winnowing the weak from its ranks, Enron was rising high on the puffery of ego and hot air – the corporation told the survivors that 'if we were smart, anything could be accomplished', says Amanda Martin-Brock, a former Enron executive. What better way to develop a distrustful work environment than to pit employees against one another and as Larry Bossidy, former CEO of Allied Signal, noted 'forced ranking promotes bad employee morale' (2002), a win-at-all-costs mentality and a willingness to cross the ethical line (Wolfe 1988; Sims and Brinkmann 2002).

The occurrence and handling of internal whistle-blowing also tells a lot about a corporate culture. At Enron, employees who tried to blow the whistle were punished, e.g. by career setbacks and hostility (e.g. not least the Enrongate website). On the other hand, those who closed their eyes to the wrongdoings were rewarded – with the words of a former Enron employee: 'It was very clear what the measures were and how you got promoted at Enron. That absolutely drives behavior ... getting the deal was paramount at Enron' (Hansell 2002). A Houston recruiter described the freedom given by Skilling when he was Enron's CEO to loyal employees metaphorically: 'Once you gained Jeff's trust, the leash became really long' (Zellner 2002).

The selection and rewards system was consistent with the culture at Enron. It promoted greed, selfishness and jealousy within the organization. Enron's executives selected those employees who shared their aggressive, win-at-all-costs mentality. Their short-term view may have prevented them from seeing what the long-term costs of this kind of personality could be on the organization as a whole.

Conclusion

What was it about the corporate culture at Enron that allowed the ethical debacle to flourish? The story of Enron sounds smart and stupid at the same time. Enron's top executives set the tone for this culture. Personal ambition and greed seemed to overshadow much of their corporate and individual lives. They strove to maximize their individual wealth by initiating and participating in scandalous behaviour. Enron's culture created an atmosphere ripe for the unethical and illegal behaviour that occurred.

Enron's house of cards collapsed as a result of interacting decision processes. The culture at Enron eroded gradually, by the trespassing of ethical boundaries, allowing increasingly questionable behaviour to slip through the cracks. This deterioration did not go entirely unnoticed. Individual employees at Enron, auditors at Andersen and even some analysts who watched the financial markets, noticed aspects about the Enron situation that did not seem right, long before the public became aware of Enron's transgressions. There were whistle-blowers but the Enron leaders did not listen.

The culture at Enron, which cultivated and nurtured the corporate wrongdoing, carries important lessons for all of us. Punishments for ethical violations were dreadfully slow. As long as people were making money for Enron, they could get away with many sins. Everybody notices when people get away with the bad stuff, and it becomes embedded in the culture.

Thoughts for future work

In our introduction we mentioned briefly Enron's image of being an excellent corporate citizen, with all the corporate social responsibility (CSR) and business ethics tools and status symbols in place. It was suggested that this was a key aspect or dimension of the Enron case, as a case of deceiving corporate citizenship and of surface or facade ethics (which also has contributed to the creation of the new word, *Enron Ethics*). As an academic field we owe the general public and the business public a thorough documentation, analysis and discussion of how Enron and other companies with a similar record and reputation could 'instrumentalize' (and thus discredit) ethics and CSR for mere facade purposes.

Such a focus deserves and requires more space on its own. Obviously, writings on Enron and similar organizations can be viewed as a start in this direction. In addition to telling the Enron Ethics story is our belief that it is worth offering some ideas on how we would structure such a criticism of 'instrumentalized ethics and CSR'.

As an extension of our reasoning above, using the Schein approach to organizational culture for a better understanding of the Enron story, we feel that a focus on the mix of formal and informal organization cultures is most promising, both for describing, understanding and criticizing organizations and their ethical climate. As a start, one can organize a draft of such future work by a simple four-cell ideal typology. The first dimension stands for the degree of ethicality of an organization culture or what has been called ethical or moral climate. As a second dimension, we suggest the degree of the presence of business ethical tools or artifacts, such as ethics officers, codes of ethics, value statements and the like.

Such a typology can be based upon a solid or at least sufficient body of literature related to each of these two dimensions (see e.g. Brinkmann 2002: 165–170 or Petersen 2002 on moral/ethical climate and tacit ethics; Crane and Matten 2004: 143–175; Fisher and Lovell 2003: 227–223; Ferrell *et al.* 2004: 176–200 or Brinkmann and Ims 2003 on functions and dysfunctions of tools; all sources with further references). If one (for practical purposes) distinguishes between low and high placement of a given culture on each of the two dimensions one ends up with a four-cell matrix as shown in Table 8.1.

As mentioned above, Enron looks at first sight like a 'type I' culture, similar to what Kohlberg might have called moral 'pre-conventionalism', like a classical business ethics case, with a typical mix of 'amorality' and 'immorality' (see for the distinction Carroll and Meeks 1999). According to headline-journalism and public opinion Enron was simply bad and rotten, and this was not realized until it was too late, which in our view might suggest an urgent need for more legislation

Table 8.1 Typology of moral culture types and transitions

	Ethicalness equal moral maturity of a given organization culture	
Presence and marketing of business ethical tools	Disputable moral climate	Positive moral climate
Lots of tools and talking	II: Window-Dressing: Morality, superficial morality	IV: Moral Role-Modelling, justified self-appraisal
No or few tools and little talking	I: Underdeveloped ('preconventional') Morality: often hurting stakeholders	III: Morality as Collective Conscience, underreported doing right and good

and emphasis on ethical organizations. Our thesis is that Enron is at least as good an illustration of 'type II', of window-dressing ethics, with talking instead of walking, ethics as rhetoric. While 'type II' looks modern or at least fashionable, 'type III' looks like the old-fashioned type of moral business, from the days before the disciplines of business ethics, CSR, marketing and public relations were invented, with morality as collective conscience (borrowing E. Durkheim's term) as consistent label and content, perhaps additionally communicating moral humbleness, with a touch of British understatement. The final 'type IV' refers to a moral role-model business culture in the age of marketing and public relations, with walking the talk, with showing and confessing openly its collective moral conscience (call it self-reassurance, or more US-style self-marketing, to put it stereotypically). In other words, we believe future writings should primarily deal with a documentation and criticism of 'window-dressing ethics', with how to further processes towards collective moral conscience, with more or less marketing of the good examples, and with how to prevent degeneration towards 'window-dressing ethics' (see, as a first critical draft of the interdependence between CSR and PR, Brinkmann 2005, to some extent based on L'Etang 1996).

In conclusion, we continue to question whether or not we would prefer honest amorality and immorality to dishonest morality. Still, we choose to read the paper title of Tonge *et al.* (2003) optimistically: 'The Enron story: you can fool some of the people some of the time …'

Notes

1 The chapter is a slightly revised version of R. R. Sims and J. Brinkmann (1993) 'Enron Ethics (Or: Culture Matters More than Codes)', *Journal of Business Ethics*, 45: 243–256. Permission granted.
2 Subsequent to filing for bankruptcy, Enron agreed to a merger with Dynergy, but Dynergy backed out of the agreement shortly thereafter.
3 For example, Enron had promised CIBC World Markets the majority of the profits from Project Braveheart for ten years, or in the event of failure Enron would be obligated to repay CIBC its entire $115.2 million investment. Not only did Enron book the earnings prematurely, but it was also forced to repay CIBC its full investment.

References

Bartlett, C. A. and Glinska, M. (2001) 'Enron's Transformation: From Gas Pipeline to New Economy Powerhouse', Boston, MA: Harvard Business School Press.

Berenbeim, R. E. (2002) 'The Enron Ethics Breakdown'. *The Conference Board*, Executive Action, No. 15, February 2002, 1–6.

Brinkmann, J. (2002) 'Business and Marketing Ethics as Professional Ethics. Concepts, Approaches and Typologies', *Journal of Business Ethics* 41: 159–177.

—— (2005) 'Understanding Insurance Customer Dishonesty: Outline of a Situational Approach', *Journal of Business Ethics*, 61, 183–197.

Brinkmann, J. and Ims, K. (2003) 'Good Intentions Aside (Drafting a Functionalist Look at Codes of Ethics)', *Business Ethics: A European Review*, 12: 265–274.

Broughton, P. D. (2002) 'Enron Cocktail of Cash, Sex and Fast Living', *Telegraph.co.uk*, Available online at http://www.telegraph.co.uk (February 13, 2002).

Carroll, A. B. and Meeks, M. D. (1999) 'Models of Management Morality: European Applications and Implications', *Business Ethics: A European Review*, 8: 108–116.

Crane, A. and Matten, D. (2004) *Business Ethics*, Oxford: Oxford University Press.

Emshwiller, J. R. and Smith, R. (2002) 'Murky Waters: A Primer on Enron Partnerships', *The Wall Street Journal*, January 21.

Ferrell, O. C., Fraedrich, J. and Ferrell, L. (2004) *Business Ethics* (6th edn.), Boston: Houghton Mifflin.

Fisher, C. and Lovell, A. (2003) *Business Ethics and Values*, Harlow: Prentice Hall.

Frey, J. and Rosin, H. (2002) 'Enron's Green Acres', *The Washington Post* (February 25).

Hansell, G. (2002) 'The Fall of Enron Pressure Cooker Finally Exploded', *The Houston Chronicle*. Available online at http://www.russreyn.com/news/newsitem. asp?news=235.

Lardner, J. (2002) 'Why Should Anyone Believe You? What Ruined Enron Wasn't Just Accounting. It Was a Culture that Valued Appealing Lies Over Inconvenient Truths. Are You Sure Your Company Is All That Different?', *Business 2.0*. Available online at http:// www.ba.metu.edu.tr/~adil/BA-web/bus%20press/BW-Why%20Should%20Anyone%20 Believe%20You.doc.

Larimer, L. V. (1997) 'Reflections on Ethics and Integrity', *HRFocus*, 5.

L'Etang, J. (1996) 'Corporate Responsibility and Public Relations Ethics' in: L'Etang and Pieczka, M. (eds) (1996) *Critical Perspectives in Public Relations*, London: International Thomson Business Press, pp. 82–105.

Pearce, J. A., Kramer, T. R. and Robbins, D. K. (1997) 'Effects of Managers' Entrepreneurial Behavior on Subordinates', *Journal of Business Venturing* 12: 147–160.

Petersen, V. (2002) *Beyond Rules in Society and Business*, Cheltenham: Elgar.

Schein, E. (1985) *Organizational Culture and Leadership*, San Francisco, CA: Jossey-Bass.

Schwartz, J. (2002) 'Darth Vader. Machiavelli. Skilling Set Intense Pace', *The New York Times*, February 7: 1–2.

Sims, R. R. (2003) *Ethics and Corporate Social Responsibility: Why Giants Fall*, Westport, CT: Quorum Books.

Sims, R. R. and Brinkmann, J. (2002) 'Leaders as Moral Role Models: The Case of John Gutfreund at Salomon Brothers', *Journal of Business Ethics*, 35: 327–339.

Sims, R. and Brinkmann, J. (2003) 'Enron Ethics (or: Culture matters more than codes)', *Journal of Business Ethics*, 45(3): 243–256

Stern, G. (1992) 'Audit Report Shows How Far Chambers Would Go For Profits', *The Wall Street Journal*, October 12: A1.

The Report of Investigation by the Special Investigative Committee of the Board of Directors of Enron Corp., February 1, 2002, Special Report, p. 3.

Tonge, A., Greer, L., and Lawton, A. (2003) 'The Enron Story: You Can Fool Some of the People Some of the Time ...', *Business Ethics: A European Review*, 12: 4–22.

Tracinski, R. (2002), 'Enron Ethics', *Capitalism Magazine*. Available online at http://www.capmag.com/article.asp?ID=1381 (January 28 2002).

Trevino, L. K., Hartman, L. P. and Brown, M. (2000), 'Moral Person and Moral Manager: How Executives Develop a Reputation for Ethical Leadership', *California Management Review*, 42(4): 124–142.

US Congressional Hearing, February 6, 2002, Washington, DC.

Willet, B. and Always, T. (2002) 'For Investors, X Marks the Spot, Whether They Choose To See It Or Not', FallStreet.com. Available online at http://www.gold-eagle.com/editorials_02/willettalway012802pv.html.

Wolfe, D. (1988) 'Is There Integrity in the Bottomline? Managing Obstacles to Executive Integrity', in S. Srivastva (ed.), *Executive Integrity: The Search for High Human Values in Organizational Life*, San Francisco: Jossey-Bass: pp. 140–171.

Zellner, W. (2002) 'Jeff Skilling: Enron's Missing Man', *Business Week Online* (February 11 2002).

9 No smoke without fire?

Corporate social responsibility and the ethics of university–industry partnerships

Todd Bridgman

Academic institutions must adhere to certain core principles. Among the highest is a commitment to open scientific enquiry. The tobacco industry is institutionally allergic to this central tenet, preferring to bury incriminating data and to obfuscate emerging truths about the toxicity of its products.

(Chapman and Shatenstein 2001: 1)

Critics of the tobacco industry fumed when a leading tobacco company, British American Tobacco (BAT) signed a deal with Nottingham University (UK) to contribute £3.8 million in establishing an International Centre for Corporate Social Responsibility at the university's business school. Universities accepting tobacco money was bad enough, they argued, but using it to fund research and teaching on corporate social responsibility was plain madness. It was equivalent, argued Chapman and Shatenstein, to oil barons sponsorship chairs in peace studies, pornographers funding the study of erotic literature and unrepentant Nazi officers donating money towards the teaching of a critical history of the Holocaust. Tobacco ethics was, they argued, a 'grotesque oxymoron' (Chapman and Shatenstein 2001: 2). In protest at the collaboration, Richard Smith, editor of the *British Medical Journal*, resigned from his post at the university, a 20-strong cancer research team relocated from Nottingham to London and a European parliamentarian gave up her roles at the university.

What was considered a publicity disaster for the university was also judged a publicity coup for BAT. It was seen as part of a strategic move by BAT to present itself as a socially responsible corporation in order to counter mounting criticism of an industry faced with lawsuits, threats of regulation and increasing restrictions on smoking in public places (Hirschhorn 2004). Critics of the deal argued that by accepting funding, the university was providing BAT with respectability by association, thereby helping to maintain the legitimacy of the tobacco industry (Cohen 2001).

BAT and Nottingham University defended the arrangement. From BAT's perspective, cigarettes are a legal product and while the tobacco business is controversial, it argued that tobacco companies could still be ethical and honest. From the university's point of view, the establishment of the centre would not have been possible otherwise and if tobacco money could be used to pursue socially beneficial research then that was a positive outcome to balance the industry's negative impacts. Of particular interest is that academic freedom was invoked by those on both sides of the debate. Critics feared that the sponsorship would constrain academic freedom by silencing those academics who would otherwise speak out on the harmful effects of smoking. In contrast, supporters argued that universities violate academic freedom when they ban the acceptance of research funds from tobacco corporations or other organizations deemed to be ethically tainted (Dalton 2003).

Whichever side one takes, it is undeniable that the issue posed an ethical dilemma for the administrators of Nottingham University's business school. This chapter does not analyse the case in depth – its inclusion serves merely to illustrate the kinds of ethical dilemmas faced by deans and faculties of university business schools. It is a useful illustration because it involves ethical dilemmas at two levels. The first concerns the ethics of accepting money from private corporations and the implications of this for the independence of the business school. Who is it acceptable to accept money from and who is it not? Does that money come with strings attached and if so, how can the integrity of the institution be preserved? The second level of ethical consideration relates to the university's ability to play an active social role on issues of ethics and corporate social responsibility (CSR). Conflicts of interest involved with private sector funding affects the ability of the university to act as a watchdog on the ethics of other organizations, a role which universities might reasonably be expected to play.

The purpose of the chapter is to examine these dilemmas and to explain why they are likely to be more common in the future. Managerial decisions take place in a context where there is widespread conflict over the nature and mission of business schools and the universities of which they are part. To understand how business school managers deal with particular ethical dilemmas, we must explore the contextual factors which give rise to them and shape their outcome. It is argued that when business schools come to be seen first as businesses themselves, rather than academic departments or teaching institutions, there are strong incentives for heads of those schools to accept endowments and enter partnerships with corporations, especially when their funding from the public purse is being squeezed. As the pressure to generate revenue from the private sector grows, those managing business schools will face difficult decisions about where to draw the line. This remains a highly controversial trend, evidenced by the furore over the BAT/ Nottingham University deal, which indicates that this commercial articulation of the business school's role is a contested one.

Business schools and CSR

The university occupies a pivotal position in the development of corporate social responsibility (CSR). University business schools have been integral in putting the CSR agenda on the radar of corporate executives through their research and teaching. What started as a critique from the margins has now become mainstream management practice, to the extent that the language of CSR has become a ubiquitous feature of management discourses. Given this influence, it is surprising that universities do not often feature in contemporary debates about CSR, which usually focus exclusively on the roles of business and government.

A survey of CSR by *The Economist* (2005) is typical of how narrow the CSR debate has become. Unsurprisingly, given the ideological commitments of this publication, the conclusion reached is that 'the business of business is business. No apology required' (p.18). According to this line of argument, managers should concentrate solely on discharging their responsibilities to shareholders by attempting to maximize profits, while leaving it to government to safeguard the public interest. This is a direct attack on CSR, which believes that managers have a duty to take account of the interests of all stakeholders, including customers, employees, suppliers and the wider public. Ironically, in pushing the argument that 'the business of business is business', *The Economist* has an ally in Joel Bakan, University of British Columbia law professor and author of *The Corporation: The Pathological Pursuit of Profit and Power* (2004) and thereafter a documentary film of the same title. Bakan shares the view that, ultimately, managers have a legal duty to serve best the interests of shareholders, which means doing whatever it can to maximize profits. Because of this pathological pursuit, argues Bakan, corporations cannot be trusted to safeguard the public interest through socially responsible practices. Instead, it is the duty of government – a democratically accountable government – to make and enforce laws that constrain the actions of corporations in a manner that benefits society.

Bakan certainly does not share the faith of *The Economist* in the virtues of capitalism, yet they reach the same conclusion – corporations do not have a conscience so it is someone else's responsibility to provide it. The institutions of government are certainly one means, but this chapter considers the responsibility of the university, which tends to be overlooked in discussions of CSR. For the university, unlike most other organizations, 'conscience' is central to its mission. Through its location as an institution supposedly independent from government and corporations, the faculty has a role to play as 'critic and conscience' of government and corporate behaviour.

In Western democracies, there is generally wide acceptance of principles such as freedom of expression, independence of the judiciary, a sovereign parliament. Each of these principles implies that democratic institutions be open to critique from individual citizens and other institutions. For Monbiot (2000) a healthy democracy is one which is open to challenge. The ideal is the creation of an 'adversary culture', where the status quo can be scrutinized and judged and where citizens are provided with cultural resources for critical reflection (Brint 1994; Keat 2000). The performance of this role of 'critic and conscience' requires freedom – freedom of the press, freedom of the judiciary and one that receives less public attention, the freedom of the university. This asserts that in a free society a university has a moral purpose, combining an intellectual purpose of free and open inquiry and a social purpose as a source of social criticism independent of political authority and economic power (Tasker and Packham 1990). If academics fail to accept this 'duty' to be critical, they become 'mandarins' who legitimate the activities of powerful institutions (Chomsky 1969).

Universities, in recent decades, have faced enormous structural change that marginalizes and threatens this mission. Two significant threats are professionalization and commodification. The professionalization of knowledge is blamed for academics abandoning their social role as critical intellectuals and becoming detached from political life (Brunner *et al.* 2000). The decline of non-academic public intellectuals has moved in step with the expansion of universities and the concomitant trend towards increased specialization of knowledge (Posner 2001). Today's public intellectuals, therefore, are likely to be 'safe specialists' residing within university departments (Posner 2001: 6). For Jacoby (1987), institutional factors have encouraged academics to specialize and write for other academics rather than the public; with career advancement based on publication in abstract and small readership journals, written in a language that deliberately obscures. Jacoby blames academics for accepting the security offered by the profession and neglecting their role of addressing the public, arguing that academic freedom not only loses its relevance, but is partly to blame for making the intellectual's existence in the university a safe and comfortable one – 'for many professors in many universities academic freedom meant nothing more than the freedom to be academic' (Jacoby 1987: 118).

A second challenge to academic freedom is from the commodification of knowledge. Universities are well positioned to take advantage of an expanding market for education 'products', but it is also a market where traditional, public sources of funding, are insufficient to compete nationally and internationally. For an increasing proportion of academics, work is undertaken in mass, McDonaldized environments (Jary 2002; Parker and Jary 1995; Parker 2002) where there are mounting pressures from the state as well as from industry to collaborate more closely, and in numerous ways, with other suppliers of funding – notably, the private sector (Craig and Amernic 2002; Willmott 2003). As knowledge is conceived to be critical to the economy, academics are urged to become more 'customer-facing' as a condition of receiving funding. It is feared that academics will hesitate to speak out where the expression of academic freedom is perceived to damage their chances, or those of colleagues, of securing and maintaining funding (Hart 1989). This is seen to compromise the 'critic and conscience' role of academics and increases the risk of socially irresponsible actions by corporations. Marginson (1997) and House (2001) refer to the biotechnology and biomedical sectors as examples of where the forging of commercial partnerships between universities and these sectors has compromised the academic's role as critic. Who will safeguard the public interest, they ask? In this commercialized context, the meaning of academic freedom becomes the freedom to be entrepreneurial and engage in commercial activities, not freedom from interference from industry and government, as originally conceived (Slaughter and Leslie 1997).

Overall, the literature is pessimistic about academic freedom and the possibilities of faculty continuing to play the role of critic in an increasingly professionalized and commodified university. The former has encouraged academics to neglect their role as 'critic and conscience', while the latter serves to devalue this role since the market would appear to attribute little value to it.

The university, therefore, occupies an increasingly contested position in relation to CSR. If the business of business is business, and the business of the state is to govern the actions of corporations to serve the public interest, what is the business of the university? Indeed, what is the business of the business school? To be a cheerleader for business or its 'critic and conscience'? These tensions have been heightened by corporate scandals surrounding Enron, WorldCom and others, which appear to place greater responsibilities on business schools to scrutinize corporate behaviour and foster a higher level of ethical conduct.

Constituting the business school and its conscience

In this chapter, the link between university business schools and CSR is examined through the lens of identity formation, drawing on the discourse theory of Laclau and Mouffe (1985). Through this lens, the business school becomes a site of contestation where various discourses are engaged in a struggle to define its role and relationship to society. For example, the understanding of the university as an 'ivory tower', where the production of knowledge takes place 'for its own sake' is seen to displace and marginalize other possible conceptions of the university, and fosters a set of relations between the university and society that promotes a relative stable identity around the notion of a 'scholar'. However, this formulation of the university–society relation is vulnerable to destabilization by considerations that it necessarily excludes, such as the university as a driver of the 'knowledge economy'. Identifications become 'sedimented' as a consequence of processes of hegemonic fixing, but they are inherently vulnerable to 'reactivation' as their taken-for-grantedness becomes problematized and denaturalized.

This understanding is then applied to an empirical study of six UK research-led business schools to explore the ways in which 'conscience' is articulated and enacted – and the various ethical and moral dilemmas that result. The archival data consists of key documents in the formation and development of the business school and subsequent government reports and white papers on higher education. In addition, 60 interviews were conducted at a sub-group of six UK business schools, being those 'research-led' as reflected by performance on the Research Assessment Exercise (RAE), which provides ratings of research quality and is used to inform funding decisions.

The first task, in analysing the data, was to identify the specific discourses that articulations of the business school were drawing on. Laclau and Mouffe's concept of *chains of equivalence*, the bringing together into relationship elements that were once isolated, is useful for analysing how particular identities and discourses combined discursively to organize social space. The interest is not just on what meanings particular articulations establish by positioning elements in relationship with one another, but also what meanings are excluded by such articulations. Discourse theory's concept of *antagonism* is relevant here, with the source of antagonism being a radical 'otherness' where every objectivity, identity or meaning exists in an antagonistic relationship to all other objectivities, identities and meanings (Laclau and Mouffe 1985). Antagonisms are centred on *nodal points* – signs that have a privileged status within a discourse and have the effect of providing a partial fixation of meaning (Laclau and Mouffe 1985). In an antagonism, other discourses compete to give these signifiers alternative meanings and an analysis of nodal points provides a useful insight into the struggles taking place over meaning. After identifying competing hegemonic articulations and analysing how they organized identity, the final task was to consider how these articulations organized social space. *Myths* emerge through structural *dislocation* and suture that dislocated space through the constitution of a new space of representation. Myths have a hegemonic effect by forming a new objectivity through the re-articulation of dislocated elements (Laclau 1990).

The analysis of archival and interview texts identified three distinct articulations that have competed for hegemony over the constitution of the business school (see Table 9.1). Each articulation binds together key signifiers in a chain of equivalence, which invests these key signifiers with meaning. Within these different articulations, the critic and conscience role is constituted in different ways.

Articulation 1: The vocational/professional school

In this articulation the business school is a vocational, not an academic, institution. Teaching takes priority over research and there are close links with the 'profession', with practitioners having a part to play as teachers. The faculty has a role as a consultant to industry, but there is no suggestion that the position of 'critic

Table 9.1 Summary of three articulations of the business school

	1	2	3
Business school constituted as …	Vocational/ professional school	Academic department	Commercial enterprise
Myth (division of social space)	Management profession	Ivory tower/real world	Knowledge economy
Subject positions (identity)	Teachers, trainers	Academics, scholars	Entrepreneurs, experts
Nodal points (discourses)	Vocationalism, practice, partnership	Academic respectability, scientific research, independence	Enterprise, partnership
Priority activity is …	Teaching	Research	Public role ('third stream activity')
Knowledge is …	Applied, transmitted	Generated	Disseminated, commercialized, exploited
Relevance means …	Practical application, training competent managers	Breaking new ground through independent research	Commercializing intellectual property

and conscience' is a legitimate one for faculty to occupy. The first articulation is represented clearly in the report of Lord Franks (1963), which led to the establishment of the UK's first business schools at London and Manchester. Franks' report is significant because it was the first 'official' articulation of the business school and its role and objectives.

The *myth* articulated by Franks is that management is a profession, equivalent in status to other professions, such as law and medicine. Franks describes management as an 'applied, professional, technological' subject such as 'law and medicine: and in recent times engineering' (p. 7). In the myth of management as a profession, the *discourse of practice* is a nodal point. Franks notes that:

> By 'business' I understand both industry and commerce; by 'Business School' an institution the primary purpose of which is practical, to increase competence in managers or those who will be managers.
>
> (Franks 1963: 3)

The Franks Report constitutes 'practice' in a way that establishes a dualism between 'practical' and 'academic'. In theoretical terms this represents an *antagonism*, a radical 'otherness' where identity exists in an antagonistic relationship to other identities (Laclau and Mouffe 1985). In the Franks Report, 'academic' represents 'the Other' which is excluded by the discourse of practice. He states that 'business management is an intelligent form of human activity, not intellectual nor academic, but practical in nature' (Franks 1963: 4).

In addition to the discourse of practice, the *discourse of partnership* is a nodal point in this articulation, signifying the link between the profession (management) and professional school (business school). Franks' vision was for 'frequent two-way traffic' (p. 6) between the business school and industry. The discourse of partnership is also manifested in both the funding and policy-making functions of the business school. Franks proposed that the costs of operating the business school be split evenly between the university and industry and its governing body should be composed of half of representatives from the university and half from industry.

In examining any articulation, insights can be gained from looking at not only what objectivities, identities and meanings are included, but also those that are excluded. First, the role of research in the mission of the business school is not recognized. Where research is mentioned, it is in reference to industry fears that the business school will become too academic.

> The university, they fear, will make the School over in its own traditional image. Instead of the School being thoroughly vocational and practical, with courses and programmes designed to help managers to be better at managing, to increase their general competence, it will become like other departments of a university, concerned with the advancement of knowledge and its communication, turning out scholars and not men better fitted for management.
>
> (Franks 1963: 7)

Second, there is no sense that faculties have a role to play as independent scrutinizers of business activity. Faculties are encouraged to perform consulting and directorship activities 'out of hours' to supplement low academic salaries. However, there is no recognition that the business school, as an institution, has a legitimate democratic function as a source of social criticism, whether it is through faculty involvement in the policy process or through public fora, such as commentary in the media.

The first articulation, then, structures a field of meaning around the signifier of the business school, temporarily fixing the identities of business school faculties and work practices in a particular way. A chain of equivalence comprises vocationalism, practicality, applied knowledge and the business school, with its 'Other' being a chain comprising advancement of knowledge (research), scholarship and university departments.

Articulation 2: The academic department

The insight of Laclau and Mouffe is that any fixation of meaning is always partial, since there is always a 'surplus of meaning' that can never be exhausted by any discourse. A second, competing articulation constitutes management as an academic field of study, the business school as an 'ivory tower' institution removed from the 'real world', and business school faculties as academics and scholars. Research takes priority over teaching, academics becomes experts within a specialized scientific field and connections with academic colleagues assume a greater importance than connections with the world of practice.

The *myth* of this second articulation is that the business school is an 'ivory tower' removed from the 'real world' of industry and commerce, where management is constituted as an academic field of study. The discourse of practice is displaced by a *discourse of science*, which privileges the role of research and the generation of new knowledge, rather than the dissemination of existing knowledge through teaching. The hegemonic effect of this second articulation is represented in the priority in UK research-led business schools given to the RAE. The RAE was criticized by many respondents for detaching the faculty from the world of practice by rewarding publication in academic journals, which are rarely accessed by practitioners.

At all schools, respondents complained that the RAE has created a 'publish or perish' mentality, which reduced the amount of time available to engage critically with audiences outside the academy. While the business school did not actively discourage such work, junior faculties simply did not have time to do it. One respondent believed the RAE was to blame for academics neglecting their duty to scrutinize developments in the corporate sector.

> In the dot com fever in the 1990s we didn't stand back and say 'there's an awful lot of things not right about this'. Academics in doing their academic work are culpable in the sense that as a community they weren't very good at standing back and looking at the practical issues of the day and saying

in knowledge terms and intellectual terms and moral terms, things aren't sustainable. And one of the reasons why we weren't doing it is the RAE. We're back up the food chain, counting the number of angels on the pin and building theoretical models. And not actually, in a systematic sense, looking at the conditions of the real world and the implications of what's going on in the real world.

Paradoxically, while the 'academic department' articulation reduces opportunities to interact with external audiences by rewarding contacts with other academic 'professionals', it does create a conceptual space for the identity of 'critic and conscience'. In this articulation, the myth of the 'ivory tower' is connected in a chain of equivalence with the nodal points of academic freedom, detachment and independence. The 'ivory tower' is detached from the 'real world', which gives faculty a privileged position from which to observe society and offer comment. In addition, the discourse of science, notably positivist science, is employed to suggest that academics have access to 'the truth' that those outside the 'ivory tower' do not possess. This privileged position needs to be protected through the institutionalized practice of academic freedom. In this articulation business school faculties are professional academics, and academic freedom is a core value of the profession, as one respondent explains:

> We are academics, we are not managers, we are not consultants, we are not salesmen, we're academics. At the end we live and die by our personal beliefs and values and complete freedom in my academic domain is an absolute precondition for me to be part of an institution

In sum, while there is a role for academics to play as 'critic and conscience' it is a circumscribed role, limited by the need to satisfy the requirements of the RAE and by the fact such activity tends not to attract institutional rewards.

Articulation 3: The commercial enterprise

This third articulation redraws the ivory tower/real world division of social space and repositions the business school as a driver of the knowledge economy. In this articulation, academic work takes on new meaning. It is not, as in the first articulation, the dissemination of existing knowledge through teaching that takes priority, or, in the second articulation, the generation of new knowledge through research. In this third articulation, priority is given to the commercial exploitation of knowledge. By contributing to economic growth, business schools can demonstrate their 'relevance' to society and justify continued government support.

In this third articulation, the university (and by implication, the business school) is constituted as a commercial enterprise within the myth of a knowledge economy. In a 2000 Department of Trade and Industry review, Stephen Byers, then UK Secretary of State for Trade and Industry said:

In the knowledge economy it is not enough to generate research – we also have to make the most of it. To turn ideas into products which can improve our lives. We have already introduced incentives for universities to develop commercial applications for their research. We will now build on this, to give universities a new mission to play an active role in the economy.

(Department of Trade and Industry 2000: 1)

A distinctive feature of the third articulation is the *discourse of enterprise*. In this discourse, higher education is a business rather than a public service and is part of a competitive marketplace where only the fittest will survive. For the university, being an enterprise means not only competing with other providers of educational services, but also commercializing their stores of knowledge.

Universities can play a central role as dynamos of growth. But they will only fulfil that mission if they match excellence in research and teaching with innovation and imagination in commercializing research.

(2000: 27)

A nodal point in this articulation is the *discourse of partnership*, which was also a feature of the first articulation. Here though, it takes on a different meaning, focusing not on the training of managers for industry, but on the development of intellectual property.

The most dynamic economies have strong universities, which have creative partnerships with business. The Government wants more UK universities and businesses to learn from the experience of universities with strong track records of commercial exploitation.

(Department of Trade and Industry 1998: 24)

This third articulation raises concerns about the future viability of the 'critic and conscience' role because of the ways in which academic freedom and the democratic function of the university are marginalized. The articulation of the 'knowledge economy', organized around nodal points of engagement and partnership, is antagonistically related to the nodal points of independence and detachment that constitute the business school as an 'academic department'.

In the 'commercial enterprise' articulation, business school faculties are repositioned as 'insiders' in the business and policy worlds. This contrasts with their positioning in the academic department articulation as 'outsiders' who conduct objective, independent, scientific research. This repositioning raises concerns about conflicts of interest and academic freedom. The fear is that business schools, by entering into 'partnership' with industry and government sponsors, lose their independence and their capacity for critique. One respondent, who is part of a research centre which is funded primarily by industry, says they work hard to retain their independence.

We receive a lot of money from the industry but that doesn't mean to say that we simply support the industry. Most of our money comes from industry but that doesn't mean we will simply support the industry line. In fact, quite recently we've found ourselves on the wrong side of that fence and we simply have to be very clear about why we've taken the position and how we can support it.

This 'wrong side of the fence' incident occurred when the respondent was invited to present a paper at an industry conference. He drafted a paper that was highly critical of a firm that he had previously provided consultancy services to. The company was a significant funder of his university and when it became aware of the criticism, it approached the head of school and threatened to withdraw its funding unless the criticism was removed. The respondent stood his ground, the funding was not withdrawn, but he has not been asked to work for the firm again.

When those moments come, you have to be prepared to stand your ground. You have to be clear what your role is and my role is to bring an independent analysis. If it doesn't coincide with their interests, that's unfortunate but that's life.

The head of school acknowledged there were potential conflicts of interest involved with external funding:

I wouldn't say we're in the business of selling our soul. We are keen to get money but for worthwhile things and we're not interested solely in money. Then again, if the amounts were big enough we would be, if one is honest about it.

While many respondents acknowledged that external work contained numerous potential difficulties and conflicts, most argued these could be negotiated in a way that protected the integrity of the individual and the institution. Above all, it was important to safeguard 'independence', since this represented a 'competitive advantage' that business schools have over consultancies and other non-university competitors. As one respondent put it:

Often now organizations are looking to academics rather than consultants, precisely because academics have independence and knowledge of business organizations and are maybe willing to be more critical.

In conclusion, three hegemonic articulations constitute the 'critic and conscience' function of the business school in different ways. In the 'vocational/professional school' there is no recognition that faculties have a legitimate 'watchdog' role as critics of corporate conduct. In the 'academic department', there is a space for the constitution of this function, but this is marginalized because conversations with other academics (measured and rewarded through the RAE) assume a greater value than connections with external audiences. Recently, a third articulation of the business school has begun to compete for hegemony. In this articulation, business schools serve the public interest by not just preparing the knowledge workers of the future, but by commercializing their stores of knowledge to generate wealth.

Conclusion

This chapter has attempted to extend the boundaries of the CSR debate by considering the university business school's role in promoting a high standard of ethical conduct by corporations. In theory, UK business school faculties appear well positioned to perform this role. The concept of academic freedom has legal status in the UK; business schools occupy a position which is largely independent from both government and business; and their faculties possess expert knowledge that can be employed to scrutinize business conduct. However, these are perceived to be intensifying threats to a critical public role for academics. These include the professionalization of the academy, which, it is held, encourages academics to withdraw from public debate and the commodification of higher education, which makes universities increasingly reliant on external sponsors and academics more reluctant to speak out on issues of social concern. The tone of the literature is highly pessimistic, placing doubt about the future of academic freedom, whatever its legal status.

There is evidence from this research, conducted at UK research-led business schools, that academic freedom, as traditionally conceived, is indeed threatened by these structural changes. As 'knowledge' is perceived to be more vital to the economy, greater value is place on academic work that has some realizable commercial value. Critical commentary on sensitive issues of business conduct is valued less in this environment and the fear is that faculties will remain silent in fear of discrediting themselves and their institutions and in doing so damaging their chances of securing external funding.

While there is reason to be pessimistic about the prospects for the 'critic and conscience' role, some contradictory evidence did emerge. The literature on commodification assumes that the exchange (or market) value of technical work activity, which reproduces and legitimates the dominant order, is greater than critical activity, which challenges the status quo and, therefore, that critical intellectual activity will inevitably be devalued and marginalized. This is not necessarily the case, since in an environment where 'independence' is commodified, there are opportunities for business schools to market themselves as 'critical' and by doing so, to differentiate themselves from the competition, especially those non-university-based competitors. In an environment where universities are anxious to raise their profile, the position of the 'critic and conscience' may indeed be encouraged. In this environment, academic freedom might not necessarily become devalued, as the literature on commodification assumes.

The message for business school administrators is that care should be taken in safeguarding the independence of their institutions. This is especially the case where CSR is concerned, as BAT's sponsorship at the University of Nottingham demonstrates. The deal was widely condemned as ethically dubious, which has a two-fold damaging effect. First, it tarnishes the university's 'brand' of independence, thereby reducing its competitive advantage. Aside from the competitive implications, it raises serious questions about the ability of the research centre to act as the critic and conscience of corporate behaviour, an important social role that is distinct to the university as a democratic institution.

There is a bigger issue here concerning the corporate takeover of ethics. Critics of CSR argue that it is ethics made safe for business, essentially being reduced to a corporate branding exercise, which is just one more attempt to maximize profits. This has removed much of its critical potential from ethics and thereby ignored the 'big picture' of the ethics of business. This results in a tendency to accept at face value corporations' claims to be ethical without questioning their less publicized profit-seeking behaviour (Wray-Bliss, 2007). Applied to the tobacco industry, the ethics of selling a product that has massive negative health effects slips from view. Companies such as BAT can position themselves as socially responsible by meeting codes and criteria for social reporting and corporate governance and for developing partnerships with institutions such as the University of Nottingham's centre for CSR.

There is consensus amongst those on all sides of the CSR debate that corporations are powerful entities whose actions shape our everyday experiences as customers, employees, shareholders and citizens. There is also consensus that government has a duty to ensure that business acts in the public interest, irrespective of the claims made by business about their commitment to CSR. This chapter has sought to broaden the terms of the debate by suggesting that the university and business schools in particular can also perform an important 'watchdog' role. The promotion and protection of academic freedom is the embodiment of the independent university and provides a valuable check and balance in democratic society. The university does not wear the legal straitjacket that corporations do, with their responsibilities to shareholders. Universities have responsibilities to business, government and to the wider public to preserve their function as 'critic and conscience' of society. Lucrative financial partnerships with industry sponsors might not necessarily compromise this, however university administrators, including those at Nottingham University would be wise to remain conscious of the popular refrain – 'where there is smoke, there is fire'.

References

Bakan, J. (2004) *The Corporation: The Pathological Pursuit of Profit and Power*, London: Constable.

Brint, S. (1994) *In an Age of Experts: The Changing Role of Professionals in Politics and Public Life*, Princeton, NJ: Princeton University Press.

Brunner, K.-M., Hofbauer, J. and Prabitz, G. (2000) 'Intellectual discourse in the academy and society: Interpretation, legitimation and the rise of management talk', in R. Brown and Y. Schubert (eds), *Knowledge and Power in Higher Education: A Reader*, New York: Teachers College Press, 70–87.

Chapman, S. and Shatenstein, S. (2001) 'The ethics of the cash register: Taking tobacco research dollars', *Tobacco Control*, 10: 1–2.

Chomsky, N. (1969) *American Power and the New Mandarins*, Harmondsworth: Penguin Books.

Cohen, J. (2001) 'Universities and tobacco money: Some universities are accomplices in the tobacco epidemic', *British Medical Journal*, 323: 1–2.

Craig, R. and Amernic, J. (2002) 'Accountability of accounting educators and the rhythm of the university: Resistance strategies for postmodern blues', *Accounting Education*, 11(2): 121–171.

Dalton, R. (2003) 'Academics fume as university refuses to reject tobacco dollars', *Nature*, March 27: 361.

Department of Trade and Industry (1998) 'Our Competitive Future: Building the Knowledge Driven Economy', London: HM Government.

—— (2000) 'Excellence and Opportunity: A Science and Innovation Policy for the 21st Century', London: Office of Science and Technology, HM Government.

Economist. (2005) 'The Ethics of Business', January 22, 16–18.

Franks, Lord. (1963) 'British Business Schools', London, British Institute of Management.

Hart, K. (1989) 'Is academic freedom bad for business?' *Bulletin of the Atomic Scientists*, April, 28–34.

Hirschhorn, N. (2004) 'Corporate social responsibility and the tobacco industry: hope or hype?' *Tobacco Control*, 13: 447–453.

House, D. (2001) 'Agent of changelessness: The development and commodification of biotechnology', *Organization*, 8(2): 251–258.

Jacoby, R. (1987) *The Last Intellectuals: American Culture in the Age of Academe*, New York: Basic Books.

Jary, D. (2002) 'Aspects of the "audit society": Issues arising from the colonization of professional academic identities by a "portable management tool"', in M. Dent and S. Whitehead (eds), *Managing Professional Identities: Knowledge, Performativity and the 'New' Professional*, London: Routledge, 38–60.

Keat, R. (2000) *Cultural Goods and the Limits of the Market*, Basingstoke: Macmillan.

Laclau, E. (1990) *New Reflections on the Revolution of Our Time*, London: Verso.

Laclau, E. and Mouffe, C. (1985) *Hegemony and Socialist Strategy: Towards a Radical Democratic Politics*, London: Verso.

Marginson, S. (1997) *Markets in Education, St Leonards*, NSW: Allen and Unwin.

Monbiot, G. (2000) *Captive State: The Corporate Takeover of Britain*, London: Pan Macmillan.

Parker, M. (2002) '"The romance of lonely dissent" intellectuals, professionals and the McUniversity', in M. Dent and S. Whitehead (eds), *Managing Professional Identities: Knowledge, Performativity and the 'New' Professional*, London: Routledge, 138–156.

Parker, M and Jary, D (1995) 'The McUniversity: Organization, management and academic subjectivity', *Organization*, 2(2): 319–338.

Posner, R. (2001) *Public Intellectuals: A Study of Decline*, Cambridge, MA: Harvard University Press.

Slaughter, S. and Leslie, L. (1997) *Academic Capitalism: Politics, Policies and the Entrepreneurial University*, Baltimore: Johns Hopkins University Press.

Tasker, M. and Packham, D. (1990) 'Freedom, funding and the future of the universities', *Studies in Higher Education*, 15(2): 181–195.

Willmott, H. (2003) 'Commercializing higher education in the UK: The state, industry and peer review', *Studies in Higher Education*, 28(2): 129–141.

Wray-Bliss, E. (2007) 'Ethics at work', in D, Knights and H.Willmott (eds), *Introducing Organizational Behaviour and Management*, London: Thomson Learning, 506–533.

10 Overmanagement and the problem of moral consciousness

Hervé Laroche

> We lie all the time, but if everybody knows that we're lying, is a lie really a lie?
>
> (A corporate executive, cited by Jackall, 1988: 121)

In the introduction to his 1988 book, *Moral Mazes*, Robert Jackall writes that he started his research with the intention to investigate 'how bureaucracy shapes moral consciousness', but that he ended up studying the 'manager's rules for survival and success' (pp. 3–4). On this journey towards the 'bureaucratic ethos', he identified the 'fragmentation of consciousness' (p. 84) imposed on managers by the 'constant state of probation' (p. 40) they endure.

> As a matter of survival, not to mention advancement, corporate managers have to keep their eye fixed not on abstract principles but on the social framework of their world and its requirements. Thus, they simply do not see most issues that confront them as moral concerns even when problems might be posed in moral terms by others. Managers' essential pragmatism stems thus not only from the pervasive matter of factness engendered by the expertise so typical of bureaucracies, but from the priority that managers assign to the rules and social contexts of their bureaucratic world.
>
> (Jackall, 1988: 112–113)

Moral consciousness may be lacking in organizations not because of intrinsic wickedness of managers, not because of intrinsic or learned indifference, not because of greed or hubris, but mainly because the very context of managerial work makes it difficult for moral consciousness to emerge, develop and be sustained. If one understands consciousness as a mental activity grounded in processes such as allocating attention, information processing, interpretating, making decisions and making sense of what is happening, then managerial work imposes specific constraints and demands on managers' consciousness, which bears heavy consequences on their moral consciousness.

I shall start with the assumption that ethics – the ability to reflect on and to distinguish right from wrong and good from bad in a particular context – relates to the consciousness of individuals in organizations. Two restrictions have to be kept in mind. I focus on managers, with a primary concern with middle managers. This is not to say that other groups in organizations do not play important roles, but I assume that, as regards the ethical positioning of organizations, managers are of the most importance. My specific intent is to draw the debate away from the usual focus on top executives or governance structures and to look more deeply into the organization's mundane work realities.

My argument is as follows: Large corporations exhibit a tendency to 'overmanagement'. Overmanagement is a pattern of self-reinforcing management practices primarily aimed at solving the basic problem of performance and control that is the very reason for management. However, these practices produce unexpected outcomes and engage corporations in a 'more of the same' vicious circle.

The overmanagement phenomenon is twofold. First, large corporations face serious difficulties in the specification of what is expected from managers at various levels. High judgemental pressure is generated in order to compensate for the lack of clarity and stability of internal agency relationships. As managers face multiple formal and informal evaluations of their actions and of themselves, they resort to various strategies to protect themselves. This results in turn in an increased need for control. Second, large organizations try to extract high levels of involvement from their members, because of an assumption that high involvement leads to improved performance. However, unrealistic demands for involvement from managers lead them to fake the desired attitudes and behaviours. In both cases, the overmanaged organization gradually becomes an unmanageable organization.

Overmanagement shapes individual consciousness in the organization. More specifically, overmanagement gives rise to opportunistic and faking behaviours, resulting in a lack of collective mindfulness and the ability of individuals to understand the ethical implications of what they do. Overmanagement leads to a levelling-down of all kinds of issues that in turn fails to give solid ethical grounds to managerial actions.

The reduction of ethical grounds is superficially compensated by various surrogates (some of them under the banner of Corporate Social Responsibility). However, it also reinforces judgemental pressure and requirements for strong involvement, thus participating in the circle described above. Overmanagement, though not being in itself an unethical or a deviant set of practices, thus limits the development of moral consciousness.

Judgemental pressure and overmanagement

Unclear and unstable mandates

Management involves getting things done: top executives give mandates to senior managers, who in turn give mandates to middle managers, who in turn give mandates to front-line managers. Whatever means of influencing behaviour is emphasized, management theories assume that bosses at every level know what they want from their subordinates and that what they want is reasonably consistent over time. Still, in the context of rapidly changing environments and shifting demands of stakeholders, there are obvious limits to bosses' competence and discretion. Consequently they may not be able to define clear mandates because of the complexity of contexts, missions, and tasks (including their own) (Hendry 2002). Their objectives can also be the outcomes of action, which can itself be the product of either rules or chance (March 1994). Apart from being confused, bosses may also show Machiavellian traits: they may use ambiguity or vagueness in order to preserve their freedom of action or to escape responsibility (Girin 1995: 257). Sometimes they need to maintain secrecy because precise specification of goals could raise controversies and opposition. Finally, confusion may arise because of complicated organizational structure. Project responsibilities, matrix structures, temporary assignments and mixed operational and development missions are common ways of multiplying mandates at the level of an individual. Thus, mandates may conflict with one another.

In short, mandates are likely to be quite 'woolly' (Watson and Harris 1999: 78). In large organizations, uncertainty and ambiguity about what is expected is likely to trickle down the hierarchical line and spread across managerial levels.

Evaluative pressure in organizations

Bosses facing difficulties in formulating clear mandates are likely to compensate by increasing evaluative pressure on their subordinates. Though most contemporary management theories and practices promote autonomy as a management value, increased autonomy of agents is counterbalanced by higher evaluative pressure. Bosses experience increased anxiety as a result of increased autonomy among subordinates and resort therefore to closer evaluation as a means of mastering situations and avoiding uncomfortable feelings of powerlessness and dependence on others. Evaluating actions and people is a key feature of modern management techniques and requires a wide variety of management tools (audit, reporting procedures, assessment, appraisal, diagnosis, evaluation, feedback, etc. (Power 1997)).

Still, neither top executives nor managers are satisfied with formal information and evaluation systems. This is highly understandable because explicit, formal systems cannot deal well with unclear objectives, hidden agendas, changing requirements and contradicting norms. In most organizations, informal or private evaluation activities develop outside official, explicit evaluation systems. In fact, formal evaluation tools are only one part of a more complex evaluative activity that I call judgemental activity. In some contexts, formal evaluation systems may even become mere bureaucratic rituals.

Bosses make evaluative judgements upon their subordinates and their actions in the light of what they find useful for their own purposes and with the intention of mastering the outcomes of these actions. Judgements may occur at any moment, but most of them are prompted by events such as meetings, reviews, deadlines, official releases of information, etc. Other opportunities for evaluating subordinates may also occur when unanticipated issues arise. Most of these are kept private or are shared within a small circle until they are absorbed into more formal opportunities for judgement at the organizational level.

Bosses are likely to prefer frequent and superficial to infrequent and deep evaluations, because it allows them more opportunities to detect and correct deviations, and to observe intermediate results. It also allows them to inject new objectives or reformulate objectives according to shifts in contexts or in their own mandates. Exercising judgement about past action is primarily an opportunity to motivate and legitimate new courses of action.

Increased frequency of evaluations, however, results in increased evaluative pressure. Frequent evaluative judgement has to rely on experience rather than on method, and on cues rather than on thoroughly assessed information. Actions may be evaluated on clues conveyed by individuals, and conversely people are evaluated through their actions, or actions that are attributed to them. For example, a project is more likely to be rated favourably because its sponsor is trusted as a clear-sighted, reliable person. Conversely, a manager may be granted outstanding qualities because of the success of his or her project.

The proliferation of cues

People in organizations are aware that judgements are made upon them and are certainly concerned about them. Evaluation pressure is frequently seen as a major cause of stress and possible psychological, behavioural or health troubles among organization members. People are not passive in the face of judgements, that is, they are not just waiting more or less anxiously for results once they have done what they feel they should do. They actively try to influence these judgements, either defensively or proactively (Tetlock 1998). Being widely aware of the volatility of the judgements they are subjected to, managers incorporate this characteristic of their context in their actions and behaviours. For example, they will select actions that are easy to justify, rather than actions that would be more efficient; or they will favour actions that demonstrate their willingness to please their bosses without committing too heavily to them.

Managers tend to select, shape, alter, dispatch and control the cues their bosses are likely to be sensitive to. These strategies imply information production or retention, communication tactics, impression management, agenda setting, etc. Their purpose may be defensive (avoiding judgements, limiting exposure or preventing blame) or offensive (boasting one's accomplishment, seeking exposure and trying to stand out). In organizations, a large proportion of information is stored and shared for justifying actions rather than for elaborating decisions and constructing options (Weick 1979). Managers produce explanations and justifications to shape judgements (Sillince 1999; Sillince and Mueller 2007). They address the problem of multiple and contradictory mandates by dispatching selected information to the various constituencies and try to build or maintain false consensus among bosses.

Internal ambiguity

Increased judgemental pressure results in implicit demands for coherence as a cue of efficiency and mastery by managers. Managerial mandates are a call for alignment between means, policies and objectives. Obviously, unclear and unstable mandates make alignment of means, policies and objectives problematic. Middle managers are explicitly or implicitly in charge of dealing with variability and heterogeneity (Malan and Kriger 1998). When bosses ignore or minimize the confusion, managers are left with the task of projecting coherence onto incomplete, loosely bundled and possibly contradictory sets of objectives, policies and means that constitute their mandate. We may view coherence as a cue that is looked for by principals, when uncertainty about what is expected mixes with uncertainty about what is done. Coherence is likely to stop judgement processes in their early stages, when lack of coherence is likely to prompt a deeper search for clues. In some way, coherence, or at least apparent coherence, constitutes a protective screen for managers.

However, managers only build superficial and provisional coherence. Because of the lack of stability, clarity and communicability of what is expected of managers, consensus can only be built on transient or ad hoc criteria and is vulnerable to the occurrence of new pieces of information, clues, and reinterpretation. Shared meanings are unable to develop and communication is both cryptic and superficial. Managers face a context of internal ambiguity that requires them to be constantly alert to the meaning of whatever information they are able to grasp.

Negative Hawthorne effect

When workers are conscious of being under benevolent attention from superiors or observers, they tend to raise their effort level. This virtuous effect of attention to people is known as the 'Hawthorne effect' (Roethlisberger and Dickson 1939), but this works only when there is little ambiguity about what is expected from the workers and about the link between efforts and results. For managers facing internal ambiguity in large corporations, efforts are diverted from producing coordinated action towards deciphering judgement situations and producing positive cues or protective justifications. The energy that managers should give to the organization is likely to disperse into unproductive defensive vigilance and might result in a waste of efforts. Instability and intricacy of judgements are thus likely to produce a generalized and unproductive Hawthorne effect.

Opportunism and expediency

On the whole judgemental pressure and the resulting strategies adopted by managers shape managerial action in ways that may produce deviations because of excessive 'alertness to expediency' (Jackall 1988: 112) and opportunistic behaviour. Expediency becomes a necessary habit when expectations, objectives, means and evaluations are not aligned, and managers are left with recurring contradictions and opacity. Managers unable to meet or to decipher demands from bosses may exploit information asymmetry and deliberately fake compliance. Such behaviour is reasonable when bosses are unlikely to seek details because they stay away from operations or when they are expected to leave for other assignments on short notice. In many cases bosses themselves are aware of the unrealistic nature of the demands they place on managers and are ready to tolerate hypocrisy, provided that cues and justifications are fitting with official demands. Though not unethical in itself, expediency certainly blurs the distinction between legitimate and less legitimate organizational goals and actions on the one hand, and between legitimate self-interest and self-serving behaviour on the other hand. Opportunism is thus likely to follow expediency. Opportunistic behaviour from bosses increases uncertainty and instability in managerial mandates, while opportunistic behaviour from managers is likely to lead bosses to increase evaluative pressure.

Such logics are self-reinforcing. An excess of management would then end up in unmanageability, which in turn would prompt more control efforts (Figure 10.1).

Strong involvement and overmanagement

Judgemental pressure develops in the hope of a tighter mastery of behaviours, actions and outcomes by managers. Still, large organizations also resort to other means for the same purpose by aiming at the psychological relationship between individuals and the organization. This relationship is described under various categories such as: motivation, commitment, loyalty, culture, or identity. Whatever the

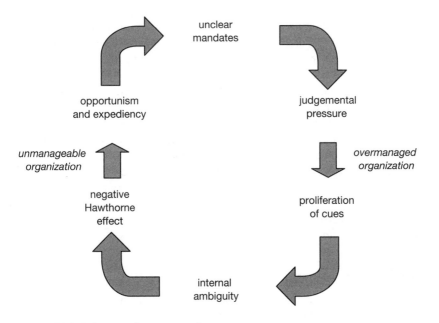

Figure 10.1 Judgemental pressure and overmanagement

category, the general feature of the required type of relationship is that it has to be strong. Strong involvement from employees is taken as a condition for performance. Building conditions for strong involvement is viewed as a reliable means for extracting efforts, producing self-sustaining momentum and obtaining reliability while lowering the costs of direct and indirect control and the levels of monetary incentives.

Such faith in the virtues of strong involvement, whether sincere or not, is backed by a huge literature produced by management gurus, consultants and academics. According to the management fashion of the time, a specific type of strong involvement provides explanations, which are taken for granted, for spectacular success stories (e.g. Deal and Kennedy 2000; Collins 2001; Kotter and Heskett 1992; Reichheld 2001). Consequently this type of strong involvement becomes the focus of corporate plans for improved efficiency or revitalization. Enthusiasm over strong involvement is fuelled by the current best sellers and included into corporate charters and mission statements. It is repeated at length in various speeches and written documents, as repetition is taken as evidence of commitment and consistency.

Negative effects of involvement

The downsides of strong involvement are much less advertised, though many of them are well known to practitioners. For example, highly motivated employees tend to make a personal case of their jobs and build their own understanding of corporate goals and missions. Such an appropriation of their position is likely to generate discrepancies between their bosses' expectations and their actual behaviour, even more so when corporate goals are unclear or shift with variations in context. 'Strong' cultures frequently produce strategic inertia or hubris, resulting in a lack of adaptation to changing conditions. They might generate 'groupthink' processes leading to major failures (Janis 1972; Whyte 1998); or, if fragmented, they might give birth to local networks that turn into defensive cliques. Identification with the organization is likely to frustrate employees when they disagree with policies or when the organization's image is engaged in public issues. Frustration might prompt them into voicing their disagreement and opposing policies or change programmes. In short, strong involvement, when it is real, generates forces that might be well beyond the reach of top management. It is often assumed to provide a means of control, and it is true, though control through high involvement has limits, given the fact that its foundation lie in the autonomy of the person involved. Once the involved person starts to exert autonomy, the organization then has to deal with an empowered individual.

Abstraction and vagueness

Calls for strong involvement are binding for top management. They have to provide reasons and motives for involvement and demonstrate convincingly that they are worth it. They have to commit themselves to support these reasons and motives, translate them into the organization's policies and incorporate them into management practices. But in the context of instability because of changing contexts, shifting ownership, stakeholder influence or unclear objectives, such a commitment exposes top management to potential discrepancies and contra-dictions. Moreover, the downsides of strong involvement listed above may well generate misalignment of strongly involved members' interpretations with top management's understanding of the implications of these reasons and motives. For example, context-conscious top managers might have a more flexible inter-pretation of values than lower ranking managers and employees, who might be tempted to take them to the letter, if not to invest them with their own meanings.

In order to prevent the dangers of being excessively committed and to counter the negative effects of strong involvement, organizational leaders tend to resort to highly abstract and vague formulations of the reasons and motives for involvement they provide to their members. Moreover, being afraid of possible unfavourable reactions from stakeholders, they seldom depart from high-con-sensus discourses. That is why most corporate mission statements are dull and cliché-ridden. Communication specialists try to compensate for this lack of meaning with beautiful colours, thick glossy papers, or other more technically elaborate tricks. Unable or unwilling to convey intensity in the substance of the reasons and motives they offer to their employees, organizational leaders develop a tight control of words and images they use, with limited connection to how organization members make sense of their jobs and of the organization.

Negative effects of abstraction and vagueness

Strongly involved employees are likely to be disappointed when they realize that their involvement is not supported by the organization, even though the organization called for it. They are disappointed and disenchanted because the words and images that the organization use to account for their efforts – being abstract and vague – do not reflect the meaning they themselves give to their own efforts. The gap between the personal meanings and the public discourse reveals the lack of commitment from top management. It is a measure of the instrumental use of words and images in order to extract additional efforts from employees without paying a price for it. Variations and shifts in acknowledgement of efforts, in rewards for involvement and in interpretation of the value of specific accomplishments may add to the disappointment because they make the value of involvement a matter of transient, subjective judgement. Whether this disappoint-ment results in employees leaving the organization, voicing discontent or retiring into a reluctant or passive loyalty depends on the conditions of the time and place. In any case, the effect is a negative one.

Employees who are not strongly involved quickly learn that the words and images that form the standard gospel of the organization are to be acknowledged but not trusted, because their meaning is too vague to provide a sound basis for their behaviour. They should be repeated but with no other purpose than to avoid using different words and images that might expose oneself to criticism. They can be used for explanations and sensemaking only in a limited way but they can be used for protection and justification. They are little or no help for solving problems but not using them is a sure way of getting into problems.

Faked involvement

Organizational leaders frequently call for strong involvement but fail to provide the basis for it. Faking thus appears a reasonable way to satisfy the organizational demand without risking the disappointment of a true involvement. Middle-managers are especially exposed to the temptation of faking because, not only do they have to exhibit visible signs of high involvement, but they also have to spell the word and obtain strong involvement from their subordinates in turn. This double pressure makes them particularly aware of the discrepancy between the strong involvement ideology and the daily practices of management. Wary of the downsides of strongly involved employees, they may subtly encourage their subordinates to engage in similar faking behaviours, or favour subordinates who have the skills to do so. What develops then is a culture of faking. This should not be understood so much as a culture of lies and misbehaviour, but rather as a culture of protection and self management. The primary goal of faking is not to obtain undue rewards, it is to avoid the trappings of contradictory demands from the organization. Still, one result is that organization members develop a distant relationship with the organization and with their action in its context. Another one is that organizational demands for performance and control are not met. A vicious circle then develops when the assumption of the need for strong involvement remains unchallenged. More demands for strong involvement lead to more faking which leads to more demands (Figure 10.2).

Judgemental pressure and strong involvement

It is hard to decipher the interactions between the logics of judgemental pressure on the one hand, and of strong involvement on the other hand. For one, demands for strong involvement may be used to cover up for judgemental pressure. The rhetoric of involvement may help to hide internal ambiguity in the hope of establishing a stabilized foundation for action. But conversely, the abstraction and vagueness of this rhetoric are likely to increase perceived internal ambiguity. Strong involvement nurtures additional expectations that managers have to satisfy, generating more faking in order to obtain positive judgement.

The main point, however, is that both logics produce the same kind of vicious circle. They are intended as solutions to solve fundamental problems of today's organizations but they put increasing strain on managers and employees. Reacting against it in an indirect manner, managers and employees dodge and escape by maintaining a distant relationship with their organization, their job, and perhaps distancing their personal identity from their professional one. Their minds take a secretive and defensive stance, carefully protected by skilful tactics of faking and expedient behaviour.

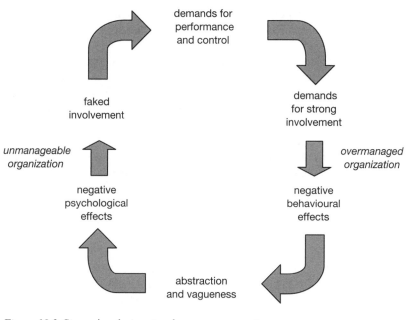

Figure 10.2 Strong involvement and overmanagement

Overmanagement and moral consciousness

Moral consciousness as process

If one accepts the overmanagement phenomenon as an accurate description of a common trait of the corporate world, then one has to assess its effects on moral consciousness in the organization. In itself, overmanagement is not an unethical behaviour and is not directed at unethical actions. One way of conceiving of its effects on moral consciousness is to measure the extent to which moral principles and ethical standards are incorporated – or not – in the judgemental activities that proliferate in today's organizations; and to evaluate the demands for strong involvement on a similar standard (do they, for example, require commitment towards ethical guidelines?). Such an approach would be a substantive one, assuming that moral consciousness would be a consequence of the proportion of moral concerns in the total mass of concerns that feed judgements and demands from the organization towards its members.

This is the way business ethics are generally framed in the literature, and especially in the literature on Corporate Social Responsibility. Surely this is important, but, as it turns out, many of the corporations that have been shown to behave badly scored very high on those criteria. The domination of a substantive view of ethics recalls the domination of the substantive view of decision making, where options are carefully and rationally assessed by a decision maker with clear and stable preferences. Particularly revealing is the fascination for ethical dilemmas depicting a more or less solitary executive facing tough decisions and painfully weighing the alternatives before sacrificing economic efficiency, or career advancement, for the sake of morality.

On these grounds, and in contrast with the substantive view, I propose a process approach to moral consciousness. Ethical (or unethical) decisions are just like other decisions in organizations: they happen more than they are made (March 1994). Action unfolds based on past action and is retrospectively rationalized through sensemaking and knowledge retention processes (Weick 1995). In this perspective, moral consciousness is not a superordinate mind frame that filters decisions based on ethical criteria but a continuous process of noticing, interpreting, questioning what is happening or not happening in the organization.

Managers' self-overconsciousness

What is of particular interest in the logics of judgemental pressure and strong involvement is not the content, but the process; not the nature of judgement criteria or the values behind calls for commitment or corporate culture charters, but the confusion or mazes (Jackall 1988 – mazes, unlike dilemmas, are unstructured) they produce; not the roots but the consequences. Overmanagement is of particular concern because it precludes the emergence of sustainable conditions for moral consciousness. By generating high levels of internal ambiguity and covering them with abstract and vague rhetoric, overmanagement diverts the limited cognitive and emotional personal resources of organization members, and especially of managers, away from moral or ethical concerns that may develop in the conduct of organizational action.

Consequently, such concerns do not appear as fully developed, well-structured issues that managers could face as moral dilemmas. Rather, they end up lurking in the flow of ordinary, day-to-day activities. Whether they will surface as problems attracting attention often depends on external events or even chance. But it also depends on the amount, the intensity and the direction of attention that managers will be able to allocate to the ambiguous cues that signal pending or growing problems. High internal ambiguity coupled with vague and abstract discourses provide no direction for attention. Instead, managers subjected to high judgemental pressure and having to demonstrate strong involvement are likely to concentrate on what is of prior importance to them – their own actions and behaviours – not as they might appear to outsiders or stakeholders in the light of more or less universal standards, but rather as they are going to be interpreted and evaluated by local judges – peers, bosses, bosses' bosses.

Managers are thus forced to develop continuous self-scrutiny, in order to protect themselves from judgements and to seize opportunities for demonstrating their mastery – a phenomenon labelled 'self-rationalization' by Jackall (1988). Beside this attention devoted to themselves, what is left of their cognitive alertness has to be allocated to the detection of opportunities to get (or keep) things going, sometimes at the cost of juggling rules and a bit of creative reformulation of policies.

In short, overmanagement induces individual overconsciousness. This has a double meaning. Individual overconsciousness is an excess of attention to oneself in regards of others and other matters, which leads to being excessively influenced by one's own interests when making choices. It is also a lack of awareness that makes it much harder to seize 'the whole picture' in complex situations, thus restricting the ability to understand situations in ways that encompass ethical or moral points of view. Individual overconsciousness is thus likely to result in lack of sensitivity to the consequences of one's actions.

The 'levelling down' of problems

As time is limited and self-interests are pressing in organizations, the complexities of problems and contexts tend to be levelled down to simple trade-offs. Jackall again puts it perfectly when he writes that:

> principles [are] turned into guidelines, ethics into etiquette, values into tastes, personal responsibility into an adroitness at public relations, and notions of truth into credibility.
>
> (Jackall 1988: 204)

Principles, ethics, values, responsibility or truth are problematic notions. In other words, they are filled with ambiguity that can only be removed through uncertain, complex, time-consuming processes of sensemaking, discussion, and reframing. But overmanagement makes managers unable to absorb another dose of ambiguity. Instead of trying to build a comprehensive view of problems and situations, they break problems into manageable pieces or shrink them to manageable pieces. Just as scientists operationalize the theoretical variables they try to assess into measurable, easy to manipulate variables, managers turn to handy notions like guidelines, rules, preferences, credibility, and so on.

'Surrogates for conscience'

Such a levelling down is supported by an objectivation of external constraints imposed upon the organization, as if organizations traded the costly effort of maintaining moral consciousness for the acceptance of externally defined boundaries to their freedom. Portions of the environment become more or less sanctified and are included in codes of conduct, mission statements, policies and performance review systems. Among these, one often finds powerful or significant consumer groups, specific stakeholders and selected parts of the regulative or normative system that the organization is facing. The organization goes to great effort to demonstrate its commitment towards the external constraints they acknowledge as legitimate, downplaying the fact that each of them has been painstakingly negotiated and is the result of a social construction in which organizational leaders (or their representatives) have played an active role. Laws and regulations, for example, are influenced by lobbying efforts, just as stakeholders are admitted to voice their concerns only after having gained credibility by getting media coverage.

Organizations certainly need such a process of internalizing external constraints to develop coordinated, consistent actions. Coordination and consistency are needed to assure sustainable ethical behaviour just as they are needed for any kind of action. The issue here is that, by legitimizing selected external constraints and claiming to comply with their demands, organizations not only develop routines and systems, but also adopt 'surrogates for conscience' (Goodpaster 2000) that are expected to fulfil all the ethical duties and solve all the ethical issues that the organization may have to face. Citing T.S. Eliot, Goodpaster suggests that organizations spend too much time 'dreaming of systems so perfect that no one will need to be good'. However, such systems do not exist because ethics cannot be outsourced or automated like other organizational functions (Goodpaster 2000: 194–195). From this, Goodpaster concludes that we have to rely on human goodness to compensate for the imperfections of the 'systems'.

In the view developed in this chapter, the quest for 'systems so perfect', has the consequence of alleviating the burden of moral consciousness for managers under pressure – though one might argue that managers are attracted to systems by many other hopes than the one of being relieved from their moral duties. Relying on systems rather than on consciousness allows organizations to go on with ethical issues without allocating too much attention to them. Awareness of ethical issues is thus limited to a set of registered problems. While 'surrogates for conscience' coupled with the practical calculus of levelled-down variables excuse organizational lack of moral consciousness, 'human goodness' needs human awareness to have a chance to develop and influence the course of organizational action.

Moral underconsciousness in organizations

The notion of a moral consciousness is only valuable if one can assume neither that the 'systems' or 'surrogates' will suffice (whatever the kind of people who operate them), nor that the goodness of people will prevail in the end (whatever the systems are). In my view, moral consciousness is a meaningful concept when applied to organizations if we give it the following characteristics: (1) it is an emerging phenomenon, not a structure; (2) it is a question more than an answer, or more precisely, it has a questioning capacity; (3) it is situated, in the sense that the forms or the processes that produce moral consciousness are not separated from the forms and the processes that produce actions, cognitions and emotions in organizations. Thus, we may hope to escape the fallacy of considering organizations as quasi-human entities (e.g. Goodpaster and Matthews 1982; Pruzan 2001) and endowing them with a rationality that even humans do not have.

Central to the perspective I have tried to outline is the idea that moral consciousness is akin to some type of attention or awareness. The management of awareness thus appears as a key issue in the organization. It turns out that awareness is seldom managed in itself. What is managed primarily is accountability and involvement. Such a conception of management priorities results in overmanagement. Overmanagement induces individual self-overconsciousness which in turn produces moral underconsciousness at the organizational level. Defensive, self-centred managers are not keen to communicate their doubts and concerns to peers or bosses, whom they perceive as competitors or judges. Self-overconsciousness lowers the level of organizational moral consciousness. Relevant information is ignored or down-played. Some problems are left unattended because of restricted access of problems to decision-making agendas (Dutton 1997). More importantly, the issues at stake are constantly restricted in order to give priority to individual preoccupations, thus hindering the development of collective mindfulness (Weick 1995), the sharing of information and knowledge and the production of refined social representations (Allard-Poesi 2001) that would allow action to unfold reliably. In other words, organizational underconsciousness results in simpler cognitive abilities, in a less versatile, less reflexive organizational mind (Figure 10.3).

It is hard to conceive of moral consciousness when so much quality and complexity is lost. Moral consciousness is more unlikely to develop when organi-zational underconsciousness is sustained by seemingly rigorous and reliable systems and when issues are dealt with in a seemingly straightforward manner. The danger here is that the very substance of problems may be lost in the systems (as 'surrogates of conscience') and the categories through which they are discussed (the 'levelling down').

Another danger, not to be underestimated, is that demands for ethical behaviour, compliance with external codes or rules and demonstration of social responsi-bility feed the vicious circles of judgemental pressure and demands for strong involvement. Social responsibility, for example, certainly adds to the instability and lack of clarity of managerial mandates. As fundamental values are at stake, often carried loudly through pompous claims, organizations are likely to request high levels of involvement on these matters from their employees. As matters

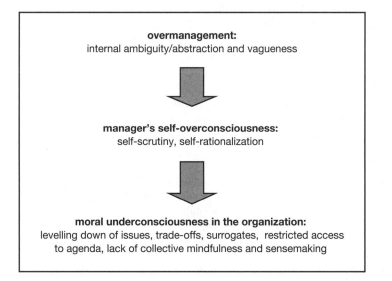

Figure 10.3 Overmanagement and moral underconsciousness in the organization

of social responsibility, apart from being intrinsically messy, are still highly debated between various constituents of society, they are likely to raise the level of internal ambiguity when entering the organization. Abstraction and vagueness are a convenient way to accommodate opposing views. In other words, there is a high probability that overmanagement feeds itself with one of its consequences, namely organizational moral underconsciousness.

Breaking the overmanagement circle

Developing moral consciousness certainly implies developing an ethical sense among organization members, recruiting executives that have strong moral commitments, and designing rules, procedures and policies to ensure that ethical principles are set in place. Still, none of these strategies are likely to succeed if some basic conditions are not met. Moral consciousness needs space to develop – cognitive space. Space must be allocated to the reflexive engagement of managers so that consciousness can rise to a level high enough to allow for some cognitive complexity. Moral consciousness as awareness arises from the possibility of not shrinking down clues, problems and issues to immediate, narrow concerns and calculus. Management practices that lead to overmanagement, however, leave no space. Overmanagement provides the illusion that organizational action, including ethical matters, is under control – whereas it is not.

There is no obvious way to break the overmanagement circle. It would be unrealistic to simply call for clearer managerial mandates and less demands for performance and control. If mandates are unclear, there are often good reasons for it. And performance and control are the very purpose of management. What should be examined more carefully and more creatively are the solutions taken for granted to these problems: are judgemental pressure and strong involvement unavoidable? Apart from harsh criticism of the pervasiveness of power structures and ideologies in capitalist organizations in particular, some thinking could be done about ways of balancing the burden of judgements and softening the call for involvement. Management scholars make few efforts in these directions, too happy to feed the corporate market with new tools and success stories or to issue virtuous but distant warnings. Organization and management scholars also have their responsibility in the perceived lack of moral consciousness.

References

Allard-Poesi, F. (2001) 'Collective representations: Decision-making in a working group', in Hellgren, B. and Lowstedt, J. (eds), *Management in the Thought-full Enterprise: European Ideas on Organizing*, Bergen: Fagbokforlaget.

Collins, J. C. (2001) *Good to Great*, London: Random House.

Deal, T. E. and Kennedy, A. A (2000) *Corporate Cultures*, (11th edn), Cambridge, MA: Perseus Books

Dutton, J. E. (1997) 'Strategic agenda building in organizations', in Shapira, Z. (ed.), *Organizational Decision Making*, Cambridge: Cambridge University Press.

Girin, J. (1995) 'Les agencements organisationnels', in F. Charue-Duboc (ed.), *Des savoirs en action*, Paris: L'Harmattan.

Goodpaster, K. E. (2000) 'Conscience and its counterfeits in organizational life: A new interpretation of the naturalistic fallacy', *Business Ethics Quarterly*, 10(1): 189–201.

Goodpaster, K. E. and Matthews, J. B. Jr (1982) 'Can a corporation have a conscience?', *Harvard Business Review*, January–February: 132–141.

Hendry, J. (2002) 'The principal's other problems: Honest incompetence and the specification of objectives', *Academy of Management Review*, 27: 98–113.

Jackall, R. (1988) *Moral Mazes: The World of Corporate Managers*, New York: Oxford University Press.

Janis, I. L. (1972) *Victims of Groupthink*, Boston: Houghton Mifflin.

Kotter, J. P. and Heskett, J. L. (1992) *Corporate Culture and Performance*, New York (NY): Free Press.

Malan, L. C. and Kriger, M. P. (1998) 'Making sense of managerial wisdom', *Journal of Management Inquiry*, 7(3): 242–251.

March, J. G. (1994) *A Primer on Decision-making: How Decisions Happen*, New York: Free Press.

Power, M. (1997) *The Audit Society: Rituals of Verification*, Oxford: Oxford University Press.

Pruzan, P. (2001) 'The question of organizational consciousness: Can organizations have values, virtues and visions?', *Journal of Business Ethics*, 29: 271–284.

Reichheld, F. F. (2001) *The Loyalty Effect: The Hidden Force Behind Growth, Profits and Lasting Value*, Boston: Harvard Business School Press.

Roethlisberger, F. J. and Dickson, W. J. (1939) *Management and the Worker. An Account of a Research Program Conducted by the Western Electric Company, Hawthorne Works*, New York: Wiley.

Sillince, J. A. (1999) 'The organizational setting, use and institutionalization of argumentation repertoires', *Journal of Management Studies*, 36(6): 795–830.

Sillince, J. A. and Mueller, F. (2007) 'Switching strategic perspective: the framing of accounts of responsibility', *Organization Studies*, 28(2): 155–176.

Tetlock, P. E. (1998) 'Losing our religion – On the precariousness of precise normative standards in complex accountability systems', in R. M. Kramer and M. A. Neale (eds), *Power and Influence in Organizations,* Thousand Oaks, CA: Sage.

Watson, T. and Harris, P. (1999) *The Emergent Manager*, London: Sage.

Weick, K. E. (1979) *The Social Psychology of Organizing*, New York: McGraw Hill.

—— (1995) *Sensemaking in Organizations*, Thousand Oaks, CA: Sage.

Whyte, G. (1998) 'Recasting Janis's groupthink model: the key role of collective efficacy in decision fiascoes', *Organizational Behavior and Human Decision Processes*, 73(2–3): 185–209.

11 Tying some ends together

Reflecting around a 'lightning rod' model of business ethics

Christina Garsten and Tor Hernes

Companies are actors in society and they observe and are themselves observed by other actors around them. Many actors in society may be considered stakeholders of the company, because what the company does matters to them, directly or indirectly. This relationship is often reciprocal, that is, what stakeholders do may also affect the company's actions. When a company launches a new service, establishes a unit to guarantee the quality of a service or obtains a certificate of high quality service, it all matters to stakeholders. Similarly, if an advocacy group pushes for information about working conditions in a production facility, this is something the company has to deal with.

Companies operate in worlds of meaning in which the words and deeds of a company carry certain values and assumptions. We may conceive of companies as nested within *discursive structures*. 'Discourse' may be taken to mean the 'thematic fields' in which the exchange of meaning takes place, as well as the movement of words and symbols that flow through these fields. In discourse, central aspects of a company are connected into a structure so that they tell something about an organization, both separately and as a whole. The word 'structure' implies that aspects make sense in relation to one another, and that they express a certain 'togetherness'. They are connected in ways that 'make sense'. An individual aspect that makes sense to stakeholders would be when, for example, a certificate of high quality service is obtained. It makes sense 'in itself' because certificates of quality are known phenomena in modern society. But it also makes sense in relation to other things a company might do, such as when it sets up a unit to guarantee the quality of its services. Whether all its services are of high quality, and whether the unit actually manages to ensure quality, may not be of prime importance, although, of course, it is not entirely unimportant.

When we emphasize that discourse consists of aspects that make sense individually and together, it is to underline that discourse is structural. By this we mean that the discourse is composed of different parts that make it appear as a reasonable, coherent whole. It is 'structural' in a way that makes sense in itself and in relation to its parts. In other words, the different components are related in significant ways.

An excellent example of the structural dimension of discourse is provided in Todd Bridgman's chapter, in which he describes the change in discourse taking place in a group of university business schools. Bridgman describes how various aspects of the school begin to resemble business practices and he gives illustrations of how this change is reflected in the ways that talk is structured around the practices. The 'talk' shows in particular how the management of the schools wanted to distance itself from a traditional academic 'ivory tower' discourse while providing proximity to a more practically oriented business discourse:

> The myth of this second articulation is that the business school is an 'ivory tower' removed from the 'real world' of industry and commerce, where management is constituted as an academic field of study. The discourse of practice is displaced by a discourse of science, which privileges the role of research and the generation of new knowledge, rather than the dissemination of existing knowledge through teaching.

The structure of talk serves to construct a meaningful whole. It provides a context for conveying information, and to some extent, sets limits for what can be communicated. Discourses are seen to influence our views on what goes on around us; they are difficult, if not impossible, to escape. In the case of the business schools, Bridgman shows how the business-related discourse reflected an emerging market-oriented culture in which the view of the schools as both research establishments and partners to business became increasingly evident.

A way to think about structure and parts may be in the sense of a string game, such as the 'Cat's cradle'.[1] Cat's cradle is one of many different possible configurations made by passing a string around one's fingers, thus obtaining the contours of a known image. For example, the Eiffel Tower is one such configuration. In a string game, it is the string that makes the pattern, or the image, whereas the fingers serve as fixed points thus enabling the string to remain in place in making up an image. Although we say that the fingers are fixed points, this does not mean that they cannot move. On the contrary, the fingers may move but as they move, they enable the image to change. In most cases moving a finger or two does not produce a recognizable image, such as the Eiffel Tower, a dog, etc. An image without a recognizable form is not very interesting, and the player may experiment by moving fingers around until a recognizable image turns up. Or, what is most likely to happen, is that fingers are moved until something emerges which is close enough to a familiar form, but does not quite fit that shape. Getting it closer to a familiar image may be done by passing the string around the fingers again or alternatively undoing it by going backwards a few steps and then to pass it around the fingers in a different pattern.

A string game is normally played to obtain a predefined image following a given series of steps. We set out to make the Eiffel Tower, and following the established sequence of steps we arrive at the Eiffel Tower image. In a sense, this is what happens when a given discursive structure is followed. For example, the unit and the certificate in our example may, as soon as they are established and are in operation, conform to a known and tested pattern.

Companies establish discursive structures which convey to the stakeholders what they do and try to do. This point is borne out by Laroche in this volume. Although not referring to discourse as such, Laroche makes the point that in modern corporations, coherence of corporate goals is necessary for evaluative criteria by which the performance of managers is judged. At the same time, however, Laroche argues that coherence becomes what he calls a 'protective screen' for managers in the sense that they can hide behind it in their everyday work, and thus avoid resolving inconsistencies in practices that might prove painful. We agree with Laroche that managers project coherence onto a world that is not coherent. At the same time, organizations depend on assuming coherence, even if the assumption is sometimes shaky. Organizational life is built around notions of stability even in a rapidly changing world. Problems arise, as Laroche points out, when employees sense too much discrepancy between the generalized discourse of top management and the information they need as a meaningful basis for their own actions. In this situation, employees may begin to fake loyalty and cheat on performance criteria. Another situation conducive to faking is when goals and criteria become so vague (i.e. incoherent) that they lose their sense of meaning.

Hence, although discursive structures may be contested among employees, we will continue on the assumption that they, when seen as coherent, form reasonably meaningful bases for action in organizations. Discursive structures do this in at least two ways. First, they reflect what the company actually does. Second, they provide the company with legitimacy in the society of stakeholders. This second function often relates to the ethical dimension of the company. It is devised in such a way that elements, when connected, channel attention so that a favourable impression of the company is created and maintained. For example, CSR measures such as codes of conduct, serve to direct attention to particular, desired values and aspirations of a company. This is what we call a 'lightning rod' structure for a company. Lightning rods serve to deflect the lightning so that is it does not hit a house. In a similar way, discursive structures serve to channel the attention of various stakeholders so that a favourable impression of the company is presented. At the end of the chapter, we discuss how Corporate Social Responsibility may be seen as a discursive structure lending the impression that the corporation is acting ethically, while it may, at the same time, remove the need for the company to deal with potentially important ethical dilemmas.

Discursive structures and how to make sense of them

Corporate actions may be considered part of discourse for two reasons. First, the action conveys something to stakeholders; it communicates an intent to accomplish a task. When a company establishes, for example, a unit for dealing with ethical issues, the establishment of that unit conveys to employees, customers, other companies and public agencies that the company considers ethical issues to be part of its normal business. The second reason why it may be considered part of discourse is that an action may be regarded as part of a larger set of actions. The action acquires meaning in the context of a larger set of actions, and it is evoked as part of this larger set. For example, a company may set up a special unit to deal with ethical issues that may produce guidelines for ethical behaviour which apply to all employees. In addition, rules may be established to delineate, identify, and provide sanctions for breaking those rules. The sanctions may be enforced by the personnel department, such as making sure that when someone breaks those rules, it is recorded in that person's personnel file. In this case, the act of establishing the unit is intrinsically linked to other acts that also make sense in relation to setting up that unit. Thus actions of a company, be they verbal or other, are enmeshed in larger discursive structures, which provide them with a composite meaning beyond the meaning of the individual actions.

The main point that we wish to make in this concluding chapter is that companies develop discursive structures in order to deal with ethical dilemmas. By this we mean that they bring to light aspects of their companies on which they want stakeholders to focus. These are aspects that make a company distinctive and recognizable. Such structures, in addition to reflecting important aspects of a company, serve to channel the attention of stakeholders in ways that help ensure a company's legitimacy vis-à-vis its stakeholders.

When we use the expression 'dealing with ethical dilemmas', we do not limit the expression to reflect that which is done when a dilemma occurs. Dilemmas may also be dealt with in such a way that they are likely to be avoided. This is precisely the idea behind Corporate Social Responsibility: By imposing rules on what is allowable ethical behaviour, companies make it less likely that non-ethical behaviour occurs. But dilemmas may also be dealt with by ignoring the problem, such as suggested by March (1988), who observes that decision makers frequently ignore problems by simply pretending that the problems are not there, and that by closing one's eyes, things appear to change and the problems go away by themselves.

A point we wish to make is that organizational actors do all of these things. They create structures that help them avoid some ethical dilemmas, but which also help them deal with other ethical dilemmas in manageable ways. In fact, CSR is an attempt to achieve both these things. First, it is a set of discursive elements developed to attract focus to specific aspects of a company's operations. For example, a company may choose to focus on selected topics such as the environment, human rights and working conditions, which means that it may exclude certain areas related to its operations. Second, CSR is a way to deal with ethical challenges in a manageable way. For example, CSR procedures may consist of standard action items, such as auditing, reporting, problem solving, follow-up and evaluation. Routines like these make difficult decisions manageable.

But, how do discursive structures operate, for example, in the handling of ethical dilemmas? We have mentioned above that structures consist of elements. Bridgman, in his chapter, uses the same term for what constitutes discursive structures, and so do Hernes, Schjelderup and Vaagaasar in their chapter. An 'element'[2] is any recurring aspect of a company that distinguishes it from other companies. When we read about a company, when it is mentioned in the media, or when we use its products or services, some things about that company are more noticeable than others.

However, what we notice about the company is a selection made available to us by the company itself. It is a selection of elements that are connected by association in a specific way. Together, the elements make up a whole, a structured totality. In the above example, we connected a quality certificate with the unit setting up a mandate and procedures to ensure that quality standards are met; thus, the actions of the unit correspond to the idea of the certificate. Note, though, that connecting processes is far from mechanical. Just because there is a unit does not guarantee that the quality standards associated with the certificate are met.

Lightning rods

As the string game mentioned above, discursive structures consist of elements that are connected to make up a recognizable structure. Thus the elements and the connections between them make up the discursive structure. The analogy of the string game brings attention to the fact that configurations vary with their elements and the connections between their elements. For example a company may commit itself to nurturing a culture free of harassment (which is the case in Steve McKenna's chapter). Harassment presents a potential ethical dilemma if cases are not handled properly. For example, what are the reporting procedures, how and by whom should cases be judged, and on what criteria should judgement be based? To handle harassment, a company would typically establish rules for personal conduct, develop procedures for reporting, prescribe steps to be taken by managers, nominate panels for investigating cases, and specify appropriate sanctions for various types of cases. All of these items are elements in a structured totality. These elements make sense when seen as a totality of measures, i.e. a structure to deal with harassment in a company.

The string game analogy illustrates well how elements connect into the whole. It illustrates less well, however, the dynamics that take place between elements. We have suggested above that companies establish discursive structures that convey to stakeholders what they do and try to do. First, they reflect what the company actually does. Second, they provide the company with legitimacy in the eyes of stakeholders. Hence, it becomes important to study *how* discursive structures actually channel and absorb attention from stakeholders. Moreover, discursive structures are not just to be seen as stable structures waiting to be activated. On the contrary, companies mould and remould discursive structures in order to channel and absorb attention from the outside world.

We will, however, use a different analogy from the string game to illustrate this phenomenon. We use the analogy of 'lightning rods' to illustrate how discursive structures channel and absorb ethical dilemmas. Lightning rods serve to conduct lightning away from buildings to protect the building from being struck by lightning. What lightning rods do, in effect, is to both deflect lightning and make it 'manageable'. We propose that, in a similar way, companies draw upon discursive structures to deflect and render manageable attention from stakeholders.

But let us first take a closer look at some of the characteristics of lightning rods;[3] a vertical, grounded metal stick with a sharp end designed to attract and lead lightning away from the buildings to the 'ground', thus protecting buildings. The lightning rod acts as a conductor of the electricity in the form of lightning. The point to be made is that a lightning rod possesses both dynamic and structural characteristics. Its dynamic characteristics describe how it 'catches' and conducts the lighting, i.e. how it actually makes the lightning 'move' through the air, via the rod and into the ground, in terms of its form, intensity and path. It is possible, for example, that the presence of a lightning rod might intensify lightning while deflecting it from the building the lightning rod is meant to protect. Thus, the lightning rod (or the ethics part of the total discursive structure) may be seen to intervene *before* the lightning becomes that intensive flash that strikes close to the building. In other words, it works in anticipation of a situation that has not yet taken place. This important point is similar to one made by Tore Bakken in his chapter, that companies establish ethics for *the world to come*. Bakken's point is that the future is basically not knowable, and in a risk society – which in many respects reflects our current society – risk cannot be calculated in advance. Thus, fear becomes an element of society, which corporate actors attempt to dampen by rendering the menace of the future 'determinable', and hence manageable. In much the same way, companies attempt to manage ethical dilemmas in advance, either by trying to eliminate them or by making them manageable. CSR, for example, can be seen as a means by which companies, by instituting a mechanism of rules, try to avoid having to deal with important and potentially delicate 'future' ethical dilemmas. In this case, CSR is part of a lightning rod structure that deflects focus from the building.

What we analogously call lightning rods are the parts of the discursive structure of an organization that specifically concern ethical issues. Lightning rods are the parts that make ethical issues appear manageable for the organization. They channel or deflect ethical concerns from stakeholders in such a way that the organization can cope with them. A question, then: What are the structuring characteristics of lightning rods in the context of discourse? We propose that they operate according to three principles.

Demarcation

The first principle is that of *demarcation*. Demarcation relates to what is included and what is excluded, in other words, which parts of the discursive structure are to attract attention and which parts are not to attract attention. Demarcation serves to set the discursive structure pertaining to a particular company separate from those of other companies. Demarcation defines what is to be 'noticed' by stakeholders about the company. A useful source for delineating, defining, etc. a company's demarcation of its discursive structure is its annual reports, which include structured accounts of the company's activities, assets and plans. Although such representations may not be shared by everyone, they represent, nevertheless, a reasonably stable basis upon which a company can be recognized.

In their chapter, Hernes, Schjelderup and Vaagaasar point out that organizations are complex, and that to make sense to their stakeholders – as well as their own managers and employees – organizational actors highlight certain areas of their practices that are representative of the organization. Without reducing complexity, an organization would cease to make sense because it becomes too difficult for anyone to come to grips with or to understand. This, then, is the primary reason for demarcating ethics-related practices of the organization to which attention should be drawn. In their chapter, Sims and Brinkmann bring up the idea of attention, which relates closely to demarcation. The very act of demarcating something is almost synonymous with drawing attention to something, as both suggest marking off that to be seen from what should not be seen. In his chapter, Bridgman brings out this point in referring to Laclau and Mouffe's observation that there is always a 'surplus of meaning' which can never be exhausted by any discourse. Hence, some articulations in a discourse need to be retained as significant and representative of the overall discourse.

An important question in relation to demarcation is: What demarcation is made to which stakeholders? In their chapter, Sims and Brinkmann make the interesting observation that Enron made a different demarcation for their employees than they did to their external stakeholders. Sims and Brinkmann observed that Enron top management communicated to their managers that only bottom line results mattered:

> The issues that capture the attention of the leader (i.e. what is criticized, praised or asked about) will also capture the attention of the greater organization and will become the focus of the employees. If the leaders of the organization focus on the bottom line, employees believe that financial success is the leading value to consider.

Sims and Brinkmann suggest that, 'In such a context, rules or morality are merely obstacles, impediments along the way to bottom-line financial success' (Sims 2003). They point out further that:

> When an instance of ethical achievement occurs – for instance, when someone acts with integrity and honour – the organization's leaders must reward it. Such an effort sends as clear a message to the rest of the organization as when an organization rewards an employee who acts unethically (e.g. Larimer 1997). Enron's reward system established a 'win-at-all-costs' focus. The company's leadership promoted and retained only those employees that produced consistently, with little regard to ethics.

While focusing inward on 'bottom line results at all costs' to the external world, Enron management cultivated an image of caring about ethical issues and having structures in place to ensure ethical behaviour among their staff. As Sims and Brinkmann point out, Enron's image was that of an 'excellent corporate citizen with all the corporate social responsibility (CSR) and business ethics tools and status symbols in place'.

When Enron burst at the seams, the rapid disintegration of the corporation may be explained by the fact that the demarcation of its discursive structure to its employees was distinctly different from that communicated to the outside world. The essence of the answer lies in the fact that the two demarcations were in complete opposition to one another in terms of the underlying values that they communicated. The internally focused structure was clearly based on ruthless drive for bottom line results without regard for even basic notions of ethical standards. The externally focused structure, on the other hand, was equally clearly based on being the good and conscious corporate citizen. Being able to keep two entirely incompatible structures apart explains the commercial success of Enron before the debacle. Alternatively, the fact that two incompatible structures were kept apart *also* explains why, once the company's practices became known, the disintegration happened as fast as it did and became such a huge scandal.

It may seem from the example that demarcation is done wilfully by a company. However, it is important to see demarcation as a two-way process. External stakeholders, such as the public, NGOs, customers and governmental agencies, by expressing their concerns, contribute largely to what areas of a company's activities are within the demarcated area. As Hernes, Schjelderup and Vaagaasar point out in relation to the dairy corporation they studied, a correlation exists between the emerging focus of attention among external stakeholders on the one hand, and the areas of the corporation's activities on which management focuses on the other hand. Attention from external stakeholders is also channelled through media, as pointed out by Grover and Moorman in this volume. They make the point that 'the behaviour of our political leaders, for example, is placed under a microscope in the media, which highlights inconsistencies or dishonesties that may not be noticed in typical business leaders'.

An additional point to be made about demarcation relates to the important observation by Spar and La Mure (also in this book) that companies may, in fact, demarcate areas *in anticipation* of reactions from external stakeholders. The observation is made from their study of how companies react to pressure from NGOs and activist groups. Spar and La Mure write that, 'If firms suspect that the activists may eventually succeed in imposing their demands upon an industry (as happened, for example, in the environmental realm), then pure strategy may dictate moving first'.

Articulation

The second principle, *articulation,* is mentioned by Todd Bridgman in his chapter.[4] Articulation may have two different meanings. First, it means the distinct expression of something. To be able to articulate is to be able to express something in such a way that it is clear and understandable. Articulation is linguistically about clarity of expression. For example, a rule of conduct that is clear, concise and comprehensible is well articulated. A second meaning of 'articulation' is similar to the physiological sense of joining different parts. A common interpretation describes articulations as joints allowing bodily parts to rotate in relation to one another, such as a knee or an elbow. A code of conduct, for example, may be joined together with other rules in such a way that they make up a coherent set of rules, in which each rule or code finds its place. Put together, these two meanings of articulation – the distinct expression of something and the joining of different parts – point towards how attention makes its way through the discursive structure of a company.

Discursive structures create meaning by relating elements to one another, as well as in articulating certain aspects. In their chapter, Hernes, Schjelderup and Vaagaasar describe how various elements of a dairy corporation's discursive structure make sense in relation to each other. For example, the corporation's products were all natural products (cheese, milk, fruit juices, etc.). Their products were consistent with a discourse on a healthy lifestyle and on being close to nature. Thus, articulation, in addition to defining elements of the discursive structure, defines coherence between elements of the structure.

Two main aspects comprise articulation in a discursive structure, both of which relate to how attention is channelled through the structure. First, coherence may vary in strength from one discursive structure to another. In the case of the dairy corporation, the coherence among the elements of the discursive structure may be described as strong. It is not difficult to see strong connections between milk and its symbolic features of health and cleanliness, and elements such as natural products and a national culture in which the idea of 'a healthy mind in a healthy body' is central. A strong coherence of the discursive structure makes for effective channelling of attention, just as the lightning rod is seen to channel lightning. Strong coherence may also give the impression to people – both inside and outside the company – that ethical dilemmas are handled well. Strong coherence may give the impression that the entire discursive structure is unitary. However, once incoherence shows up in a company's operations, strong coherence of structure may prove disadvantageous, because incoherence may then appear all the more dramatic. When it became known that the dairy corporation described by Hernes, Schjelderup and Vaagaasar had tried to bribe a store chain not to sell products from the dairy corporation's main competitor, the story took on huge proportions in the media. Thus the image of the corporation, which one year earlier had been judged as one of the most attractive companies among business graduate students, plummeted in esteem, not just among graduates, but also among customers.

A second aspect of coherence relates to what articulations show as compared to what they do not show. Articulations position elements of a discursive structure in relation to each other in such a way that attention is channelled between them. While highlighting connections, articulation, by the same token, highlights absence. This is a point made by Bridgman in his chapter: 'The interest is not just on what meanings particular articulations establish by positioning elements in relationship with one another, but also what meanings are excluded by such articulations'. Companies do not articulate their discourse in such a way that their practices are displayed in an unfavourable light. However, they cannot always be masters of all the articulations pertaining to their practices. Thus in their chapter, Spar and La Mure make the pertinent point that external stakeholders, such as activist groups, may seek to influence discursive structures to a company's disfavour in order to focus public attention on particular aspects of the company's practices. The way in which they do this is, according to Spar and La Mure, by connecting a target company to a problem that stands the best chance of attracting external pressure:

> On closer examination, the causal chain runs as follows: an NGO identifies a problem that it and its supporters feel passionately about redressing. In an effort to gain maximum impact from their finite resources, they select a target with the greatest potential to affect the problem at hand and the greatest susceptibility to external pressure. In many cases – natural gas firms in Burma, apparel makers in Indonesia, diamond brokers in Sierra Leone – this target is a firm rather than a state, a market player with purported political clout. Target in hand, the NGO then strives to communicate the link between its issue and the chosen firm (or firms). By taking the issue public and connecting it with a well recognized, usually well heeled, organization, the NGO effectively attaches a tangible target to a broader cause.

Visibilization

The third principle is that of *visibilization*. Whereas demarcation marks off the parts of the discursive structure available and articulation is used to focus on how different parts are defined, constituted and fit together, visibilization directs focus on how attention flows through the structure. Companies connect elements dynamically to maintain, or focus, attention on parts of their discursive structures. They may, for example, hold seminars with invited specialists on specific topics related to their core products or services in order to highlight their research and development efforts. This means that they show the articulation between their research and their products or services by means of public display. This is to enable actors to observe articulation in the structure.

By visibilization we mean the process of making something seen, visible, in a dynamic sense. Making something visible means having it repeatedly activated so that it stays in people's memory. A structure that is not activated ceases after some time to capture people's attention, and thus to make sense to people. A set of rules, like a code of conduct, only has an impact if it is repeatedly made visible and taken into account by managers and employees. If it is not continuously placed in the limelight, it is easily ignored or forgotten.

Visibilization is a way to bring to light elements and their articulations.[5] This can be done in a number of ways, but common to all these ways is that they involve repeated actions. Visibilization implies activation, without which discursive structures would fade away. Actions serve to remind people and organizations of elements and their relationships. To take an example from this volume, which shows how this works, Steve McKenna tells how a company had rules of appropriate behaviour. These rules may be seen as elements in a discursive structure. McKenna writes:

Within its broad code of business principles, Compco has a statement on *standard of conduct* and specific sections on dealing with employees and customers. The code of business principles is comprehensive in its coverage. On paper it appears impressive; for example, the statement on the standard of conduct is: 'We conduct our business with honesty, integrity and transparency. We respect the rights and interests of our employees. We also respect the interests of other stakeholders with whom we have relationships.'

With respect to employees, the code of conduct states specifically: 'No employee shall endure harassment, physical, mental or other form of abuse'.

However, the point that McKenna makes is that serious harassment took place in the company. There was not a visible organizational structure in place through which a person subjected to harassment could channel his or her complaint.

CSR is largely about making visible, or choosing not to make visible, certain aspects of the company's actions and priorities. As shown by Garsten and Lindh de Montoya in their chapter in this volume, CSR and its associated set of terms, like transparency, is closely related to the act of making visible:

Much of the potential and power of transparency tools and practices in organizational life is related to transparency being a mechanism for revelation, disclosure, and visibilization. We may also see transparency in corporations as something communicated and constructed – or not – from the moment of its birth. The pioneers of a company determine the level of public and private information in practice, and it is then communicated to succeeding generations of workers. In this way, the hidden and the transparent become communal work, not just the responsibility of management. Furthermore, it becomes closely linked to the image and brand of the company, a linkage that is also continuously worked on.

CSR standards can potentially provide a great deal of information about the company's priorities, decisions, and undertaking – information that may assist management in handling ethical dilemmas. For example, certification and verification procedures can help make sure that stakeholders get the information they need in an understandable form. Complex processes can be made visible and hence manageable. However, just as the discursive structure of a company may make certain elements visible it may just as well shield others.

Conclusion

Companies, like all social collectives, are places where people's views, priorities, interests and values collide. They are arenas for the continuous negotiation, confrontation and evolution of different perspectives and sets of meanings. And many of these are to do with what is right and wrong, good and bad in a particular situation and according to a particular logic or reasoning. By definition, there will always be ethical dilemmas involved in organizing processes.

The key idea of this concluding chapter is that companies develop discursive structures to deal with ethical dilemmas. They bring to light – demarcate, articulate and visibilize – aspects of their companies on which they wish stakeholders to focus. These discursive structures, apart from contributing to the positioning and branding of a company, serve to channel the attention of stakeholders in specific ways.

Dilemmas, being problems that defy a satisfactory solution, will continue to puzzle management in corporations. There will be ever new 'solutions' and 'tools' invented to help find ways out or avoid dilemmas. Management will continue to invent ways of handling dilemmas that take them closer to, or further away from, the real problem.

Notes

1 Donna Haraway (1994), a social scientist, describes the string game as follows: 'Cat's cradle is about patterns and knots; the game takes great skill and can result in some serious surprises. One person can build up a large repertoire of string figures on a single pair of hands, but the cat's cradle figures can be passed back and forth on the hands of several players, who add new moves in the building of complex patterns. Cat's cradle invites a sense of collective work, of one person not being able to make all the patterns alone. One does not win at cat's cradle; the goal is more interesting and open-ended than that. It is not always possible to repeat interesting patterns, and figuring out what happened to result in intriguing patterns is an embodied analytical skill...'.
2 'Element' is a term used in an influential book on discourse by Laclau and Mouffe (1985).
3 Benjamin Franklin (1706–1790) – an American scientist, inventor, political theorist, politician and diplomat – is credited with the invention of the lightning rod in the 1750s. Václav Prokop Divi, a Czech, apparently also devised a lightning rod in Vienna at about the same time as Franklin.
4 'Articulation' is a principle that was central to the thinking of Heidegger (1927) and used by Laclau and Mouffe (1985).
5 Heidegger, discussing discourse, suggests that phenomena (entities) are what lie in the light of the day or can be brought into the light of the day. Making sense of phenomena implies 'letting entities be perceived' (Heidegger, 1927: 34).

References

Haraway, D. (1994) 'A game of cat's cradle: Science studies, feminist theory, cultural studies', *Configurations* 2(1): 59–71.
Heidegger, M. (1927) *Being and Time*, Oxford: Blackwell.
March, J. G. (1988) *Decisions and Organizations,* Oxford: Blackwell.
Laclau, E. and C. Mouffe (1985) *Hegemony and Socialist Strategy: Towards a Radical Democratic Politics*, London: Verso.
Larimer, L. V. (1997) 'Reflections on ethics and integrity', *HRFocus* (April): 5.
Sims, R. R. (2003) *Ethics and Corporate Social Responsibility: Why Giants Fall*, Westport, CT: Quorum Books.

Index